What do you do
when there's no justice
at the Justice Department?

A True Story

1612 K Street, N.W.
Suite 400
Washington, D.C. 20006
October 24, 2001

United States Congress
Washington, DC

Open Letter to the U.S. Congress,

I am an FBI agent. My superiors have ordered me to lie about a criminal investigation I headed in 1989. We were investigating the US Department of Energy, but the US Justice Department covered up the truth.

I have refused to follow the orders to lie about what really happened during that criminal investigation of Rocky Flats Nuclear Weapons Plant. Instead, I have told the author of this book the truth. Her promise to me if I told her what really happened was that she would put it in a book to tell Congress and the American people.

Some dangerous decisions are now being made based on that government cover-up. Please read this book. I believe you know what needs to happen.

Respectfully,

Jon Lipsky

The Ambushed Grand Jury

How the Justice Department
Covered Up
Government Nuclear Crimes
And How We Caught Them
Red Handed

by **Wes McKinley** and **Caron Balkany, Esq.**

The Apex Press
New York

The authors are donating all of their profits from the sale of this book to anti-nuclear groups around the country.

Library of Congress Cataloging-in-Publication Data

McKinley, Wes.
    The ambushed grand jury: how the Justice Department covered up government nuclear crime: and how we caught them red handed / by Wes McKinley and Caron Balkany.
      p. cm.
    Includes bibliographical references.
    ISBN 1-891843-29-X (alk. paper) — ISBN 1-891843-28-1 (pbk.: alk. paper)
    1. Offenses against the environment—Colorado—Golden. 2. Rocky Flats Plant (U.S.)—Management—Corrupt practices—Colarado—Golden. 3. Rockwell International. Rocky Flats Plant—Corrupt practices. 4. United States. Dept. of Energy. 5. Rockwell International—Trials, litigation, etc. 6. United States. Dept. of Justice—Corrupt practices. 7. Justice, Administration of—Corrupt practices—United States. 8. Corruption investigation—United States—Citizen participation. 9. Radioactive waste disposal—Colorado. 10. McKinley, Wes. I. Balkany, Caron. II Title.

HV6404.C6M35 2004
364.1'42—dc22

                                                      2004041051

Published by The Apex Press,
an imprint of the Council on International and Public Affairs,
located at 777 United Nations Plaza, Suite 3-C
New York, NY 10017

Its publications office may be reached at (800) 316-APEX (2739)
P.O. Box 337, Croton-on-Hudson, NY 10520

e-mail: cipany@igc.org.
website: www.cipa-apex.org.

Text design and production by Jim Mafchir, Western Edge Press
Cover design by BoulderBookworks

Back cover photo of Wes McKinley courtesy of *Daily Camera*

Printed in the United States of America by
Capital City Press
Montpelier, Vermont

Table of Contents

Foreword by John Nichols

Author of *The Milagro Beanfield War*, *The Sterile Cuckoo*, and other literary works

The Ambushed Grand Jury **is a fascinating,** scary, very important story. In an age of increasing environmental collapse and "terrorist" danger, our government's careless and illegal actions at the Rocky Flats Nuclear Weapons Plant outside Denver should prompt all of us to become activists on behalf of our own future. This book is a chilling account of nuclear danger perpetrated *by* the United States *against* the United States.

As foreman of the Grand Jury that investigated nuclear crimes at Rocky Flats, Wes McKinley is a truly courageous American, and a fabulous character. The whistleblower, the FBI agent, and the lawyer who joined Wes in the drawn-out Citizens' Investigation of Rocky Flats, at clear danger to their own lives and livelihoods, deserve the Medal of Honor for their refusal to back down.

When everyday common citizens have the guts to stand up against the monolith, at great risk to themselves, the rest of us need to listen. Their perseverance is remarkable. In lucid exciting prose, *The Ambushed Grand Jury* unweaves a tangled web, giving us extraordinary insight into the Chinese puzzle of nuclear weapons development, nuclear waste disposal, and our government's complete disregard for the well-being of its citizens. More to the point, the book itself is a true act of hope in a cynical universe.

Whoever dreams of a better earth should take this story to heart. In such dangerous times, we all need to become activists, and here is a blueprint to get us started. I predict that someday, *The Ambushed Grand Jury* might become a film to join the ranks of movies like *The China Syndrome*, *Norma Rae*, *A Civil Action*, *Silkwood*, and *Erin Brockovich*. It is that engaging and inspiring.

A Note to Our Readers,

whom we call on to act as a Citizens' Grand Jury

In this book, you, the readers, will receive evidence showing how the US government and its defense contractors covered up dangerous environmental crimes at Rocky Flats Nuclear Weapons Plant, suppressed the indictments demanded by a federal grand jury, and threatened those jurors with jail if they spoke out; so that now, you as Citizen Grand Jurors can consider all the facts and render your own decision in the court of public opinion and before the Congress of the United States of America.

A Lawyer's Opening Statement

Members of this Citizens' Grand Jury:

This is an opening statement, what lawyers call their roadmap. An opportunity for us, a group of outraged fellow Americans, to tell you a little bit about what the evidence in this Citizens' Grand Jury Investigation is going to show. And to ask you—the reader and Citizen Grand Juror—these fundamental questions:

> *What do you do when you find out someone is committing a deadly crime? Usually, you go to the police. And then the government will enforce the law. But what do you do when it's the US Government and its corporate contractors committing the crimes? And another part of the government is covering it all up?*
>
> *What happens when citizens investigate the crimes of their own government?*

The roadmap for this Citizens' Grand Jury Investigation is pretty scary. It takes us to Rocky Flats Nuclear Weapons Plant, just 16 miles upwind from Denver. One of the most contaminated places in the country. We're worried about elevated cancer rates and increased infant mortality levels in the communities adjoining Rocky Flats. And about new government plans that will expose even more people to the dangers of hidden radioactive contamination.

So we formed a Citizens' Grand Jury Investigation to investigate the US government. We caught the government red handed in a dangerous nuclear deception. It's one that puts the public health at risk.

We've written this book to provide you, the Citizens' Grand Jury, with the proof of that government cover-up. And to request you to help us do something about it.

Who are we, these four Citizen Investigators? And why are we asking you to sit as a Citizens' Grand Jury to judge government nuclear crimes?

Jon Lipsky is an FBI agent. In 1989, he led the historic FBI raid on Rocky Flats Nuclear Weapons Plant, the first time the FBI ever served a search warrant on the US government. But a decade later, Special Agent Lipsky wrote the letter you see in the front of this book.

Why would the FBI order Special Agent Lipsky to lie about the FBI's Rocky Flats criminal investigation? Why is Special Agent Lipsky instead helping the Citizens' Investigation uncover the secrets of Rocky Flats?

Jacque Brever was a plutonium worker who blew the whistle on secret midnight plutonium burning at Rocky Flats. In 1989, someone tried to kill her to stop her from testifying to the federal Grand Jury investigating evidence of nuclear crimes by the government and its defense contractor, Rockwell International. They intentionally contaminated her with deadly radioactivity. She testified anyway, spending two days behind the closed doors of the Grand Jury chambers. And then, afraid of the continuing assaults on her young daughter and herself, she fled Colorado and disappeared for almost ten years.

In failing health and still fearful of the dangers that almost killed her, Jacque has now come out of hiding to join this Citizens' Grand Jury Investigation.

Wes McKinley, a Colorado cowboy, was Foreman of the 1989-1992 federal Grand Jury that investigated the nuclear crimes at Rocky Flats. Wes says the US Justice Department ambushed the duly impaneled Grand Jury and sealed the Grand Jury Report detailing the evidence of nuclear crimes and lethal contamination. And threatened the Grand Jurors with prison if they talked about it. Wes says the US Justice

Department lied to Congress and the public about what the US Energy Department and Rockwell International had really done at Rocky Flats.

Wes McKinley is as patriotic and law-abiding as they come. He's never even had a traffic ticket. But he's been under FBI investigation since 1992 for trying to find a way to warn Congress and the American people about the nuclear dangers the Justice Department covered up at Rocky Flats.

I'm their volunteer lawyer. I've been representing citizens' groups for over two decades.

Why have we formed this Citizens' Grand Jury Investigation? Why is Jacque Brever again risking her health, Jon Lipsky his career and maybe more? Wes McKinley does not lightly take on the US government. Grand Jury secrecy rules prevent him from talking about what really happened behind the closed doors of the Grand Jury chambers. Violation of Federal Criminal Rule 6(e), as it's known, can lead Wes to a prison sentence. An indefinite prison sentence, based on how badly he ticks off the judge.

But we have no choice *except* to form a Citizens' Grand Jury Investigation. The public health is at stake. Because now, a decade later, unaware of what really happened at Rocky Flats, officials have announced that the former nuclear weapons plant can be partially cleaned up, turned into a national wildlife refuge, and opened for recreation. Horseback riding, hiking, and children's school trips are planned for these radioactive fields.

This Citizens' Grand Jury Investigation isn't just about Rocky Flats. It isn't just about a Justice Department cover-up. The government has plans to turn toxic and hazardous waste sites throughout the entire country into recreation areas. They say they'll clean them up. But after you hear the evidence of the cover-up at Rocky Flats, you decide whether you can believe what the government says about how it cleans up its own toxic mess.

Members of the Citizens' Grand Jury, we need your help. We need you to weigh and evaluate the evidence we've presented in this book. There's a "Citizens' Grand Jury Indictment" in the very back of this book. Have we proved that the government covered up nuclear crimes at Rocky Flats? Have we proved that Rocky Flats is no place for recreation?

You decide.

Please fill out the Citizens' Grand Jury Indictment to indicate your decision. You can sign your name, or simply say "A Citizen Grand Juror." Then please cut out the Indictment and mail it to us at the address on the form. Or go on-line at Ambushedgrandjury.com, and fill out the

Citizens' Grand Jury Indictment you'll find on the web page. We will compile the Indictments and get them to all of the members of the United States Congress.

We've asked Congress to conduct an investigation into the government's criminal acts and the plans to open former toxic and hazardous waste sites for recreation. These Citizens' Grand Jury Indictments will let Congress know what you and other citizens want them to do.

Members of the Citizens' Grand Jury, don't be deceived by people who tell you it's wrong to criticize the government. The most unpatriotic act in the face of a known government wrong is standing silent.

The United States Constitution provides no vehicle for citizens to judge the criminal actions of our government. Congress can impeach elected officials and judges in some instances. But impeachment is a decision by Congress, not by us. Citizens can vote elected officials out of office. But that only occasionally is related to criminal actions.

When there's evidence that the US Energy Department and its defense contractors have committed dangerous nuclear crimes and the US Justice Department has covered them up, there's nothing to do *except* form a Citizens' Grand Jury Investigation. Especially when the public health is at stake.

When the Justice Department convenes a Grand Jury, after reviewing the evidence, the federal Grand Jurors decide whether there's enough evidence to believe that crimes have been committed. If so, an indictment issues, and the defendant stands trial for criminal charges in a court of law.

Here, the trial will take place in the court of public opinion. Perhaps where it matters most.

Ladies and gentlemen of the Citizens' Grand Jury, what will you do?

Part One

"Operation Desert Glow"
Rocky Flats Nuclear Weapons Plant
Golden, Colorado, 1989-1992

THE FBI RAID HAD BEEN SET UP AS A STING.[1] How else would the FBI serve a surprise search warrant on a government nuclear weapons plant? The security guards protecting Rocky Flats Nuclear Weapons Plant had shoot-to-kill authority and surface-to-air-missiles, too. The FBI couldn't just fly in with choppers over the incinerator smokestacks and shuttered buildings, or knock down the gates with their guns drawn.

So the FBI made up a story about needing to brief the weapons plant management about some recent eco-terrorist activity. The ruse had gotten them past the heavily guarded gates and the miles of barbed wire fence surrounding the 6,550 acre concentration camp-like site 16 miles west of Denver.

They'd been invited inside the gates, and *then* they'd served their search warrant.

The deception was just beginning.

CHAPTER ONE

The FBI Raids Rocky Flats, June 6th, 1989

Jon Lipsky was driving fast, hurrying to meet the rest of the FBI agents waiting to start the raid of Rocky Flats. He'd just gotten the search warrant signed. As soon as he could get it out to the weapons plant to be formally served, the raid would start.

The FBI is good at stings, but this would be the first time the FBI had set out to sting the US government.[2] And it wasn't drugs or guns or dirty money the agents were searching for. This time, the FBI had set out to investigate potentially deadly environmental crimes at a US nuclear weapons plant.

Rumors had come to Special Agent Lipsky from more than one source. Leaking barrels of toxic waste contaminating the nearby drinking water reservoirs. Ash and smoke from secret midnight burning of lethal plutonium. Enough weapons grade materials gone missing to supply the secret dreams of every terrorist on the planet. Accidents with dangerous materials on a regular basis.

Dr. Carl Johnson, the health director for Jefferson County where Rocky Flats is located, had issued repeated warnings about increased cancer and infant mortality rates in the surrounding neighborhoods.[3] The Colorado Committee for Environmental Information, a group of scientists and radiation experts based in nearby Boulder, publicly announced that plutonium had escaped the Plant and contaminated the surrounding areas.[4]

Even the federal government was worried about Rocky Flats, admitting in a 1988 study that the groundwater contamination was the worst in the entire weapons complex.[5]

Lipsky and the other agents were understandably nervous. This was a place so secret, so used to making its own rules, that employees of the private defense contractors which ran the Plant for the US government actually blindfolded the Environmental Protection Agency regulators when they came in trying to conduct inspections. And the EPA was so weak, they'd put up with it.[6] The US Energy Department—under the shield of "National Security"—answered to no one. Even Congress got the runaround from the nuclear industry.[7]

Rocky Flats did top secret national security work, building the plutonium triggers for nuclear weapons. The grapefruit-sized "pits" of highly radioactive metal form the cores of nuclear bombs. In 1989, Rocky Flats was run by Rockwell International, a Fortune 500 defense contractor, under contract to the US Energy Department. The Energy Department may have owned Rocky Flats on behalf of US citizens, but Rockwell International ran the show. For huge, huge profits.

Rocky Flats was Colorado's seventh largest employer. And perhaps the dirtiest, most polluted place in the State.[8] Yet, since it opened in the 1950s, Rocky Flats had seemed impervious to any kind of environmental oversight, even by the EPA. Something the raid was about to change.

Lipsky accelerated as he neared the foothills. It was still early, but he hated being late. Then he smiled, looking over at his brief case. Well, they can't start the raid without me, he thought.

He slowed as he approached the large white sign:

Lipsky was waved past the gates after presenting his identification. Plant management was waiting for him for a security briefing, he told the guard, who confirmed it on his clipboard and called ahead by walkie talkie to the next set of guards.

The investigation leading up to the raid had started in 1987 when Lipsky and William Smith, an agent from the EPA's National Environmental Enforcement and Investigation Unit, had begun a small, discrete inquiry. Both Lipsky and Smith were based in their agencies' local Denver offices.[*] But, still, it wasn't easy working up leads. There were many local environmental groups who could have helped with information and inside tips: among others, the American Friends Service Committee, the National Toxics Campaign and a coalition of groups those two led called Citizens Against Rocky Flats Contamination. But after years of secrecy at Rocky Flats, a no-access rule, and repeated violations that the government refused to discuss or remediate, the environmental community was extraordinarily distrustful.

Lipsky had spent a lot of time trying to talk to local activists, listening to their concerns and hoping for leads. He was a former Las Vegas street cop. He had an air of sincerity and real concern for the environment. But still, he was an FBI agent, and as far as most activists were concerned, the FBI had been sitting around on their duffs for decades while Rocky Flats contaminated the countryside. Despite his big grin and earnest manner, most of the environmentalists didn't trust him.

Adrienne Anderson, then heading the western regional office of the National Toxics Campaign, thought Lipsky was a plant and was misleading the activist community into thinking the FBI was serious about prosecuting environmental crimes. But Bonnie Exner, another local activist, decided to trust him.[10] She knew a lot about what had been happening at Rocky Flats. She started providing leads.

Exner introduced Lipsky to Jim Stone, a utility and ventilation engineer who used to work at Rocky Flats.[11] Stone was a bald, portly gentleman in his 60s. He usually wore a fedora, spoke slowly and politely, and knew the Plant inside and out. Many years earlier, he'd helped design some of the ventilation systems.

---

[*] The EPA and the Energy Department are both Cabinet level departments headed by Presidential appointees. The EPA helps develop and enforce regulations which implement the environmental laws enacted by Congress. Among other missions, the Energy Department develops and oversees the nation's nuclear weapons programs. The Energy Department has historically disputed the jurisdiction of the EPA and the States over environmental compliance by the nation's nuclear weapons labs.

He'd written enough letters about safety concerns at Rocky Flats to get himself fired. He had nothing to lose by talking to an FBI agent. Jim Stone became a whistleblower. He agreed to talk with Special Agent Jon Lipsky.

Lipsky slowed to look at the peaks of Colorado's famous Front Range towering behind the 152-foot smokestack of the Plant's plutonium incinerator. The view made him pause, and slow down, and wonder how the government could have allowed Rocky Flats to contaminate an area so lovely it almost took your breath away.

He sped up again. It was a long drive through the Plant grounds to the administration building where the rest of the team was waiting for him. He gave a last look towards the aging plutonium incinerator, its malfunctioning smokestack, and the dangerously contaminated ventilation system inside the building that whistleblower Jim Stone had described.

Plutonium work is done in gloveboxes or other containment areas because it's so dangerous. Even a microscopic speck of it's deadly, Stone had explained. There are filters and ventilation systems and exhaust systems running throughout Building 771. They supposedly protect the workers and the public by filtering the air before it's exhausted out the smokestack. It looks impressive. But it doesn't really work.

Stone was exasperated as he repeated to Lipsky a story he'd been telling Rockwell, unheeded, for years.

The workers tamper with the filters in the plutonium incinerator, or simply remove them, because they slow down production. Worse, the filters just aren't capable of withstanding the kind of use they get. So plutonium, in the form of fine particles, deposits in the ventilation ducts. Lots of it. The Plant is supposed to keep track of all the plutonium, according to the Energy Department's own rules, because it's so dangerous and expensive. But a lot of it's missing. And because the Energy Department basically just reports to the Energy Department about anything nuclear—claims of "National Security" again—there's no external regulation or oversight to force the Energy Department to fix the problems.

The missing plutonium is probably in those ventilation ducts, Stone insisted. And blowing around outside in the dust. It's incalculably dangerous. There could be an accidental criticality.[*] A fire could cause

---

[*] A criticality is a nuclear chain reaction that could result in bursts of lethal radioactivity.

the whole Plant to blow, contaminate the entire city of Denver. They'd already come close to catastrophe with two fires in the 1950s and 1960s.[12] But no one would listen to Stone. He was frustrated, and scared.

Lipsky remembered how he'd taken notes, and kept on looking. Plutonium incinerator? Why would they burn plutonium so close to Denver? And 16 miles directly upwind at that? Stone's information had been riveting, but he hadn't worked at Rocky Flats in several years. Lipsky needed someone still on the inside who'd point them towards the evidence and be willing to explain it to the Grand Jury.

In 1987, Lipsky and Smith had taken the fledgling investigation to the office of the United States Attorney for the District of Colorado and sat down to talk with Ken Fimberg.[*] Fimberg had been a logical choice for Lipsky. Fimberg was a Harvard trained lawyer with a boy-next-door smile who'd gone to college in Boulder, right outside Rocky Flats. Before coming to the US Attorney's Office, he'd worked for an environmental protection organization. He'd done missionary work with his church during his high school summers. He considered himself a liberal, and an environmentalist. And Lipsky knew he was a good, aggressive lawyer.

Fimberg, Lipsky and Smith kept investigating and in October 1988 brought the case to US Attorney Michael Norton.[13] Norton had twice run unsuccessfully as the Republican candidate for Congress from Colorado. President George HW Bush had appointed Norton as US Attorney despite his complete lack of any prior criminal experience. He had plans to run for Governor.

Norton was still waiting for his Senate confirmation as US Attorney when Lipsky, Fimberg and Smith first told him they wanted the FBI to raid Rocky Flats. Lipsky had been worried that Norton wouldn't take them seriously and would never take the political risk of authorizing a full-blown investigation of a US nuclear weapons facility. But an accident at the 771 plutonium incinerator, one of several in recent months, had provided the impetus to convince Norton to agree.[14]

This time, the accident contaminated an Energy Department

---

[*] The US Attorney's Office and the FBI are both part of the Justice Department. Each of the 50 states and the US territories has one or more US Attorney representing the federal government's legal interests. The US Attorneys and the FBI report to the Attorney General of the United States, as the head of the US Justice Department.

employee, not Rockwell's plutonium workers who usually got the accidental doses. From headquarters in Washington, DC, the Energy Department had ordered the aging plutonium incinerator, and the entire Building 771, closed down. Both the Energy Department and Rockwell publicly promised that it wouldn't re-start until the safety problems were remedied.

The shutdown order was a perfect opening. At this point, "Operation Desert Glow" had only a small investigation team—Lipsky from the FBI, Smith representing the EPA, and Fimberg as the attorney supervising the investigation on behalf of the Colorado US Attorney's Office and the US Justice Department. Within a few days of the accident at Building 771, they'd assembled to try to convince Norton that now was the time to go forward with a raid of Rocky Flats.

Lipsky had explained the idea.

Rocky Flats has accumulated so much hazardous and radioactive waste they'll have to keep burning it in the incinerator, in spite of the Energy Department shutdown order, he told the group. Letting that contaminated waste accumulate is illegal. And making bomb triggers creates even more contaminated waste. Rockwell International gets its bonuses from the Energy Department based on bomb production, so we think their usual greed is going to compel them to keep on burning that waste in spite of the shutdown order.

Bill Smith from the EPA had chimed in.

We have the technology now to catch them if they're burning that contaminated waste. Forward Looking Infrared. Contaminated waste streams give off heat. We go up in a plane at night and use infrared photography to tell us whether there's anything thermally hot. If they're burning that contaminated waste, we can nail them.

To Lipsky's surprise, Norton had agreed almost immediately. He contacted his higher-ups at the Justice Department in Washington, DC for approval. He authorized Lipsky and Smith to develop an investigation plan, including infrared aerial surveillance of the 771 plutonium incinerator.

It had taken six more months before they were ready to raid Rocky Flats. And by that time, they'd found their smoking gun, the evidence that was going to make all the difference in the world to the Grand Jury about to be impaneled: the FBI's aerial infrared tape of secret midnight plutonium burning at Rocky Flats during the time the 771 incinerator was supposed to be shut down.

Lipsky was thinking about Fimberg as he neared the administration building at the Plant. Fimberg would be the lead prosecutor on the case and would present the investigation findings to Colorado's first Special Grand Jury. They would be impaneled under a federal statute that authorized the Grand Jury to write a report of their investigation.

Thinking about the facts the FBI had already uncovered, Lipsky was sure it was going to be one heck of a Grand Jury Report.

Lipsky glanced at the barbed wire fencing as he parked the car. He knew the security cameras were trained on him, the guards having shoot-to-kill authority. He had his own .357 in a holster on his belt. Same side as the search warrant. The two symbols of his authority to start this raid made him smile.

Ken would be inside waiting. He never carried a piece; most Assistant US Attorneys didn't. Jon grinned, thinking about Ken sitting calmly in the Plant's conference room, pretending it was just a briefing about terrorists. After several years of working together, Ken was like a brother to him, and he knew Ken was excited, too. After all the years of preparation, the raid was finally going to happen.

Lipsky was looking forward to the upcoming face-to-face with the weapons makers.

Let's see how cocky those guys are when they see our badges, he thought with satisfaction. Their little game is over. No more hiding behind claims of "National Security" whenever there's an investigation into the accidents they keep having and the laws they keep breaking. That just won't cut it with the FBI.

Deep inside the sprawling weapons plant, workers went about their dangerous business, oblivious to the impending raid. In the conference room, suited FBI agents, badges dangling from cords around their necks, met quietly with officials from Rockwell International and the Energy Department.

The conference room was calm. The FBI agents were arrayed on one end of a long table, their backs to the wall. There were maps of the huge facility, flow charts, and stacks of papers next to plates of coffeecake on the table. The men were all relaxed and chatting comfortably across the table. The whole group was smiling, coffee cups were steaming, and it looked like it would be a pleasant enough meeting.

The FBI had told the Rocky Flats officials they were coming to give a briefing on a potential terrorist threat from EarthFirst, a group the FBI had labeled as eco-terrorists. Several members of EarthFirst had been arrested just days before on charges of conspiring to blow up several facilities they said were giant polluters. Rocky Flats was one of their targets, the newspapers had claimed.

Jon Lipsky knocked twice and entered the conference room without waiting for a reply. He nodded casually at the assembled group, then sat down next to his boss, Special Agent in Charge Tom Coyle. Lipsky caught his eye and nodded almost imperceptibly, signaling that the judge had signed the search warrant and they were good to go.

Dominick Sanchini, Rockwell's Manager of Rocky Flats, arrived late for the meeting, a respirator dangling from around his neck. He'd obviously come from one of the contaminated areas. He was breathing hard as he sat down facing the suited visitors. He had a look of irritation on his face, as though he had much more important things to do.

Sanchini tried to get the meeting started, but the FBI agents seemed to be stalling. Sanchini looked at the visitors expectantly, waiting for them to begin. He nodded and smiled at the FBI suits. No one returned his smile. Sanchini started looking uncomfortable, and glanced quickly around the room. His polite smile started to fix on his heavily jowled face.

No one spoke.

Then there was a nod from the agent closest to the door. The outside teams were in place. The FBI raid of Rocky Flats Nuclear Weapons Plant officially began.

The assembled Rockwell personnel were stunned as, in the somber monotone they'd probably heard only in police movies, they were officially advised that 90 FBI and EPA agents were assembled at the gates, ready to enter Rocky Flats to begin an official investigation of environmental crimes by Rockwell International and the Energy Department.

The US Justice Department has ordered this investigation.
You will remain in this room. The agents are approaching the
gates now. You will inform your guards. . . .

Lipsky had been responsible for developing the factual basis for the 116 page affidavit that had convinced the judge to sign the search warrant. It was Lipsky's signature at the end of the affidavit alleging ongoing environmental crimes at Rocky Flats. He watched with satisfaction as Sanchini got the bad news.

Outside at the perimeter gates, the raid began in earnest. Security guards rushed to the phone, sending furtive glances at the teams of FBI agents. They peered worriedly at the string of vehicles loaded with FBI and EPA agents, and the laboratory vans just outside the gates.

The agents fanned out. Plant workers gasped as the FBI and EPA agents burst into room after room, holding up their badges and motioning the startled employees aside. Other agents headed straight to the offices and storehouses, and started confiscating boxes of documents.

Agents entering the rooms housing the sinister-looking gloveboxes, barrels of radioactive waste, and the other paraphernalia of a nuclear weapons factory wore full-face respirators and white Tyvek personal protection suits. They took samples from barrels marked RADIATION HAZARD, swipes from the plutonium manufacturing equipment. And then they ordered the workers to close the equipment down. They moved awkwardly in their radiation protection garb, and their eyes behind the facemasks were grim.

———————

Lipsky spent the rest of the day clearing the hurdles Rockwell and the Energy Department tried to put in front of the FBI as they attempted to execute the search warrant.

First, Rockwell and the Energy Department told the FBI they'd need special gear to go in some of the rooms.

FBI Special Agent in Charge Tom Coyle told them no problem, the FBI was prepared and had the gear.

Sometime later, one of the Energy Department men told them the agents couldn't go in certain areas because the work being done there was classified.

The FBI had taken care of that, too.

The next excuse was that the Energy Department couldn't get the badging requirements met for a few days. Visitors to nuclear weapons plants have to go through a security check and get issued an Energy Department badge before they're allowed in restricted areas. The FBI would have to wait.

Lipsky almost smiled as Coyle explained they weren't visitors.

It took a while, but finally, after almost a full day of stalling, the agents were fully engaged in the search.

Many of the FBI agents, including Lipsky, as well as lead Prosecutor Ken Fimberg, did not wear radiation protection garb when they started the raid. When later asked why he hadn't suited up, Fimberg looked uncomfortable, shrugged and said, "Well, I'd never been on an FBI raid at a nuclear weapons plant."

Neither had anyone else.

———————————

Lipsky was riding high the first day of the raid. This was a bench-mark in his career, something he'd worked on hard for more than two years. And it was going to prove to the environmental community that the FBI could be serious about its new mission of prosecuting environmental crimes.

As the first day's excitement degenerated into tedium and fatigue, Lipsky tried to push aside some nagging concerns. FBI agents were spread throughout the huge facility, confiscating documents and trying to get the workers to talk with them. EPA agents were testing barrels of contaminated waste, taking water samples from contaminated streams.

Lipsky, as he supervised them, was being followed by Plant security guards, tailed wherever he went. It gave him an uneasy feeling, despite the search warrant and his gun. The guards still had their shoot-to-kill authority and a nasty attitude about the influx of EPA and FBI agents looking for evidence of criminal conduct. That kind of situation was a powder keg.

At five o'clock the afternoon of the first day of the raid, Lipsky took a break. He'd been going at it since early that morning. He was now supervising parts of the search from a room in Building 111, near Sanchini's office. And he finally had a desk and a phone. He planned to remain on-site for several weeks of probably 18-hour days, until they were through.

He sat down and took a deep breath. Got a big smile on his face and picked up the phone.

He called Bonnie Exner, the local activist who had trusted him enough to introduce him to whistleblower Jim Stone. "Hey Bonnie," said Special Agent Lipsky with a satisfied grin. "Guess where I am."

———————————

Lipsky finished the first day of the raid tired but satisfied. The FBI and EPA agents were hauling away hundreds of boxes of documents. They planned to take samples of hazardous and radioactive waste, and they'd started interviewing reluctant and for the most part uncooperative Rockwell and Energy Department employees. Another team was conducting a simultaneous search of the Energy Department's regional office in Albuquerque that's supposed to oversee Rocky Flats. There were also many documents there.

Later that night, when Lipsky finally got home, he and his wife watched the late night news together. Folks are probably shocked about the raid, he told Patti, who nodded in agreement. Their hulking neighbor to the west had been shrouded in secrecy for so many years, it would have been easy to believe that even the FBI couldn't penetrate the barbed wire fences surrounding the 6,550 acre Plant.

Lipsky had a hard time falling asleep that night, late as it was. Now comes the really hard part, he kept thinking. Would the workers talk to them? The investigation desperately needed someone on the inside— workers, managers, anyone with first hand knowledge—who would tell them how the Plant really worked. Someone who'd be willing to stand up to the anger of their fellow workers and break the code of silence.

The ruse about eco-terrorists had gotten the FBI past the gates. The search warrant had gotten them inside the buildings. Now they needed to find the rest of the evidence. And that meant witnesses who'd be willing to talk. Hopefully, the FBI's image would scare the workers into realizing that the Energy Department and its contractors weren't in charge here any more.

Patti Lipsky had stayed home with their three daughters while Jon worked the long hours leading up to and during the raid of the Plant. She was supportive, as always, of his work. But even she had some questions. Jon didn't mind talking about his work when he could, but she didn't want him to think she was complaining. The second night of the raid, over dinner, a late one as had become usual, she finally asked.

Why does the FBI even have to raid Rocky Flats? I mean, it may be run by a defense contractor but the Energy Department owns it. Why can't the Justice Department just pick up the phone and ask the Energy Department what's going on at Rocky Flats? Why would one US government agency raid another?

Lipsky grunted. We wouldn't be able to believe anything they said, Pat. The Energy Department is in this up to their ears.

The FBI suspected both Rockwell and Energy Department officials of knowingly breaking environmental laws. The few rules there were about worker safety and exposure levels for the surrounding neighborhoods slowed down production of nuclear weapons. And Rockwell got their bonuses based on the number of bombs they built, not on whether Rocky Flats had complied with environmental and safety laws. The Energy Department, too, wanted to build as many nuclear bombs as possible as quickly as possible.

Among the crimes being investigated at Rocky Flats were:[15]

- *illegal incineration of hazardous and radioactive wastes;*
- *illegal storage of hazardous and radioactive wastes;*
- *illegal discharges to Walnut Creek and Woman Creek;*
- *false statements to the EPA and to State officials;*
- *secret midnight plutonium burning in violation of a government shutdown order.*

We can't tip our hand, Lipsky had explained to his wife that night. We have to keep the focus of the investigation secret until we can get our hands on the evidence and get the witnesses to talk to us.

But the following night when he left the Plant at the end of another long hot 18 hours, Lipsky was furious. So mad he could hardly speak. In an unexpected and highly unusual move, on instructions of United States Attorney General Dick Thornburgh,[*] the Justice Department had unsealed the Affidavit and Application for Search Warrant.[16] The focus of the investigation and the evidence it already had collected were no longer secret.

Lipsky couldn't understand what was going on. They'd gone to a lot of trouble to get the search warrant affidavit sealed. It was incredibly detailed; it laid out almost their entire investigation.

Rockwell attorneys are reading it right now, Lipsky realized, blue eyes drilling into the dashboard as he headed home. And so is the Energy Department. The evidence we'd planned to get by this "surprise" raid is probably fast disappearing.

They'll know how to prep the witnesses and what documents we really need, Lipsky fumed. Why did Justice do that?

The official explanation made no sense to him.[17] Attorney General Thornburgh's press release stated that although it was a "highly unusual step," he had authorized public disclosure because the search will be a matter of public record and because the public needed to be reassured that ". . . this investigation does not signal any major new environmental or safety concerns."

That *really* makes no sense, Lipsky thought, remembering the evidence they'd already collected.

---

[*] Thornburgh had been governor of Pennsylvania at the time of the nuclear power plant accident at Three Mile Island.

As the raid continued over the next 15 days, Lipsky grew increasingly worried.

The FBI and EPA agents were having trouble getting workers to talk to them. Almost as soon as the search warrant allegations had become known, Rockwell started intimidating the workers, the people the FBI was counting on to tell them about the wrongdoing at Rocky Flats.

Whistleblowers will be dealt with severely, Rockwell warned at a June 13th employee meeting. We will provide you with legal counsel, paid for by Rockwell, to make sure your legal rights are protected.[*]

The employee rumor mill was working overtime. They're looking for someone to blame things on, the workers warned each other during breaks and over the hum of machinery. Watch yourself, or it might be you.

The FBI was losing the momentum of the first days of the raid. If we don't get a break soon, Lipsky worried, we'll never get anyone to talk with us.[18]

———————————

Rockwell's Dominick Sanchini was the highest ranking potential target of the raid.[19] He was a bald man with glasses, a lawyer and a scientist. He'd been Rockwell's Manager of Rocky Flats for three years by the time of the raid. Before that, he'd done a lot of work on NASA contracts for Rockwell.

When the FBI agents had started to search Sanchini's office at the Plant, Sanchini had barred their way. He quickly found his lawyer and started claiming a right of privacy to the office he used on government property. The FBI sealed the office, posted agents outside the door, and called Assistant US Attorney Fimberg. Lipsky didn't hear about what happened until later.

It's standard practice for the FBI to call in Justice Department lawyers when someone refuses access despite a search warrant. But what isn't standard practice is the deal Prosecutor Fimberg cut with Sanchini's lawyer that morning.

The FBI agents were armed, had a search warrant, and could have simply moved Sanchini aside and entered the room. Had him arrested if necessary. Handcuffed him if they wanted.

That would have been interesting, Lipsky thought. Arresting the

———————————

[*] Actually, paid for by taxpayers. The Energy Department's contractual indemnification provisions may require taxpayers to foot the bill for Rockwell's legal expenses incurred in trying to thwart the investigation. For both the corporation and its employees.

head of a nuclear weapons plant for interfering with a search warrant.

But Fimberg had decided to be cooperative with Rockwell and the Energy Department. Fimberg gave Sanchini permission to go in and out of his office, even though the FBI had sealed it, until the court ruled on Sanchini's claim that the office was private and couldn't be searched. In turn, in a "handshake agreement," Sanchini promised he wouldn't remove anything from the office until the court ruled.[20]

Who knows what that guy is taking out of there? Lipsky protested when he found out about the "handshake agreement." Who knows whether he's complying with the agreement? And it sends the wrong message to the workers. We need their cooperation, but if they think the Energy Department and Rockwell are still in charge, not us, we'll never get anyone to come forward.

But Fimberg insisted to Lipsky that he "had to work with those guys."

Lipsky shut up about it because it was already done. But he couldn't stop worrying.

What's that "handshake agreement" all about? he kept asking himself. Is this an FBI raid, or not?

Once it was decided that the FBI had the right to search his office, Sanchini had stayed at his desk, watching while the search was underway. Looking through some file cabinets, the FBI agents found a stack of memo pads full of handwritten notes.

Those were about his NASA days, Sanchini told the two FBI agents. He was planning on writing a book. Nothing to do with Rocky Flats.

The agents had moved on and were searching a cabinet near the corner of his office when Sanchini started explaining how there was nothing in there about Rocky Flats, either. It was more old stuff from his NASA days.

While the nervous Rockwell Manager was still talking, an FBI agent located Sanchini's Rocky Flats memo pads underneath a pile of folders. Thirteen memo pads in Sanchini's handwriting. They were a day by day account of activities at the Plant, including names and dates, kept by Rockwell's head of Rocky Flats.

The two FBI agents were sure they'd uncovered a gold mine.

From the beginning, Lipsky had worried about whether high-level officials at the Plant had been given advance notice of the raid. The FBI wanted to find the illegally stored barrels of hazardous waste. But with enough advance warning, it would be easy to hide things. Rocky Flats was a huge facility, over a hundred buildings sprawling over the barbed wire enclosed complex, with underground vaults and intimidating radioactive warning signs throughout.

And the year before, when US Attorney Norton had decided to alert Justice Department headquarters in Washington about the investigation, so many highly-connected political people had gotten involved that Lipsky's gut told him that somehow, some of the bigwigs knew they were coming.[21]

First of all, the Justice Department's Criminal Division in Washington insisted that they tell the Energy Department about the planned raid, even though high-level Energy Department officials were suspected of criminal acts. The prosecutors alerted the Energy Department Office of Inspector General, the ones who should have been doing something about the problems at Rocky Flats but apparently hadn't.

The investigation team also alerted Admiral James Watkins, Secretary of the Energy Department, the nuclear scientist President George HW Bush had hand-picked and touted as the man who was going to finally clean up the country's nuclear weapons plants.[22] Rocky Flats had the potential to make him and his boss, President Bush, look like failures.

Admiral Watkins had been given a draft of the detailed search warrant affidavit at least three months before the raid actually started. His second in command, Deputy Secretary of Energy Henson Moore, had even been present at Rocky Flats with the FBI agents when they first started the sting. And two months before the raid, the highest level Energy Department official on site at the Plant had been transferred to headquarters in Washington, DC.[23]

The whole thing struck Lipsky as just plain wrong.

Drums of hazardous waste had started moving before the FBI cars had even pulled up at the gates.[24] A shell game, one of the workers later told Lipsky, so the FBI would never know how much illegally stored waste was really there.

The woman had laughed when Lipsky asked her point blank if anyone at Rocky Flats had known in advance about the raid.

"Of course they did," she'd laughed sardonically. "It was like a Laurel and Hardy movie in there." As FBI agents would enter one room, workers would have just left with barrels of hazardous waste. As soon as the FBI exited the room, someone would scurry back in with a load of barrels.

Since one of the main search warrant allegations was that Rocky Flats was illegally storing hazardous waste in excess of the regulatory limits, moving the drums around to interfere with the FBI's count would also have interfered with evidence gathering and may have been an obstruction of justice.

Lipsky added this to his ever-growing list of possible crimes for indictment. And he stepped up his efforts to find an insider who would tell the FBI what really went on at Rocky Flats. The FBI established a hotline with a toll free number so anyone, anywhere could call in with tips.

Thousands of documents proving mishandled waste streams were necessary to a case, but without a live witness, the prosecutors were going to have a hard time trying to put anyone in jail.

And that, at least, was Lipsky's goal: enforcing environmental laws against the government and its defense contractors just like they're enforced against the guy on the street.

CHAPTER TWO

The Whistleblower,
June 15th,1989

Jacque flopped onto her living room couch across from her friend Karen. They'd been talking for hours, but always came back to the same thing.

What's the worst thing they can do to us, anyway? What can the FBI do to us that could be worse than what Rockwell's going to do?

Karen had waited in the living room while Jacque went off to put her 7-year-old to bed. Jessica had fussed a little, as though sensing her mother's tension. Karen was rubbing her lips together nervously when Jacque finally came back. They picked up the conversation they'd been having over and over for the last three days, ever since they'd learned that the overtime Sunday they'd worked on the Building 771 plutonium incinerator might be part of the focus of the FBI criminal investigation.[25]

Both women were chemical operators at the weapons plant, reprocessing radioactive waste. It was done with hazardous chemicals and heat, fluorinators, calcinators, and gloveboxes. They worked with nitric acid, caustic scrubbers, incinerators and lethal radioactive materials.

They had high paying jobs and they loved their work, dangerous as it was. It was challenging and exciting. But now they were scared to death of their employer.

Jacque took a deep breath. She *had* to talk Karen into it.

Look, Karen, we're screwed. Rockwell's got to have someone to throw to the FBI and we're it. We worked that incinerator during the Energy Department shutdown and no one's going to believe Ron never told us there was a shutdown order.

She was wondering privately if Ron had set her up. Ron Avery had disappeared a month before the raid. Just given up his foreman's job less than a year from retirement, sold all his stuff and moved to Florida. Would he really have set her up just because she'd broken up with him?

19

She didn't say anything to Karen, who hadn't liked Ron to begin with. But it made their dilemma even more painful, thinking he might have wanted this to happen.

Karen just shook her head, rattling the ice in her glass of pop. The last thing in the world she wanted to do was go squeal to the FBI.

Jacque wasn't happy about it, either. But they had no choice, she felt.

If we help the FBI, they'll protect us from Rockwell, it's just as simple as that. If we don't go to the FBI, we've had it. We'll be Rockwell's sacrificial lambs. All we have to do is tell the truth and we'll be OK.

Jacque kept repeating it in her mind as she smoked nervously, staring at her new floral patterned loveseat where Karen was sitting, looking at her grimly.

If we just tell the FBI the truth, we'll be OK.

But she and Karen both knew Rockwell and the FBI weren't their only problem. If their union brothers and sisters found out they'd talked to the FBI, there'd be hell to pay. Workers in the chemical operations have a tradition of harassing each other over even the most minor problems. Some of the "chem ops," as these plutonium workers were called, had been known to glove themselves, stick their fingers in the drains where the highly radioactive waste was collected, and flick the deadly contamination on someone they were pissed at. They didn't do it very often, but if you found yourself "hot," "crapped up," contaminated, under circumstances you couldn't explain, the first thing you did if you were a chem op was try to figure out who you'd pissed off.

As Jacque had made dinner for herself and Jessica, waiting for Karen to show up, she'd been distraught, trying not to show it, not really listening to her daughter's prattling. She'd tried hard to pay attention, knowing she was both mother and father to the energetic seven-year-old. But the fact that she was really thinking about squealing to the FBI about her boss and her co-workers was utmost on her mind.

What was she getting herself into? The rest of the chem ops would go wild if they ever found out. They were always worried that someone was going to close down Building 771, that they'd lose their high-paying jobs.

What was going to happen to her and Karen if word got out they'd co-operated with the FBI? Would the feds be able to protect them? Because surely Rockwell and the union members would both be after them.

Jacque tried hard to blow her cigarette smoke away from Karen, but saw it circle back towards her friend's dark-haired flip. Karen was quiet, seemingly less worried. Jacque wondered whether that was true, or if she

moke and ash went pluming out towards Denver and the
ighborhoods.

or maybe because of the sinister atmosphere inside the
always did full make up and hair before she came to
... uig blond fluffy hair. Eyeliner, mascara and eyeshadow all went on
at home. Once inside Building 771, she and Karen would change into
thick white cotton long-sleeved coveralls, safety boots, booties. Plastic
gloves. They looked like a strange combination of factory worker/ astro-
naut/ showgirl.

Jacque sometimes laughed at all the work she put into making up her
face and hair, only to ruin it under half masks, full face respirators, and
skullcaps. They were even supposed to wear underwear provided by
Rockwell. But it was just too gross. So the women chem ops wore their
own underwear, then washed it in the shower after work and left it dry-
ing in their lockers.

Once they'd badged into 771 and gone through the airlock doors,
they weren't supposed to have any street clothes on, and once they went
back through the airlock door and badged out, they weren't supposed to
have any more contamination on them. Strip off the coveralls, take a
shower, change back into your street clothes. Put your make up back on,
do your hair.

Once inside 771, big hair or no, you were part of the tightly knit
group of chem ops. Mostly male, mostly macho, they were performing
dangerous work which was supposed to help the nation's security by
building plutonium triggers for nuclear bombs.

Karen and Jacque, despite their feminine looks, had to be as macho
as the men. They could become contaminated at any moment, in small
amounts that would affect their health over time, or in a dose strong
enough to kill them within months. They had to have an attitude to deal
with the risk and with the men, and the attitude they both chose was to
become as macho as the guys, be the best at their jobs, talk tough, and
stick tight to their union brothers and sisters.

Safety precautions were necessary for everyone's health, but the
workers all knew a deadly truth: there was little that was safe in Building
771. Built in the 1950s, it was falling apart. It had none of the modern
safeguards. It was patched together with spit and duct tape, and it was
in constant need of repair. But the Energy Department and Rockwell
didn't want to spend the money. It was in need of replacement, but for
years the Energy Department and Congress had been trying to decide
what to do about it. It needed to be moved farther away from a huge

population center like metropolitan Denver, but nobody else wanted it near them either.

The building was in need of being shut down for good. They all knew that. But this union of working class men and women would never be able to earn the same big bucks on the outside. The retirement benefits were great, too. So they kept their mouths shut about the dangers, turned a blind eye to the leaking pipes and spills throughout the Plant, and did their work with a macabre sense of humor that served to bind them even closer together.

Jacque had started working at Rocky Flats in 1982. She'd started in the cafeteria while she was waiting for her security clearance to come through. She'd dropped out of high school at 15 to help support her mom and family of four brothers and sisters when their dad had left. She was 24 when Jessica was born.

When she'd first landed her job as a chem op in 1984, Jacque was elated. Higher pay, higher status. And a much more interesting job. Chemistry turned into her new passion, and she had quickly become one of the most respected chem ops at the Plant.

She and Karen Pitts became friends and were often assigned to work together. They operated the gloveboxes, airtight boxes with access through built-in gloves that went up to the shoulders so the operators could manipulate contaminated items in a sealed container without directly touching them.

They both learned how to operate the incinerator in Building 771, used to burn plutonium-contaminated trash. They learned to clean up the liquid and solid wastes that resulted from a burn, operating pipes and tanks, adding acids and other chemicals, working the gloveboxes. The incinerator exhausted to the outside air through two banks of filters on the second floor. Building 771 had an exhaust stack 152 feet high. Incinerating radioactive and hazardous waste was a dangerous, leaky process that spewed radioactive exhaust and would never qualify for a permit under modern environmental laws.

The Rockwell workers used to laugh about that. Most of Building 771 didn't comply with environmental laws. But it had never seemed to matter. Rockwell told Jacque and Karen and the rest of the workers to just sign the papers that said they'd read the environmental laws and watched the little video, and not to worry about it. The US Justice Department had never placed a high priority on enforcing environmental laws against the US Energy Department and its defense contractors.

For the first few days after the FBI raid, the workers had watched management hurry tight-lipped through the Plant. So far, no one from Rockwell or the Energy Department had bothered to give the workers many details. All they knew was that the FBI agents had flooded into the Plant one day in their blue jump suits with big orange FBI letters on the backs and started hauling away boxes of paper and taking control of the Plant. Everyone was in an uproar, not just in Building 771, but throughout the entire hundred-building weapons plant.

Karen and Jacque had joined in the gossiping but hadn't been particularly concerned about the raid. Until June 10th, when Jacque picked up *The Denver Post* and learned what was in the search warrant. It had been unsealed the previous day at the government's request. She read the article quickly, sitting at her kitchen table, starting on her third cup of coffee. She was usually slow to wake up, but what she read that morning woke her up fast. She read the article again. Then again.

The FBI was focusing on an allegation of illegal secret midnight burning in the plutonium incinerator in Building 771.[26] In October, 1988, Energy Department headquarters in Washington, DC, had announced that the 771 incinerator would be shut down until some recurring safety problems could be remedied. Energy Department officials had made several official statements assuring the public that there was no danger and that the plutonium operations would not re-start until the Energy Department could assure itself that everything was safe.

But the FBI believed it had caught Rocky Flats illegally operating the 771 incinerator during this shutdown period. The FBI and the EPA had conducted three surveillance flights over the Plant, on the nights of December 9th, 10th and 15th, 1988 using an FBI Night Stalker aircraft complete with infrared cameras. With FBI Special Agent Lipsky aboard, they'd taken infrared videotape of what the FBI and the EPA claimed was clandestine and illegal burning from Building 771. They'd done it again in February, 1989, after the Energy Department announced that the problems were fixed and the incinerator had been restarted.

The heat signatures on the two infrared videotapes looked the same.

The FBI had caught Rocky Flats secretly burning plutonium under cover of darkness.

Jacque started shaking. She got mad. She got scared.

She and Karen had worked on the incinerator sometime in December, 1988. She realized it was probably during the time the FBI was now investigating. She hadn't known about any shutdown order.

Jacque worried about the FBI investigation all weekend. Then she went to work on Monday the 12th of June, determined to get some answers.

It may have been the nature of their jobs that made them a little brash—they risked their lives and health every day they worked in Building 771—but when management refused to tell them what the raid was all about, some of the chem ops decided to take matters into their own hands. They broke into a Rockwell management office and stole a copy of the search warrant and the affidavit of Special Agent Jon Lipsky. Management had gotten a copy the day before, as soon as the court had unsealed it at the request of the Justice Department.

Huddled together in a dark side room, they tried to piece together what the FBI investigation was all about. What was the FBI really looking for? The chem ops only had a few minutes to review the thick document, and the legalese was daunting. Jacque was surprised the FBI had provided so much detail to Rockwell and the Energy Department. It showed them right where the investigation was heading. Jacque was sure the Rocky Flats management was hurrying around this very minute, hiding the evidence, figuring out their best defense. Deciding who to blame, what it would take to get the FBI and the Justice Department off their backs. Who to use as a sacrificial offering to the big FBI machine that would need some victims because of all the publicity of the raid.

The next day, Jacque came home from work even more shaken than she'd started out. She couldn't sleep, and late that night she finally sat up in bed to write in her journal.

> *June 13th: All personnel in Building 371 were to attend a meeting in the cafeteria called by [the plutonium operations manager]. The purpose of the meeting was to give an overview of the FBI investigation. The manager was asked if all of this had anything to do with engineer Jim Stone, who was "making big noise" about the problems at Rocky Flats. The manager said, Whistleblowers will be dealt with severely and completely. Everyone knows the incinerator did not run between October 7, 1988 and February 25, 1989. Karen spoke up in the meeting and said if the FBI came to interview us, then we would tell the truth. That we would "not go down for any of the dumb butts."*

The meeting had scared both Karen and Jacque. Rockwell's manager of plutonium operations was really high-level. And Karen and Jacque now knew there had been a government-ordered shutdown in December 1988, although they hadn't known about it when they'd worked the incinerator that December. And after the June 13th employee meeting, Karen and Jacque both felt their boss had been trying to intimidate them and the rest of the workers into lying about it.

Karen and Jacque went to talk with their union steward, another Rockwell chem op. Jacque had been visibly shaken during the meeting, and the union steward was concerned because he knew she was usually emotionally unflappable and her current state was out of character.[27]

We've got to get the paperwork, Jacque whispered to Karen the next day at work. They were both starting to show signs of worry, dark circles under their eyes that the make up didn't hide.

If we have the paperwork, we can prove we weren't hiding anything, just doing our jobs like we usually did.

But they were both sure Ron Avery had gotten them into some big trouble.

Out of desperation, they started asking Rockwell management for their time cards, the documentation they'd signed the night they'd worked the overtime shift on the incinerator. The logs that would show the dates of the incinerator operation they'd worked. The labels for the drum barrels of contaminated waste they'd removed from the piping and gloveboxes and filter canisters that overtime Sunday could also be tracked.

Rockwell's response frightened them even more. First, management wouldn't give them the paperwork. And then started trying to convince the two women that the night they'd worked the incinerator was in February, after the shutdown was over, not in December.

Karen and Jacque looked at each other. Rockwell was asking them to lie to the FBI. And if they didn't, they knew they were goners.

Even if we lie like they want us to, Jacque thought as she drove home from work, that's still no guarantee that Rockwell won't throw us to the wolves anyway. And then we'd be guilty of lying, too.

She and Karen were desperate. They didn't know what to do or who to turn to.

On the car radio, Jacque heard the announcements about the FBI hotline asking for tips about crimes at Rocky Flats. She made up her mind. We really don't have any choice, she kept saying to herself. We've got to go to the FBI, no matter what the rest of the Plant thinks. It's our only chance.

It had taken the rest of the day to convince Karen to go along.

June 16th, the day after she and Karen had called the FBI hotline, the day after they'd spent hours in private with the two FBI agents, giving them statements about the overtime Sunday they'd worked on the incinerator, Jacque watched in horror as an FBI agent approached her in the cafeteria. In front of everyone, he asked her to come to the office the FBI had set up at the Plant. Her face burning, feeling the stabbing looks of her co-workers in her back, Jacque followed the agent slowly out of the room.

Soon it was all over the Plant. Karen Pitts and Jacque Brever were cooperating with the FBI. Everyone was going to lose their jobs because those two loud-mouths had decided to testify to the Grand Jury.

Karen and Jacque couldn't believe the two FBI agents who'd been debriefing them were so dumb they'd revealed the identities of their two inside informants by accident.

They did it on purpose, Jacque realized. They probably think it will make someone else come forward.

Now, when she woke up in the middle of the night, anger at the FBI was seething right alongside the worry about whether Rockwell was going to try to blame the crimes on her and Karen. But Jacque and Karen had no choice. They had to keep on cooperating. The FBI was all they had.

The hang up calls started. The muttered curses and threats from the other workers. Shut up, or we'll all lose our jobs. Damn bitch.

One night, several cars pulled up in the driveway and shadowy figures started throwing rocks at the house. Jacque flipped on the outside lights, pulled the curtains and double locked the doors. She was heading into the kitchen, determined to call the FBI, when she noticed Jessica's curly head at the living room window. Jessica had pulled aside the curtains and was staring out into the driveway, tears running down her chubby cheeks.

As Jacque hurried to pull her away from the window, she glanced outside. There, among the other chem ops tossing rocks at the house, was Jessica's father, also a Rocky Flats worker. He was staring at them with hatred, throwing rocks hard and intently at the window.

———————————

Around July, 1989, just a month after they'd called the FBI hotline, the harassment had escalated to the point that Karen and Jacque were afraid for their lives. Jacque wrote in her journal:

By this time, I had lost every friend I had in the world, except Karen and Mark. My family refused to associate with me or have any contact, with the exception of my mother, who is worried beyond belief. My seven-year-old daughter is an absolute basket case. Karen is in the same predicament, only she has two older daughters (ages 13 and 15) and her husband is working in the radioactive area on a daily basis. We mutually decided to stick very close together at work and watch each others' backs. We could not help Mark (Pitts), as he had been moved down to Building 771 in NDA.

Our children went to school and daycare with children of parents who both worked out here and other places, but were very uneducated about what was happening at Rocky Flats. One aide at the day care approached my daughter as she was getting a drink of water from the drinking fountain. She told her, You'd better not drink that water. It's poisoned and your mom did it. Karen's daughters "friends" were not much better.

August 22: My daughter had fallen at the day care and split her head open. No one gave me any message. I did not know until I went to pick her up at the regular time, after work. She now has a small scar across her forehead. I spoke with an aide at the day care. She said that she called the Plant dispatch number at X2444. She was told that I didn't work there and was hung up on.

The harassment continued. Jacque got more and more worried. She and Karen continued their usual work with the dangerous radioactive material, facing the glares from their co-workers, wondering what was going to happen next.

September 14: Karen and I reported to work for four hours early over-time. I thought it was unusual that I was asked for overtime out of spread, but I accepted anyway. I also thought it unusual that I should be assigned to work with Karen in the same room, since she usually ran one operation and I usually ran the other. And considering the harassments we were receiving and all the unusual circumstances of the morning, we carefully smeared and checked around the glove and bag ports before beginning operations.

Karen and I started repack operations. I reached my arm in the glove to move a bottle. As soon as I did, the alarm sounded. Karen donned her respirator as she was just standing next to me. I pulled my arm out of the glove and monitored my hand. My glove was hot, so I removed it. I donned my respirator and we headed for the combo to monitor ourselves and leave the room. As I walked by, another alarm went off. I told Karen that it was one of us. She monitored herself out. She was OK. It was I who was contaminated. This was approximately 0600 hours. Karen went to phone the monitors to tell them that I was contaminated. She returned to the doorway, but could only watch helplessly as I stood with a contaminated respirator on my contaminated face and I could not move, as my sleeves, hands, and coveralls were contaminated and any movement would have only exacerbated the situation. Ten or 15 minutes later, a monitor came lazily yawning and stretching down the hall.

While I was standing in the doorway, waiting for [the radiation monitor] to do all this in the room 3206, [two chem. ops] came down the hallway. They saw me and started laughing. They came over and one of them said, "Well, that's what you get for making waves."

The radiation levels the monitor read on Jacque were higher than the machines were able to count. She'd been totally contaminated. And she knew it was her union brothers and sisters who had done it. Jacque was now petrified. The chem ops had known the dose they'd given her could be lethal. And they'd done it anyway. She wasn't going to die immediately. Maybe months, maybe years. But they'd known it was a deadly thing to do and they'd done it to her anyway. One of their own.

Jacque and Karen were angry and distrustful of everyone by now, including the two FBI agents who'd used them as bait. But there was nowhere else to go for help. They stormed the office of lead FBI agent Jon Lipsky.

Special Agent Lipsky looked furious when Jacque tracked him down and told him out about the contamination incident. And even more furious when he found out the two FBI agents had been telling everyone they interviewed that "Jacque and Karen say. . . ." His concern had made Jacque feel a little better. But it didn't make them any safer. Together, they called the lead prosecutor at the US Attorney's Office, Ken Fimberg. Fimberg wrote to Rockwell, insisting that Karen and Jacque be transferred to the "cold side," away from the dangerous radioactive work. The two women waited anxiously. They were afraid Fimberg's efforts were going to make things worse.

October 4th: I was startled to notice a huge, odd shaped bruise on my right arm. It didn't hurt and I couldn't remember hitting it. Upon further inspection, I noticed that I had small versions of this all over my right leg and upper torso.

Jacque's hair was starting to fall out and the green and yellow bruises were spreading up and down her arms. She was waiting for the next attack. She couldn't quit her job, though, sick and scared as she was. The mortgage payment, Jessica's private school. But she knew the other chem ops wouldn't stop until she and Karen quit. Every time the two of them went to work, every time they went into the locker room, down a dark hall in the snake pit, they were in danger. A pinprick hole in the glovebox again. A little "radioactive surprise" left in their street clothes.

They've already done it once, Jacque thought. They've decided we're the enemy. Those high-paying jobs are so important to them they'll close their eyes to all the safety problems, all the crimes and environmental damage and just pull their paychecks. Anything, anyone that threatens their jobs is the enemy.

Jacque and Karen grew more and more afraid at work. The other chem ops wouldn't talk to them, wouldn't look them in the eye. They were totally isolated. It occurred to Jacque more than once that she didn't have to testify to the Grand Jury, she could back out of the whole mess. But she knew it was all over for her at the Plant. They'd never let her back in the fold after what she'd already done. She really had no choice except to go forward.

Then they got the good news. Fimberg had pulled it off. They were immediately transferred away from the radioactive side of the Plant.

Jacque was so grateful she could only shake her head and squeeze back tears. They weren't going to be totally safe, but at least they wouldn't be working with the dangerous stuff anymore. Contaminating her again would be a little bit harder.

The transfer to the "cold side" came through the day before Jacque Brever went downtown to testify to the Grand Jury.

CHAPTER THREE

The Grand Jury,
August 1st,1989

Black-robed Federal Judge Sherman Finesilver swore in the 23 Grand Jurors who would investigate Rocky Flats on August 1st, 1989. He was formal and severe, looking down at the seated Grand Jurors over his half-rims, leaning on his big wooden desk.

"Ladies and gentlemen of the Grand Jury, you have now been impaneled and sworn as a Grand Jury. . . . The government attorneys cannot dominate or command your actions. . . . In performing your duties, you are free to exercise your own judgment without fear or favor and shall not be deterred or influenced by the criticism of the public, the prosecutor or the court. . . . It is every person's duty to conform his acts to the laws enacted by Congress. All are equal under the law, and no one is above the law. . . . The Special Grand Jury may submit a report to the court. Through the vehicle of this Special Grand Jury Report, the public may be assisted in learning of the facts as they relate to Rocky Flats."[28]

When Wes McKinley received the summons to serve on what came to be known as the Rocky Flats Grand Jury, he'd had to drive 40 miles into town from his ranch south of Walsh to ask the barber, who'd had some experience on a Grand Jury, to explain.[*] Wes didn't have a TV, didn't often leave the ranch his granddad had homesteaded in southeastern Colorado near the Kansas and Oklahoma borders, and had never heard of Rocky Flats Nuclear Weapons Plant.

He started learning fast. Almost immediately, the prosecutors and the judge had started talking to the Grand Jury about writing a report, in

---

[*] A Grand Jury's primary function is to determine whether there is enough evidence that a crime has been committed to support bringing criminal charges (probable cause). If so, a criminal prosecution and trial by a regular trial jury normally follow.

addition to issuing criminal indictments. That's one of the reasons for impaneling a Special Grand Jury; a regular Grand Jury doesn't write reports. Also, they were to concentrate only on Rocky Flats, not hear all sorts of cases like a regular Grand Jury. They'd be in Denver for a week each month for as long as it took, and they were cautioned that it might take a very long time.

Wes could have been excused from serving on the Grand Jury. It was a five hour drive from Walsh to Denver, and spending a week each month away from the ranch made more work for everyone else. It was hard to be away from Jan and the kids, and he wasn't used to the big city. They were really isolated out there in Walsh.

But he was intrigued. He remembered back to his civic classes in grade school. A one-room school house for all eight grades. He'd joined the other kids pledging allegiance to the flag every day in the dusty schoolyard. And they'd all meant it, he was sure.

Wes was as patriotic as the next guy, but he never thought he'd be called on to do more than vote, raise his kids right, and work hard. Then came the summons from the Denver Federal District courthouse to serve on the Rocky Flats Grand Jury.

Polio had kept Wes from Viet Nam, but Grand Jury service was something he could do for his country. Wes became the foreman of the Rocky Flats Special Grand Jury after three other Jurors dropped out.

Late in the afternoon of that August 1st, Jan McKinley came in from feeding the horses. The light was settling over the Colorado grasslands. She wiped her forehead, her shirt sticking to her back. It was a plain looking kitchen, but clean and homey, and Jan moved efficiently in the small space. She switched on a table lamp and pressed the button on an old-fashioned phone answering machine.

The corny phone machine greeting was sung slightly off key in Wes' Colorado cowboy twang. Jan moved about the kitchen, preparing supper, waiting for the end of his recorded message. There was some cowboy guitar music first.

MACHINE: The phone is ringing
It's ringing off the wall.
So please won't you tell me
What is the purpose of your call?

Children came and went and were put to work helping with the chores. There were two teenage girls, Toni and Tamra, still at home. Slim was already away at college.

When the greeting ended, there was a brief silence before the caller's message. It was Wes, in the same cheerful cowboy twang as the recorded greeting.

MACHINE: Howdy, dear ones. Made it up here fine.
Took five hours and the pick-up only needed water twice.

Jan smiled knowingly as she listened to the message, shooing the kids around the kitchen as they set the supper table.

MACHINE: Still don't know why a Grand Jury is investigating Rocky Flats Nuclear Weapons Plant—whatever that is—or what I'm supposed to be doing on the Grand Jury, but I guess I'll find out. Tell you all about it when I see you.

Tamra was using her kid-size cowboy hat to chase some clucking chickens out in the yard beyond the kitchen door. The kitchen noise got louder, and Toni went over and turned up the volume on the answering machine.

MACHINE: Truth is, it really doesn't sound that interesting. But I got picked, so I guess it's my duty to serve.

The voice got a little louder, and slower.

MACHINE: Kids, don't forget your homework.
I'll finish helping you when I get back.
Don't forget to water your mother's roses.

The two girls nodded seriously, as though their dad were in the room. The voice returned to normal speed and twang.

MACHINE: You help your mother with my part
of the chores, and all of you say your prayers and be good.

The voice changed yet again, this time a little huskier.

MACHINE: Janice, darlin', see you tonight in my dreams.

Jan turned red and flustered and hurried to shut off the answering machine. Toni and Tamra elbowed each other, giggling.

———————————

After lunch that first day of Grand Jury session, Wes walked slowly back up the long concrete walkway to the courthouse entrance. He'd spent the lunch hour roaming the streets of downtown Denver, watching peoples' faces, listening to them talk as they hurried about their business. It was a different kind of stimulation for Wes, who was used to spending most of the day outside, with just his horses, the cattle, and his dogs. Wes had gone to college in a small town in western Oklahoma with no more than a few hundred people. He'd taught high-school physics for a while. But he'd preferred being outside, so he turned to ranching fulltime.

Wes was sorry to have to go back inside. It made him feel cooped up, being indoors all day. As he headed up to the revolving door, he paused to look curiously at a small crowd of protesters gathered near the steps.

Must be some of those hippies, Wes thought with interest. They stared at him as he walked past, his cowboy boots thudding dully on the hard concrete.

One man with a long beard and no shoes looked a little different than the rest. While the others chanted, and waved their signs, he just stood there quietly holding his sign in front of his chest. He looked Wes in the eyes and smiled peacefully. Wes returned the smile and tipped his hat. Then, from the corner of his eye, he noticed some hurried movement in his direction. He turned to find Assistant US Attorney Fimberg striding towards him.

Better just ignore these protesters, Fimberg advised as he urged Wes to join him back inside. It's better if you don't pay them any attention.

Wes was surprised, but followed the prosecutor back into the Grand Jury chambers.

Fimberg's the government lawyer, so he must be right about steering clear of the protesters, Wes thought. But something didn't sit right about that, so privately he made up his mind that he'd stop back by another time and just listen to what those folks had to say. They'd been standing outside in a hot summer sun, so it must seem important to them, if not to the prosecutors.

The Grand Jurors went home after that first week in August without hearing any testimony. And the September session was cancelled. But on

October 15th, 1989, Wes rode the bus the five hours up to Denver and checked into La Quinta, ready to start his first week of Grand Jury testimony the following morning.

Wes watched Jacque Brever walk nervously into the Grand Jury room. Looks to be almost 6 feet tall, Wes thought to himself. Tall enough to be a little less scared of a bunch of lawyers.

It never occurred to him that it might be the Grand Jury the witness was afraid of.

Actually, the whole process was a little intimidating. The witness was directed to a high-backed chair surrounded by a low railing on the ground level of the room. The seats rose up the wall in front of her like an amphitheater. The Grand Jurors were spread out in front of her, almost all looking down at her, eyeing her with curiosity. In the back, at the top row, in the center of the room, sat Wes McKinley. He was about as far away from her as he could get, yet somehow she kept looking up at him where he sat, his chair sort of cocked back against the wall, cowboy hat on his knee.

She was dying for a cigarette, he was dying for a chew. But they were stuck in the Grand Jury chambers without a break for the next four hours.

First time this gal's probably ever sat in a witness stand, Wes thought suddenly, realizing why she might look so nervous when the prior witnesses had not. After all, that guy Lipsky's an FBI agent, and he's probably testified a million times before.

Wes softened a little, and watched with interest as the frightened young woman settled in and looked nervously around the room.

It was hard to imagine her working with things like that caustic filtering process. She looked so feminine sitting in the witness chair in her white crepe blouse and black skirt. She even had a manicure and her blonde hair was done to fall in curls around her face.

An attractive woman, Wes thought. She probably had a mite of trouble in there with all the men.

She had a soft little girl voice that surprised him from such a tall woman. But she knew her job; you could tell that from what she said.

Jacque explained that she and her friend Karen Pitts had been asked by a foreman, Ron Avery, to work an overtime Sunday sometime around Christmas, 1988. She wasn't sure of the exact date, but she knew it was right before Christmas. It was frosty cold that Sunday morning. She, Karen Pitts, and another worker had needed to borrow parkas from Building 371, where they'd changed into their coveralls, for the walk to Building 771. She had teased Karen and Al about the frost that was forming on their faces as they walked down the hill to the 771 incinerator building.

Another foreman directed Jacque and Karen to the incinerator and told them they'd be taking it down. Taking it down meant cleaning up after the incinerator had been run. They could tell the incinerator had been run by the mess in the burn box. In fact, the incinerator was still hot from being run the night before, and they'd had to wait several hours while it cooled down. The color of the sludge on the filter flywheel also clearly showed that the incinerator had been burning.

Jacque had made hourly notes, as required, of the temperature reading on the burn box. Meanwhile, they cleaned up the other processes that get fouled when the incinerator is fired up, using the gloveboxes and periodically checking the temperature of the burn box to see when it would be cool enough to sweep out.

Later, through a glovebox, she and Karen broomed the contaminated ash from the burn box into a pile and packaged it for disposal. They'd marked the drum with a label and signed off and dated other paperwork that was supposed to account for the burned plutonium residue.

They'd thought nothing further about the burn until they read about the search warrant in the paper. They hadn't known Rockwell had been ordered to shut down the incinerator.

At the end of the day, the exhausted witness had left the witness box and the Grand Jurors sat silently looking at each other. There was a somber mood that day after Jacque Brever left. Wes thought some of the Jurors looked frightened, others angry. Though they didn't talk much, they were all worried about the same thing.

What else were they lying about at Rocky Flats?

At the end of that first session of Grand Jury testimony, Wes left the rest of the Grand Jurors at the front of the courthouse and hurried to catch the bus home to Walsh. During the long trip, he started a journal. The witness Brever had been reading from one, and he thought it was a good idea.

Wes' journal Oct. 24, 1989: Jacque Brever: Sincere and sometimes frightened, but at all times she seemed truthful. Blonde, not too big, not too bold and not too beautiful. She cried sincerely, her emotions were open. She seemed to want to save the world and America in particular from RF. I could see how she could alienate her co-workers, because when they did things wrong, she was quick to run and tell. This may not be a fault when you're working with nuclear weapons. In open court, the prosecutors told us we were impanelled to investigate allegations of environmental crimes being committed at RF. After listening to this lady all day, looks like I can expect a short tenure as a Grand Jurist. It hasn't taken them long to prove environmental crimes were probably committed.

Wes' journal Oct. 26, 1989: Karen Pitts. Tough, tough. Even dressed in red. If I had any doubts about Jacque's story, I can lay them to rest. Karen verified Jacque's frightening story. The newspapers had printed stories of illegal burnings and today after Pitts, it looks like the newspapers can actually print the truth every once in a while.

Jon Lipsky wasn't allowed in the Grand Jury Room while Karen Pitts and Jacque Brever testified. Even Rockwell and the Energy Department weren't allowed in. Only witnesses, Grand Jurors, the court stenographer, and the prosecutors. So Lipsky was eagerly waiting to hear how things went. The midnight burning charge was important to the case. It wasn't the worst environmental crime they'd be focusing on, by any stretch of the imagination. The routine incineration of plutonium-contaminated trash that had been going on for decades was a much greater public health risk. The Bureau was looking at that, too.

But despite the fact that the secret midnight plutonium burning involved only a few nights of illegal plutonium incineration the FBI happened to catch with their spy plane, it was still important.

They'd caught Rockwell lying to the government. And lying to the government could result in debarment,[*] something Jon Lipsky was look-

---

[*] A formal process by which the government decides not to do business with a company, usually because of fraud or other forms of cheating.

ing at hard. If Rockwell had been lying to the government—and from what he'd seen so far, that was something they'd have little trouble proving—the huge and powerful defense contractor would never get another government contract again. Lipsky wanted to send a message to the other defense contractors, too. He wanted to put an end to the good old days where environmental crimes were just ignored.

Lipsky heard about Brever and Pitts' testimony from Prosecutor Fimberg.

They weren't very reliable, Fimberg announced.[29] The Grand Jury hadn't believed Karen Pitts and Jacque Brever; they'd come across like troublemakers out to get Rockwell.

Lipsky had been surprised; he'd met the two women and found them to be very believable. And they were important witnesses. In fact, they were the only eye witnesses the FBI had to the illegal midnight burn.

But the determination of whether a witness is to be believed is up to the Grand Jury, he reminded himself, not me. Lipsky had no reason to doubt Fimberg's assessment of the Grand Jurors' reaction. Lipsky figured the next witness, the infrared analyst, would do the trick. He was to testify about the FBI's nighttime infrared overflight video, which had caught Rockwell in the act of the secret midnight plutonium burning.

During the pre-raid investigation, the EPA in Denver, working with the FBI, had arranged with the EPA in Las Vegas to analyze the nighttime infrared surveillance films from the Night Stalker over-flights at Rocky Flats. Selected black and white stills were made from the videotapes, and a photographic interpretation expert had reviewed and compared them to a photo of the site layout. He annotated a written report showing which areas of the Plant were thermally active, or hot, in December, 1988, and which were not.

The infrared film read in black and white. White means hot, black means cold. According to the infrared expert, on December 9th, 10th, and 15th, 1988, the 771 incinerator was white. Hot. The incinerator was operating on December 9th, 10th, and 15th, 1988, during the time it was supposed to be shut down.

The infrared evidence was objective proof. It was what prosecutors want when presenting evidence to a Grand Jury: an actual picture of the crime. The FBI had used it to support the sworn statements in the search warrant affidavit.

Rockwell howled in the newspapers and to Justice Department headquarters in Washington, DC that the secret midnight burning had never happened. Rockwell could lose its multi-billion dollar defense contracts if caught doing something like that.

But Fimberg and Lipsky had talked with the infrared expert together, before he went into the Grand Jury room to testify. They were both satisfied he'd provided the evidence needed to support the search warrant allegations.

Lipsky was eagerly anticipating the news from Fimberg after the infrared analyst testified to the Grand Jury. He talked to Fimberg later the same day.

The witness changed his mind, Fimberg told a stunned Lipsky. The infrared expert had done a complete flip-flop. Some of the Grand Jurors, especially Peck[*] had asked some pretty pointed questions.

The infrared expert had testified that he really couldn't say how hot the incinerator was, just that some heat was coming out of the stack.

Well, was the heat just the same as normal room temperature?

The witness couldn't answer.

How hot was it? How could he tell it was hot enough to prove the incinerator was operating?

He couldn't say.

The one-two punches were hitting Lipsky hard. First, the Grand Jury dissed the only eye witnesses to the illegal burn. Then the main technological expert changed his mind.

What's happening here? Lipsky asked himself after Fimberg had delivered the bad news about the infrared expert. What's happening to the investigation?

Lipsky heard only Fimberg's version of the events in the Grand Jury room; he hadn't heard the infrared witness testify. But Lipsky knew there was other evidence that the secret midnight plutonium burn had occurred. Putting aside his concern over the unraveling investigation, he decided he'd keep on investigating, put together whatever other evidence there was, and let the Grand Jurors make up their minds about whether and what to indict.

But Jon Lipsky, Jacque Brever and Wes McKinley were all in for a surprise. Each of them, separately, opened their newspapers and saw Mark Obmascik's article in *The Denver Post* on November 30th, 1989,

---

[*] Grand Juror Ken Peck is a Denver attorney.

two weeks after the infrared expert had testified to the Grand Jury.

"Illegal burn didn't occur, officials say."

Governor Roy Romer and US Representative David Skaggs said they believe that no midnight burn took place. Romer said that after talking with Rocky Flats officials and federal investigators, "I have concluded that it didn't occur. For that incinerator to run at midnight without any people knowing it would be virtually impossible."

The Governor said he has told several federal officials that he considered the charge to be "unfair and bad government." He said the accusation caused needless public worries about dangerous pollution from Rocky Flats, located 15 miles northwest of Denver.

Skaggs, a Boulder Democrat whose congressional district includes Rocky Flats, said his own personal investigation supported that conclusion.

"I have spoken to many people involved in that FBI investigation, and from what I can tell, I just don't think that the facts are going to substantiate some of the more spectacular allegations the FBI made in its affidavit," said Skaggs.

Lipsky was so angry he could barely speak. This was an obvious leak of secret Rule 6(e) Grand Jury information, a federal crime punishable by a prison sentence. And it was clear from the newspaper article that the leak had come from the US Justice Department.

Why had they done it? The article clearly signaled that the US Attorney's Office was dropping the midnight plutonium burning charge. It was bad enough to break the Grand Jury secrecy rules, but to so clearly signal to Rockwell and the Energy Department that the charge was being dropped. . . .

Lipsky just couldn't understand it. He hadn't been consulted. If Ken Fimberg and Mike Norton had asked his opinion, he wouldn't have agreed.

Too soon, he would have told the two prosecutors. It's too soon. We haven't finished the investigation yet. There's lots of other evidence out there. It's only the second session of Grand Jury testimony. Let's wait. If the rest of the evidence doesn't pan out, we'll use it as a bargaining chip. . . .

Nobody at the Justice Department had bothered to let Jacque Brever
know they'd decided the secret midnight plutonium burning hadn't happened. Jacque was bewildered when she read the newspaper article, then
she started getting angry.

How can they say it never happened? I was *there*. I saw the incinerator. Karen saw it, too. How can they just decide it never happened? Just
like that!

Why did I risk everything? she fumed. Everything!

Karen, too, was beside herself. The two women discussed it end-
lessly, but could make no sense of it.

Why would Lipsky and Fimberg go to so much trouble for us? Take
our side against management? They probably saved our lives getting us
transferred out of plutonium operations. Why'd they do all that if they
didn't believe us? the two wondered.

After a while, Jacque couldn't stand to think about the midnight plutonium burning anymore. It was me, she concluded miserably. The Grand
Jury didn't believe me. I guess I didn't explain it right. I remember they
just kept staring at me while I was testifying. I was so nervous, I must
have really blown it.

Jacque's mom had an entirely different attitude. You should be
relieved, she said earnestly. You and Karen don't have to testify again.
Maybe the other chem ops will let it drop. Maybe you can both go back
to the way it was before.

But Jacque just shook her head. You think the midnight burning was
the only crime out there? she snorted. I've been keeping a journal of
safety problems for years. I've given it to the union, and to Rockwell
management, too, but they've just ignored it. So I gave it to the Grand
Jury. There's so much criminal activity, so many safety problems, this is
our chance to have someone from the outside make them fix it. We've got
to keep feeding the FBI information.

Jacque's mom was incredulous.

You're going to keep helping the FBI after they dumped on you the
way they did? They've hung you and Karen out to dry. Everyone will
know the FBI and the Grand Jury didn't believe you. And you're going
to keep helping them?

But Jacque was determined. She and Karen Pitts continued their
interviews with the FBI, telling them more and more about the environ-

mental crimes at Rocky Flats.

The harassment from their co-workers continued. Jacque and Karen begged the FBI to come to the Plant site with them, to show the other Rockwell workers that the FBI was still around. To offer them a little protection.

The FBI said that wasn't possible.

Jacque and Karen were on their own.

Wes McKinley read the news later than Jacque Brever and Jon Lipsky. Newspapers weren't delivered to his ranch outside Walsh. Wes saw the article by chance, when Jan brought a stack of used newspapers back from school.

His face darkened as he read the news that the Justice Department had talked about the secret Grand Jury investigation with the Governor and a Congressman. And then those two politicians had talked to the press.

Wes jerked his coat off the hook by the kitchen door and stomped out into the cold and windy dusk. The Grand Jury investigation is supposed to be confidential, he kept muttering to himself as he finished the last of the chores. The judge told us it's up to the Grand Jury to decide whether there's enough evidence to indict about the midnight plutonium burning, not those politicians, not the FBI, not the US Attorneys, not whoever it was who was talking out of school about secret Grand Jury proceedings.

Why'd they do it? he kept thinking. That's not the way it's supposed to work.

Wes started watching Ken Fimberg even more closely after *The Denver Post* article came out. He was getting suspicious. Why would the Justice Department breach Grand Jury secrecy rules? But he kept his thoughts to himself. Wes brought some flip top steno pad notebooks to take notes of the evidence. He saw with satisfaction that several of the other Grand Jurors had also brought paper and pen.

Good, he thought. Otherwise, when we write our report, we'll have to rely on the attorneys to remind us what the evidence was. They may be government lawyers, but the judge's instructions were to not give up our independence to anyone, including the prosecutors.

When the Grand Jury was in session, Wes frequently got to the chambers early. He was used to getting up before dawn at the ranch and saw no reason to change that habit just because he was spending his nights in a tiny Denver hotel room. He would often roam the early morning streets of downtown Denver, waiting for Grand Jury session to start, watching people start their city lives, so very different from his. Being outdoors helped him think, even if it was only in a city.

When the courthouse finally opened, he'd go in and make coffee and get the evidence files out of the sealed vault, so everything would be ready when the rest of the Grand Jurors arrived. Ken Fimberg was often in the Grand Jury chambers early, too, sitting in a corner at a table, working quietly on his voluminous files.

Fimberg and McKinley didn't do much other than nod at each other in the beginning, but then there had been some casual conversation at the coffee machine. Wes had gotten to know the lead prosecutor a little, but still felt he was a puzzle. And after the Justice Department broke Grand Jury secrecy to say in the newspapers that the secret midnight plutonium burning hadn't happened, Wes was puzzled *and* worried.

He doesn't look like a snake in the grass, Wes thought several times after Fimberg left the coffee machine chat and went back to his files. But then, they hardly ever do.

We'll just have to wait and see, Wes thought to himself, and then the Grand Jury will decide about all this.

CHAPTER FOUR

The Justice Department Ends the Grand Jury Investigation, March 26th, 1992

Jacque Brever went to work every day at Rocky Flats, wondering when one of her co-workers was going to get her again, trying not to think about the Grand Jury investigation. Every time she remembered the newspaper article saying the midnight plutonium burning had never happened she burned with humiliation and sadness.

The Grand Jury didn't believe me, she thought miserably. I'm too stupid to make them understand.

Her mom was pushing her to quit. They're going to come after you, again, Jacque. Why don't you just leave? she insisted.

Jacque shook her head and kept her chin down. She was thinking about the mortgage payments. Where else can I earn enough money for me and Jessica without even a high school diploma?

So she kept trying not to think about it, avoiding her co-workers and the "hot" side of the Plant. It's hard for them to get to me here, she tried to reassure her mother. But she knew if they wanted to get her, they would.

On March 26th, 1992, Jacque picked up the newspaper. The Grand Jury investigation came back to her like a bad dream. The Justice Department had ended the Grand Jury investigation, deciding to settle the case instead of going to trial. The prosecutors announced their plea bargain proudly,[30] asserting that the $18.5 million fine against the Rockwell corporation was a new record.

But Jacque was stunned to read the details. There had been no real off-site harm caused by Rocky Flats, the prosecutors insisted. US Attorney Mike Norton's public statements were even broader. "I know of no evidence of any physiological or environmental damage *at all* from the operations of the facility."[31] And not enough evidence to charge any individuals with crimes, either from Rockwell or the Energy Department. Instead, the corporation would plead guilty, mostly to some minor charges, and pay the fine.

No off-site harm? Jacque was incredulous. Everyone at the Plant knew the water they were discharging off-site was contaminated. Everyone knew about the radioactive ash from the incinerator blowing around in the dust, on and off the Plant.

But what really hit her the hardest was the Plea Agreement the prosecutors filed to record the official language of the deal with Rockwell. In it the Justice Department had officially announced that there'd been no secret midnight plutonium burning. It wasn't just speculation in the newspapers anymore, now it was official.

Jacque started shaking. It's a total cover-up, she thought, panic rising in her like an uncontrollable flood. Rocky Flats has cut a deal with the US Justice Department and now everyone knows they can get away with murder.

Jacque Brever resigned from Rocky Flats and went into hiding.

Jon Lipsky knew about the plea bargain before it was announced in the newspapers. Still, he gripped the paper angrily when the story of the plea bargain broke.

If they want to cave in and settle it, go ahead, he thought bitterly, but why lie about it? People are going to rely on what this investigation says about the dangers of Rocky Flats, and it needs to be the truth.

Norton and Fimberg were publicly lauding the plea bargain. It wouldn't have helped to take the case to trial, they told the court and the public. If we'd won and the court had imposed a fine against Rockwell, the taxpayers would probably have ended up paying Rockwell back.[32] That's in Rockwell's contract with the Energy Department, they kept repeating. But in the settlement, Rockwell agreed to pay the fine.

And Norton and Fimberg both emphasized that the problems at Rocky Flats hadn't been that bad after all. The sentencing memorandum, filed to convince the judge to approve the plea bargain, insists:

> *Based on the evidence gathered in this investigation, and to the best of the Justice Department's present knowledge and information, the conduct to which ROCKWELL has pled guilty did not result in substantial physiological harm, or the threat of substantial physiological harm, to members of the public residing and working outside Rocky Flat's boundaries. Environmental*

impacts appear to have been substantially limited to inside the Plant's boundaries.

Lipsky remembered back to the search warrant affidavit, full of many of the important facts he and his team had uncovered before Justice Department headquarters got involved. The search warrant had detailed some of the off-site impacts from Rocky Flats: "documented releases of plutonium and tritium . . . hazardous waste and constituents are also being released from the site. . . . Volatile organic compounds have been detected in groundwater in concentrations up to 16ppm of tetrachloroethylene. . . . The liquid portion of the exposed wastes evaporates, leaving the radioactive wastes to be carried by winds to other, including off-site, areas."

Jon Lipsky hadn't been consulted about the plea bargain. The prosecutors knew he didn't agree with what they were doing, so they cut him out of the negotiations almost from the beginning. When he heard the bottom lines of the settlement, he was bitter, but resigned. Headquarters had decided to take a plea, and there was nothing he or anyone else could do to change their minds. The investigation was over, the crimes had been hidden from the public, and no one was ever going to know about it.

Jon Lipsky believed in the Bureau, believed in justice and the legal system, and kept hoping somehow, someone was going to rescue this investigation he'd worked his heart out for.

It wasn't going to be Ken Fimberg, he knew that. Ken had fought hard in the beginning, but recently, he'd given in. It had strained their friendship to the point of breaking.

Lipsky thought back to his last real conversation with Fimberg. He'd stopped the harried prosecutor in the hall, and asked for a word, and from the look on Fimberg's face when he nodded, Lipsky knew his friend was not looking forward to the exchange. But he'd been honest that one last time, Lipsky remembered.

You're right, Fimberg had told him, sitting across from Lipsky at the cluttered desk. We should have indicted the individuals. There was more than enough evidence. I tried to convince them, but I was outvoted by the other prosecutors.

When is someone going to catch them at it, Lipsky wondered? When is someone going to look at that search warrant affidavit again, listen to the drivel the Justice Department is spouting, and start asking some hard questions?

Lipsky asked himself that same question over and over, but got no answer.

Then, slowly, word started to leak out that the Grand Jury had written a report and wanted to speak publicly about it. Lipsky held his breath. What could the Grand Jury do? He knew about their report, he'd even seen a copy someone from the Justice Department had pilfered from the Grand Jury vault. It was a bombshell, all right. But what could the Grand Jurors do? They were all under orders never to talk about the Rocky Flats Grand Jury investigation, or face prison for contempt of court.

Lipsky became increasingly despondent. He went to work, did his job, but was almost numb. He'd always wanted to join the FBI. But not to be used like this. Not to be totally and completely used in the name of a cover-up.

Wes McKinley had started reading the newspapers regularly towards the end of the almost three-year Grand Jury investigation. Ever since the Justice Department convinced the Governor and Congressman Skaggs that there'd been no secret midnight plutonium burning, he'd been worried about what the prosecutors were up to. He knew for sure they were doing something different from what the Grand Jury had voted on. So when the Grand Jury, over opposition from the Justice Department, had written up its findings, he'd taken pains to get the Grand Jury's documents to the judge, instead of leaving them with the prosecutors.

And when Special Grand Jury 89-2 had been discharged two days before the plea bargain was filed, the 23 Colorado citizens agreed to keep in touch by phone until they knew for sure what the judge was going to do.

On March 26th, 1992, two days after the Grand Jury had been discharged, Wes read the news of the Justice Department's plea bargain in the newspaper Jan brought home that day from school.

No mention of our Grand Jury Report, Wes muttered. The judge is probably still reading it. Wait till he sees what the Justice Department did to us. Wait till he sees what a fraud that plea bargain really is.

But it was hard for Wes to wait. The prosecutors were busy convincing the public that Rocky Flats hadn't been all that contaminated after all and that the Grand Jury agreed with the plea bargain.

We're not allowed to say anything, he told Jan, even though the Justice Department is lying.

We'll just wait, Wes told the other Grand Jurors. When the judge reads our Grand Jury Report, and releases it to the public, it'll all be clear.

The prosecutors tried to run all over us, was all he would tell Jan. I'm not allowed to talk about it. But you'll see what they're up to when the judge releases our Grand Jury Report. Rocky Flats is one of the most contaminated places in the country. Don't let that hogwash from the Justice Department convince you otherwise.

But a few months later, after waiting patiently for the report to be released, Wes picked up *The Denver Post* and learned that Judge Finesilver had ordered the Rocky Flats Grand Jury Report sealed from public view.[33]

Wes and Jan had been sitting together as usual at the kitchen table, the kids in bed, the chores done or delayed. It was the quiet time of the evening, so Wes' fist slamming on the table startled Jan. She looked up to see him clutching the newspaper, his jaw working spasmodically. Before she could even ask, Wes was up and out the door, not even putting a coat on, trying hard not to slam the door behind him.

When he came back in a while later, Jan was waiting patiently. She knew he'd cool off and come back and explain, but that was the maddest she'd ever seen him.

He read the article to her, his voice steely. "The court is not satisfied that the report of the Rocky Flats Special Grand Jury meets the statutory standard for release as a public record," Finesilver had written in a four-page order. "The report is ordered sealed and it shall not be filed as a public record."

The judge took a very public swipe at the Grand Jury. "It is with great regret that the court notes that the Grand Jury, having the opportunity to inform the public of the facts of Rocky Flats, failed in its duty."

We asked the judge to help us, Wes told Jan firmly. We asked him more than once. But he never would. He's got no call to be complaining about what we wrote. And when he wouldn't help us, Peck went back to his law office and looked up the statutory standards, and we followed them. The Justice Department just doesn't want the public to know the truth about Rocky Flats. *That's* why the judge is sealing our report.

A few weeks later, someone leaked the sealed Grand Jury Report to a local newspaper. The article by Bryan Abas in *Westword* stunned the Denver area.[34] Not all the report was included. But the public now knew that the Grand Jury had written indictments of high-level Energy Department and Rockwell officials. And that the prosecutors had refused to sign them. Now people knew the Grand Jury felt the prosecutors had lied to them and obstructed their work.

Judge Finesilver's reaction was prompt and to the point. On October 16th, 1992, he issued a request that the Justice Department investigate the 23 members of the Rocky Flats Grand Jury for violation of Rule 6(e) secrecy requirements.[35] Norton asked the FBI to get involved in the investigation.[36]

Suddenly, the Grand Jurors, not the government polluters, were under investigation.

Wes' journal Nov. 1992: I don't like the idea of being a sitting duck, waiting around for the FBI to come and take shots at us. Peck was the Grand Jurist I talked with the most about this. Peck and I decided to play Norton's game and seek some media cover.

Peck and I got together and came up with the idea of contacting newly elected president Clinton and enlisting his help. We realized we would never get him on the phone and we have no money to fly to Washington, and if we did the chances of meeting with him would lie half way between nil and none.

We decided to hold a press conference on the federal court house plaza and read a letter we will write to president elect Bill Clinton asking him to investigate the Justice Department he has just inherited.

Bill Clinton had campaigned as the environmental President. His running mate, Al Gore, had been in Denver campaigning before the election and had said the Grand Jury Report should be released.

The local TV stations have been clamoring for me to go in front of their cameras and in their words "be a talking head." The press conference will give them the opportunity they ask for and by reading the letter I can be their talking head and hopefully not say anything that will violate the Grand Jury rule of secrecy and get me thrown in jail. The judge is mad enough to throw me in, all he needs now is an excuse.

Peck and I decided if we were going to be investigated by the Justice Department, then we should have the Justice Department investigated, too. We composed the letter asking the new president to investigate the judge and the prosecutor's mishandling of the Rocky Flats environmental violations. Eleven other jurors signed it. We sent out notices to all the Denver media and prepared a pile of newspaper clippings we sent to everyone who requested them. *NBC Dateline, ABC Inside Edition, Frontline PBS*, and the major magazines and newspapers requested our press packet.

Wes' journal The Grand Jury Press Conference

Nov. 19, 1992: This morning, early, I went to Peck's downtown office, a block down and within sight of the courthouse, where we put the finishing touches on our letter to Clinton. Peck and his secretary manned the phones and kept the reporters away while I practiced my letter reading.

A few minutes till high noon. Time to go forth. Peck came in. When he asked, I told him I was ready. We took the elevator down and stepped out on the sidewalk. I expected a crowd of reporters and flashing lights from cameras with people waiting and shouting questions. No one was there.

I had shaved, washed and combed what little hair I have left. We walked down the block, turned the corner to the courthouse. They were there. The federal courthouse plaza was filled with people. Reporters, TV camera crews, ordinary citizens who support the Grand Jury's efforts, a few thrill seekers wanting to see me arrested, enough government agents to keep order and several FBI agents with warrants for my arrest.

I walked up to the bank of microphones and began my speech. I thanked the good folks for coming out here today, and started right in reading our letter to president-elect Clinton. I thought about telling the crowd if I had known there would be such a large gathering I would have sprayed my underarms with something powerful smelling, but I refrained from doing so.

The cameras flashed. TV crews jockeyed for position. Somehow, I got through it. My letter read, I asked if there were any questions. There were many. The reporters wanted to know if the report that was printed in the *Westword* article was the real Grand Jury Report and they wanted to know about the indictments of Rockwell upper level personnel and Energy Department officials.

I knew the answer to these questions but I could not respond to them because to do so would have been a violation of the Grand Jury secrecy rule. The FBI agents, warrants in hand, waited for me to make one slip and reveal information that could only have came from behind the closed door of the Grand Jury room. Had I done so, they would have thrown the cuffs on me and off to jail I would be marched.

I very carefully gave answers that were not in violation of the secrecy rule, then turned and walked back toward Peck's office. A hoard of reporters and TV camera crews followed me. I glanced to the rooftops a few times, expecting to see a sniper with his rifle sighted on me but saw no one up there.

Back at Peck's office there were numerous reporters waiting for an interview. Most were kind folks who respected my desire to not say anything that would get me charged with contempt of court.

There was one TV news reporter who kept trying to trick me into saying something about the report or the indictments that would have been a violation of the secrecy rule. He was unsuccessful.

I had planned on coming home immediately after the press conference but the many interviews lasted till well after dark. I didn't have a lot of faith in the ability of my old pickup to light the three hundred mile path to the ranch and three hundred miles was not a drive I wanted to undertake at this late hour anyway. I stayed in Denver that night.

I arrived home Friday evening. Jan was glad to see me, for a short time. Her happiness at my return soon turned to anger. We had no television, therefore Jan had not seen any of the news programs but her family and our friends had been calling her and reporting on the news stories that were being shown on the Denver stations. Many of the news reporters, while on the air, had speculated on the probability of me being thrown in jail because of the public statements I had made.

Jan was very worried. I had not called her while in Denver so naturally she suspected the worst. By the time I got home, her concern had turned into outright anger. There was also a message on my answering machine which really fueled her concern.

My answering machine was an old one. It had a four minute message capacity. My youngest daughter Tamra had helped me compose the message. It said: "Howdy folks, your efforts today have enabled you to contact Wes McKinley and Kirkwell Cattle Co. Now, if you are a tool salesman, you can forget about talking to me. For you see, everything around here is broke down and beyond repair. If you are trying to collect a bill, well my friend, prosperity is going to shine my way some day soon and then you will be the first to be paid. If you are from the IRS then you can forget about it. I no longer exist. All you other folks leave a message. Remember now, keep your powder dry and may your horse remain upright while on the trail."

Jonathan Turley, Professor of Law at George Washington

University back east, had left this message:

You had better reconsider what you are about to do. There are 5,000 Justice Department attorneys out there and every one of them wants to water down your powder and shoot your horse.

Jan interpreted Turley's message to mean someone wanted to shoot me. After hearing this message I understood Jan's anger and I was truly sorry for not making more of an effort to contact her.

I called Turley the following week and we had a good visit. He had obtained one of our press packets and through research done by his students he was up to speed on the Rocky Flats issue.

Turley impressed upon me the very real possibility of me going to jail for violating the Grand Jury secrecy rule. I told him I had no fear of prosecution for my actions of last week. I had read the newspaper story where Judge Finesilver had requested the Justice Department to investigate the Grand Jury for violating the secrecy oath and I was confident no Grand Jury would indict me for telling of the vile deeds the United States Government had done to our country. If I was charged with a crime because of my efforts to preserve my country's environment, I was quite confident no jury would ever convict me.

Turley enlightened me. I would not have the benefit of a Grand Jury; I might not even get a trial jury. Violation of the Grand Jury secrecy rule was a crime against the courts and it might be solely at the discretion of a judge as to whether or not I was guilty of committing a crime. The judge would also decide the penalty to impose on me, and I would not be eligible for parole.

I could be imprisoned for as much as 20 years or longer. Whatever the judge decided to do with me he could well do and Turley assured me the judge was sure enough very pissed off and could throw me deep within the bowels of the jail for violations of the Grand Jury secrecy rule.[37]

Dateline, Frontline and *Inside Edition* all ran pieces on the Grand Jury. There was coverage in *The Washington Post, The Wall Street Journal, The New York Times.* The local papers were full of articles about the now-famous Rocky Flats Grand Jury.

The Grand Jurors and their new lawyer, Professor Jonathon Turley, went on a quest for congressional immunity so they could talk without fear of prison about what the Justice Department had done behind the closed doors of the Grand Jury chambers. The Grand Jurors were taking risks every time they appeared in public. They were careful not to talk about Rule 6(e) confidential Grand Jury information. But each time they went in front of a camera, trying to draw attention to their concerns about obstruction of justice, each time another important person took up their cause—Vice President Al Gore, Congresswoman Patricia Schroeder, to name just two—each time another article appeared about the Rocky Flats Grand Jury, these 23 Colorado citizens were taking a risk that the Justice Department might make good on its threat to throw them in prison.

Wes' journal: The Grand Jury and Professor Turley decided to approach Congress for immunity, so we would be free to tell Congress what the prosecutors had done without worrying that someone would throw us in prison.[38] We almost got immunity. But then the big defense contractors started lobbying hard, and at the last minute, when the whole congressional committee was ready to give us immunity so we could tell them what the prosecutors had done and what really had gone on at Rocky Flats, one congressman killed the whole deal.

None other than Congressman David Skaggs, from Boulder. The same one decided there had been no midnight plutonium burning back when we were still investigating that very issue. His letter to Congress said it would be unconstitutional for Congress to give us immunity.[39]

Why didn't he pay more attention to the Constitution when he was talking to the press about the Grand Jury's secret investigation into the midnight plutonium burning?

So if Congress doesn't want to hear from us, who does? What about the indictments the Grand Jury wrote? What about all the things the prosecutors did wrong in the Grand Jury room? Who's going to do anything about that? And what about the fact that the investigation wasn't finished? There were still many things we wanted to investigate about the environmental crimes at Rocky Flats. We wanted to know the extent of the contamination. We wanted to make it public in our report. But the prosecutors wouldn't let us. They refused to bring in the witnesses or the evidence, refused to allow the Grand Jury to complete our investigation.

From what we saw, the Justice Department has no call to be saying there's no public health danger at Rocky Flats.

How can I just let them get away with this?

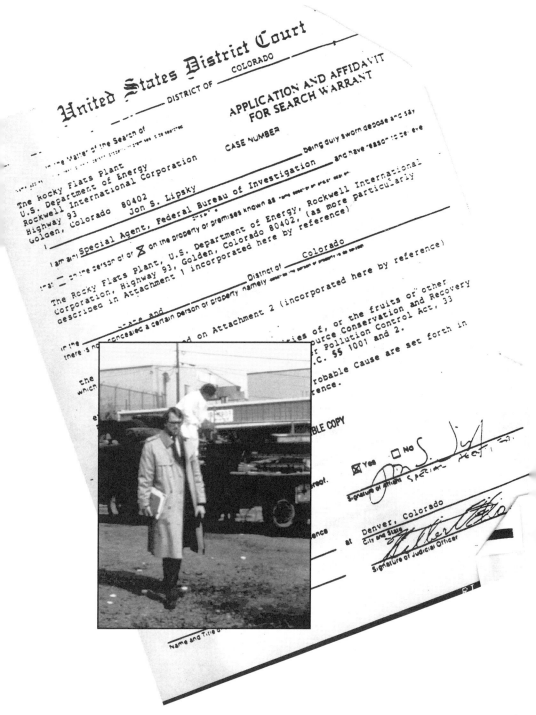

United States District Court

DISTRICT OF _____ COLORADO

APPLICATION AND AFFIDAVIT
FOR SEARCH WARRANT

In the Matter of the Search of

The Rocky Flats Plant
U.S. Department of Energy
Rockwell International Corporation
Highway 93
Golden, Colorado 80402

CASE NUMBER

Jon S. Lipsky

I am a(n) Special Agent, Federal Bureau of Investigation

The Rocky Flats Plant, U.S. Department of Energy, Rockwell International
Corporation, Highway 93, Golden, Colorado 80402, (as more particularly
described in Attachment 1 incorporated here by reference)

District of _____ Colorado

on Attachment 2 (incorporated here by reference)

☒ Yes ☐ No

Signature of Affiant   Special

Denver, Colorado
City and State

Signature of Judicial Officer

Special Agent Jon Lipsky, Denver, 1989.

Application and Affidavit for Search Warrant, Rocky Flats Nuclear Weapons Plant,
June 6th, 1989.

57

Above: Unidentified plutonium worker using glovebox similar to those used by Jacque Brever. *Photo courtesy of the Energy Department, Rocky Flats Nuclear Weapons Plant.*

Below: Building 771 glovebox. *Photo courtesy of the Energy Department, Rocky Flats Nuclear Weapons Plant.*

A "button" of weapons grade plutonium, later used to make a "pit" or "trigger," the core of a nuclear bomb. *Photo courtesy of the Energy Department, Rocky Flats Nuclear Weapons Plant.*

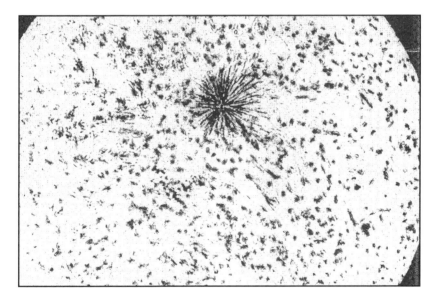

"The black star in the middle of the picture shows the track marks made by alpha rays emitted from a particle of plutonium-239 in the lung tissue of an ape. The alpha rays do not travel very far, but once inside the body, they can penetrate more than 10,000 cells within their range. This set of alpha tracks (magnified 500 times) occurred over a 48 hour period." Robert del Tredici, *At Work in the Fields of the Bomb*, (1987), plate 39, photographed at Lawrence Radiation Laboratory, Berkeley, California, (9-20-82). *Courtesy of LeRoy Moore, PhD., "Risk from Plutonium in the Environment at Rocky Flats," (November 5, 2002), Rocky Mountain Peace and Justice Center.*

Jacque Brever, Rockwell International plutonium worker, whistleblower, and Grand Jury witness, and her daughter Jessica, *circa* 1988.

Wes McKinley, Rocky Flats Grand Jury Foreman, 1989-1992. Grand Jury press conference, Denver, Colorado, Nov. 19, 1992. *Photo courtesy of Daily Camera.*

Rocky Flats Nuclear Weapons Plant, with residential communities in background.
Photo courtesy of the Energy Department, Rocky Flats Nuclear Weapons Plant.

Rocky Flats Nuclear Weapons Plant (closed) and buffer zone, showing adjoining residential communities. © 2003 Colorado Aerial Photo Service.

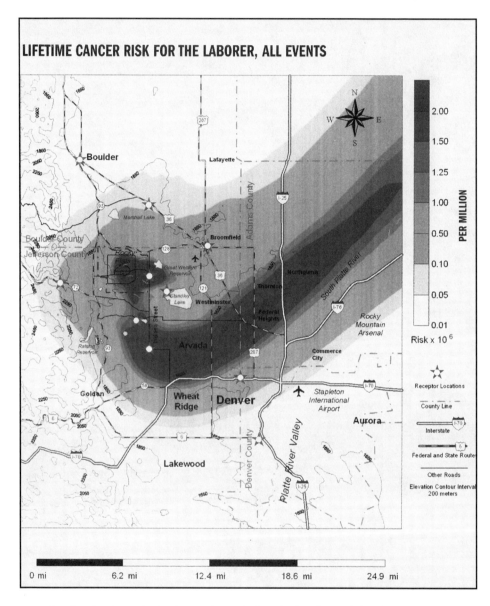

LIFETIME CANCER RISK FOR THE LABORER, ALL EVENTS

Graphic showing path of airborne plutonium from Rocky Flats and the risk of cancer to a laborer in the affected areas as a result of the Plant's operations from 1953-1989. *Courtesy of Colorado Department of Public Health and Environment, Summary of Findings, Historical Public Exposure Studies on Rocky Flats. (August, 1999)*

Wes McKinley, *circa* 2003. *Photo courtesy of Lisa Law.*

Jon Lipsky at work on the Citizens' Investigation, *circa* 2003. *Photo courtesy of Barry Curtis, AllSportsPhoto@AOL.com.*

Above: Unidentified protestors and law enforcement at Rocky Flats, *circa* 1960s. *Photo courtesy of Westword.*

Below: Protest sign, New Mexico, potential site of Rocky Flats II, the "Modern Pit Facility," *circa* 2003. *Courtesy of Lisa Law and Benjamin Forde.*

Wes McKinley, Jacque Brever and Jon Lipsky together after proving the cover-up.
Photo courtesy of Caron Balkany.

Part Two

The Citizens' Investigation Begins, 1997

CHAPTER FIVE

The Cowboy Gets Legal Counsel, 1997

Images of Rocky Flats swirled around him like fine dust as Wes McKinley galloped his four-year-old paint towards the approaching sunset. More than five years had passed since those prosecutors had ambushed the Grand Jury, but he still couldn't get it out of his mind.

The afternoon was fine, but Wes had been so busy with the ranching chores this had been his first ride of the day. And all the while, thinking about Rocky Flats. All the while, trying to make up his mind.

Is this really worth doing jail time? McKinley stared across the Colorado grasslands. The thought of being locked up turns my insides liver-green-white. I've never been arrested in my 52 years. Yet here I am planning to knowingly do something a federal judge, the US Attorney for Colorado, and a passel of lawyers have all told me could land my ass right in jail for contempt of court.

McKinley rode harder, hoping the thud of hooves on hard-packed dirt would clear his mind the way it always had. The afternoon was cool, hints of early autumn snow off the mountains despite the day of sunshine. He'd done his ranching work without conscious thought, thinking back to the trip to Santa Fe.

The drive to see the lawyer had taken him five hours, through the northern New Mexico mountains and over the pass at Raton near the New Mexico-Colorado border. He'd been thinking hard the whole drive back from Santa Fe, and on into the night, and through the routine of his morning ranching chores.

He'd got himself a lawyer. A volunteer. And they'd started to figure out a plan that might let him do what he needed to do without landing in jail. Still, it was a considerable risk he was taking, and she'd asked him to go home and think about it before finally making up his mind.

It pissed him off to be in this position just because a few chicken shit government lawyers thought they could make him be an unwilling accomplice to their cover-up scheme. McKinley remembered back to when he first got the summons to the Colorado District courthouse 303 miles away in Denver. He hadn't even known what a Grand Jury was. Now, he knew only too well. And what he'd found out in the Grand Jury room was about to land him in some significant trouble.

Pounding hooves weren't helping. Wes felt his jaw clench, the reins tighten in his hands. He was just as angry as the first time he realized what the defense contractors and their buddies in the US government were up to. Just as angry, just as frightened. And talking to Jan about the lawyer's plan wasn't going to be easy, either.

Lawyer's Notes

Meeting Wes McKinley was certainly interesting, but taking him on as a client seems such an impossible task. I'm a trial lawyer, used to litigation: if my client is wronged, I go to the courts for a remedy. But the wrong Wes has suffered isn't going to be remedied in any court.

According to Wes, the US Energy Department and its defense industry contractors had violated environmental laws for decades at Rocky Flats Nuclear Weapons Plant, contaminating the suburbs and the Denver countryside with lethal radioactive and hazardous waste. And then government lawyers at the US Justice Department manipulated the legally mandated secrecy of a federal Grand Jury to cover it all up.

Just what was I supposed to do? Grand Jury secrecy rules meant Wes could go to prison if he talked about any of it.

But now the government was planning to turn Rocky Flats into a national wildlife refuge, then open it to recreation. "Believe it or not, the clean-up standards for Rocky Flats are less because it's going to be a wildlife refuge - with children playing there—than if it's going to be developed for industry," he told me during that first meeting.[40] "They're talking about opening it for horseback riding, hiking, kids' school trips.

"How can I keep quiet?" Wes finished. "They don't even know how contaminated Rocky Flats really is because the Justice Department covered up most of the evidence."

We sat outside on the wide portal of the house, looking out over the mountains towards Los Alamos, where the nation's nuclear weapons legacy had begun during the Manhattan Project of World War II. Los Alamos National Laboratory sent out a faint glow over the mountains. The glow was only from the lights; I knew radioactivity was invisible. But since I'd started volunteering as an attorney with local nuclear safety groups, the symbolism had struck me as appropriate.

Wes talked casually for a while about the many things he'd tried to do since the Grand Jury had been dismissed in 1992. I was impressed with his determination and the many varied efforts he'd made—none breaking Grand Jury secrecy laws, he assured me—trying to get people to demand that their elected officials do something about Rocky Flats.

I made a note to get some more specifics later about what he'd actually said. Although he assured me he'd not broken the Grand Jury secrecy rules, I wanted to see for myself whether he'd given the Justice Department anything to hammer him with.

He'd spoken at press conferences, Rotary Clubs and church groups. The list went on and on. Activist groups and coffee club meetings. He'd tried them all. But the truth about Rocky Flats is still hidden, he told me.

He'd also been talking to some college classes in environmental ethics at the University of Colorado in Boulder. It was taught by Adrienne Anderson, an environmental health and safety advocate he'd met after the Grand Jury had been dismissed. Wes spoke regularly at her classes, trying to motivate the students to look carefully at the data provided by the Energy Department, to look for the real facts, not just accept the government's conclusions.

And he urged them to be very suspicious of any plans the Energy Department came up with for handling nuclear waste or turning the former Rocky Flats Nuclear Weapons Plant into a wildlife and recreation area.

But he'd had to talk in generalities, couldn't give any specifics or he could end up in jail for violating Grand Jury secrecy laws. And this had bitten him bad, worse than a blue fly on a mule's hindquarters, he told me.

One of the college students had kept pushing him.

"He knew I couldn't talk about it," Wes said, "And I knew right where he was headed."

Wes looked sort of sheepish as he told me what had happened.

"'So what did you find out in the Grand Jury room that's so important, Mr. McKinley?' the kid kept insisting."

Wes was almost philosophical about it now, but I could sense his frustration. He continued the story in a calm voice.

"When I repeated that I wasn't allowed to talk about Grand Jury matters, the kid just stood up, shrugged his shoulders and turned to the rest of the class.

"'Where's the facts?' the kid asked, looking around at his classmates. 'We need the data, like he keeps saying. Otherwise how can we accept his conclusions?'

"Of course the kid was right," Wes said ruefully. "And I had to admit that to the class. They were real polite about it but the kid was right."

He shook his head.

"Not everyone I talked to was as pushy as that boy," Wes told me. "But after that college class, I felt a fraud, telling people to insist on getting the facts when I couldn't give them any myself.

"So that's why I decided to find a lawyer," he said quietly. "How can I stay quiet if people are going to be hurt?"

The chill off the mountains sent us inside. Wes limped slightly as he walked up the steps to the front door and wiped his cowboy boots carefully on the outside mat.

A case of childhood polio, I found out later. And it was coming back. Post-polio syndrome. Wes tried to ignore it, but as I got to know him better, I could see he was often in pain, and his limp got worse over the following years.

We continued talking over coffee as the light settled into late afternoon. The light in Santa Fe is a constantly shifting thing. It attracts artists from around the world. It seemed to mesmerize Wes, and me as well. He stared out the big glass windows as he continued his story, sitting in an overstuffed leather chair.

Still had his hat on. Must be bald, I thought to myself. He's otherwise really well-mannered, in an old-fashioned Western sort of way. Much later, when I saw him unhatted for the first time, I learned I was right. But I also learned that, out West, cowboys leave their hats on even inside.

"You're still under FBI investigation, right?" I asked.

He nodded without looking at me. He seemed indignant. This man had never even had a traffic ticket. His early education had been in a one-room schoolhouse in conservative southeastern Colorado ranching country, pledging allegiance every day to the flag of the United States. He was a law-abiding, committed citizen, as stiffly conservative in his politics and lifestyle as I was unbendingly progressive.

"The Grand Jury secrecy rule, Criminal Rule 6(e), prohibits you from talking about what went on in the Rocky Flats Grand Jury room, right?" I continued.

He nodded again.

"You could land in prison if you violate Rule 6(e), you know that?"

"I know it," he stated solemnly.

"You don't even have anything we can use to prove what the Justice

Department did to the Grand Jury, do you?"

Wes was still silent, but this time he didn't nod.

I stared at him, and slowly he looked at me out of the sides of his light blue-green eyes. He started to grin. But then he turned serious, and silent.

I wasn't going to get an answer to that question. Not yet. Didn't quite trust me enough to tell me what he had. But he must have something, I thought.

As we said goodbye, I told him I'd think about what could be done. And he agreed to talk with his wife about whether they really wanted to take on the United States government.

McKinley Ranch, 1997

Wes and Jan found little time to be alone together. So many kids— theirs, the foster kids, the adopted kids. But not surprisingly, when it came time to do the ranching chores, Wes and Jan somehow were able to find a little privacy.

They hadn't brought up Rocky Flats directly. They were just doing their ranching chores, enjoying each other's company. Or so he thought.

Out of nowhere, Jan spun on her heel and glared at him.

"Are you going to at least tell her about the danger you all are in?"

It took Wes a minute to gather that the "her" Jan was talking about was his new lawyer.

"*Might* be in," Wes inserted gently. He'd never really worried about the same things that worried Jan.

She just stared at him.

"OK, OK, I'll tell her," Wes agreed. "But what am I supposed to say? It's not just the FBI you might have to watch out for? Someone might be following us? Strange hang up calls? Check if your phone is tapped? You want me to tell her about that bozo's story about the dead bodies? She'll think I'm crazy. There's nothing to all that nonsense."

Jan stood there as though she hadn't heard him.

"Isn't that up to her to decide if she agrees to help you with this?" Jan's voice was grim.

"Isn't that what you're always saying, Wes? Give people the facts about Rocky Flats and let them decide for themselves. Can't let the government do the deciding for you. Aren't you always saying everyone has that basic right, Wes? And duty?"

She snorted and turned away.

"Everyone except me that is. Being married to a crusading fool has dragged me up on that soapbox right with you."

Wes pulled her back and into his arms. They were standing beside her rose bushes, the garden she spent so much time in. Despite the dryness of their land, she'd made those roses bloom. The air was filled with their scent as he held her silently. She was breathing hard.

Wes spoke softly into her hair.

"Jan, we can't let them get away with this. We did the research on this together. You were as upset about it as I am."

Jan said nothing, but he knew she was remembering back to that day they'd spent in her school library, using the computer to research the health effects from radiation.

It was long, long after the Grand Jury had been dismissed. Wes had been trying to explain to her some of the reasons he just couldn't drop his fight against the Rocky Flats cover-up. Jan had been shaking when they closed down the computer that summer afternoon.

"You read those reports, Jan. Kids are more vulnerable to radiation than adults. Their cells are still dividing, their bones are still growing, their teeth, too. Their bodies just absorb the stuff, and most of it stays in there for the rest of their lives.

"Radiation can be deadly for adults, too, especially old people and sick people. But to make a playground for kids out of a nuclear weapons plant? It's just crazy. And I know you agree, Jan. We can't let them get away with this."

Jan was quiet for a while, and Wes just held her.

"Who is this woman anyway?" Jan said into the front of his work shirt. She hadn't returned his embrace, but she was still standing there. That was a good sign, Wes thought as he looked down at the top of her head and slowly answered.

"She's a volunteer attorney for some of the anti-nuke groups, Jan. She's been doing it for a while now. One of the guys from Concerned Citizens for Nuclear Safety down in Santa Fe recommended her."

Jan wasn't convinced. She shrugged off his embrace and stepped back a little.

"And that's a reason to trust her, Wes? You could end up in prison doing what you two are planning. Or worse. . . ."

Wes pulled her gently back.

"They won their lawsuit against Los Alamos, Jan. Just a bunch of ordinary citizens made the government obey the law. I don't really trust any lawyer, you know that. Especially after what those government lawyers did. But I can't do this by myself. I need a lawyer, and if she's willing to help, I'm going to at least try."

Jan was still mad, he could hear it in her voice.

"But *why* is she willing to help, Wes? She doesn't even live in Colorado. She's not charging you any money. What's in it for her?"

Wes sighed.

"I asked her that myself, Jan. She looked at me sort of funny and then she told me her sister had died of breast cancer right before the Grand Jury was discharged. She'd lived in Boulder, and then Denver, close to Rocky Flats.

"Caron told me her sister had fought the disease for over five years, always wondering whether Rocky Flats was the reason. She was only 41 when she died, leaving behind her 12-year-old son, and Caron said it had been a sad and painful fight."

"Caron told me, 'My sister died asking me whether Rocky Flats had done this to her, Wes. I guess I'm trying to answer her question.'"

Jan stared up at him.

"Wes, you have to tell her about the danger, even if you don't believe it."

"OK, Jan. OK, I'll tell her," Wes said quietly.

He felt her arms go around his back and knew she'd relented. At least for a while. He stared out over her head at the grandkids playing with the horses in the back pasture.

Lawyer's Notes

It wasn't until the very end of a long afternoon conference that I realized why Wes had felt he needed to come down to Santa Fe again so soon after our first meeting. When he was finished talking, I just sat there. I was shocked, and then didn't know why I should have been. I'd known there was danger involved in what we were doing, but I hadn't really thought about physical danger. It was the danger of Wes going to prison, the danger to my law license that I'd been thinking about. Now I found there was other danger, too.

Wes had started out telling me about the speech he'd given in Los Alamos at the request of the local anti-nuke groups. He was rambling a little and then he'd sort of dropped into the conversation that there'd been talk that some people had died checking out rumors of radioactive waste from Rocky Flats being secretly dumped off-site.

"Whoa," I interrupted, surprised at myself for already picking up his cowboy jargon. "Hold on there just a second, Wes. What do you mean some people died?"

Wes looked at me sheepishly, as though he wished I hadn't heard.

"It's nothing proved, Caron, just a story someone told me."

"Well, did this someone say it was a true story?" I pressed.

"Yeah, he said it was true."

I stared at him until he continued.

"He said two men had been investigating rumors about illegal dump-ing of radioactive waste from Rocky Flats in an abandoned mine in a nearby town. They supposedly were killed. The police found one body, shot in the head. The guy's dog, too. But the other man's body's never been found. They weren't together when it happened. The first man and his dog went missing first. The second man went looking for them and never came back.

"At least, that's the story this guy told me."

Wes looked at me sideways for a while. He must have been able to tell by my face that I didn't take it quite as lightly as he had.

"Guess you're going to have to check it out some more," he said rue-fully. "Hope I didn't scare you. I think it's a bunch of bull."

I didn't let on to Wes how much the story about the dead men in the mining town had worried me. And I didn't know whether any cowboy machismo was masking a concern of his own. But I'd been a volunteer nuclear safety lawyer for quite a while before I'd met Wes, and I'd heard some pretty scary stories.

There'd been a lot of money made building nuclear weapons. And lots of bureaucratic power concentrated in the Energy Department. These were high-powered folks we'd be investigating. Rockwell International is a Fortune 500 company, with years of contacts and con-tracts with the government and the military. And the government wasn't likely to turn over its secret files at the drop of a Freedom of Information Act request.* How were we supposed to prove this cover-up? How were we supposed to do it without attracting the wrong kind of attention? Especially with Wes under FBI surveillance?

Wes must have noticed my pensiveness, because he quickly changed the subject. "There was a mess of publicity about the Rocky Flats inves-tigation back in 1992," he told me. "Information got leaked from the Grand Jury room."[41]

* The Freedom of Information Act (FOIA) is a federal law requiring the government to give citizens access to government records upon request unless certain exemptions apply.

"I don't know who leaked it," he added. "Then there was a congressional investigation of the Justice Department. A Congressman from Michigan—Howard Wolpe—held hearings to find out what the Justice Department had done to our Grand Jury investigation. They wrote a report about it. But Congress never talked to *us* about what the prosecutors had done, so they still don't know about what went on inside the Grand Jury Chambers, what the prosecutors did to us."

"Well," I started. "Then it's not as though Congress doesn't know *anything* about this Rocky Flats cover-up. What's so important that you have to risk prison to talk about it?" I asked as gently as I could.

Wes was silent for a long time. When he finally answered me, his voice was calm, but I could sense it was an effort for him to keep it that way.

"They used us. The US government manipulated the whole Grand Jury system. They made us part of their cover-up, part of a lie," Wes answered. "And it's a lie that could expose people to hidden radioactive dangers. I can't let them get away with that. They used our Grand Jury investigation to convince people that Rocky Flats hasn't caused a public health threat or any dangerous off-site contamination. That things aren't as dangerous and polluted as people had thought. And that's just not true.

"Rocky Flats is so contaminated they'll never be able to clean it up safe enough for kids to play there," he said. "And now they're going to turn Rocky Flats into a wildlife refuge with public recreation.

"If I stay quiet and let them get away with that, I'm a bigger criminal than they are."

Wes was pacing now, his slight limp seeming worse as he swiveled in his cowboy boots on the brick floors of the living room.

"They're gonna pretend like nothing bad was ever done there. Property values are skyrocketing around Denver. It'd take some pretty strong political guts to just fence off the place forever and not let anyone go anywhere near the contamination.

"They've got no interest in looking at how badly it's contaminated. The more contamination they find, the more money it's going to cost them to clean it up, no matter what they do with the place."

He sighed. It was a lonely, desolate sound.

"It's much more profitable to pretend Rocky Flats wasn't so bad after all. I know the Justice Department used the FBI raid and the Grand Jury investigation to cover-up the contamination at Rocky Flats and the surrounding neighborhoods," he repeated. "But if I talk about it, they'll throw me in prison."

He stared at me.

"An old cowboy buddy of mine asked me, 'Where do you go if there's no justice at the Justice Department?'"

He had a real problem.

This was an intriguing problem for me, too. As a lawyer, I couldn't divulge any Grand Jury Rule 6(e) information Wes told me as part of our confidential attorney-client relationship. Or assist Wes in anything that might be illegal.

"So, what do you want to do about it?" I asked.

"I don't know," Wes stated quietly. "But there has to be something we can do."

I noted the "we" without comment.

Wes started speaking quietly, almost to himself.

"If you saw someone strangling a baby, could you just sit there and not do anything?"

He looked down at my big old Lab lying lazily at our feet.

"Or if someone was hurting your dog? Could you just sit back? Why is it any different if it's the government doing the strangling? What would have happened if more of those Germans had tried to do something when they saw the Jews being carted off to concentration camps? It was legal, it was the government doing the carting off. Didn't make it right.

"It's un-American to sit back and let your government break the law," he finished, and then swiveled his chair so his back was to me, sitting quietly in the oncoming dusk.

"You want me to help you find a legal way to talk about what you aren't allowed to talk about, is that it?" I asked quietly.

He nodded.

"You want to stop them from letting kids play at Rocky Flats."

He nodded again.

"What if the FBI investigation heats up? If they haul you off to jail? If they try to set you up?"

Wes was staring at Los Alamos.

"Gotta do what I can, Caron."

His words dropped into the silence between us, and I knew I'd help him, whatever it took.

So Wes and I, an unlikely duo if there ever was one, started a Citizens' Investigation. The conservative cowboy and his liberal progressive counsel investigating the US Justice Department's cover-up of government nuclear crimes. Hopefully, others would join us along the way.

We'd write it up. Send it to Congress. If we could prove there'd been a cover-up, if even part of the Justice Department's investigation had been a cover-up, it would call into question other things the Justice Department had done and said about Rocky Flats. And telling the real Rocky Flats story might persuade Congress to re-open the investigation into the whole mess.

If they did, I was sure there wouldn't be any children playing in the dust at a former nuclear weapons plant. And if Congress ever really understood that citizens are not going to accept the amount of cheating and deception practiced *on* the United States *by* the United States government when it comes to anything nuclear, maybe we wouldn't continue to build those nuclear weapons after all.

The 1992 congressional investigation was the place to start. The first of the eight recommendations in the Wolpe Report to Congress about the Justice Department's Rocky Flats Grand Jury investigation was that Congress should investigate whether the Justice Department's handling of the Rocky Flats case had been ". . .based in whole or in part on a desire to protect the current administration from evidence that it had not changed an 'Energy Department culture' that has encouraged rampant and continuing environmental violations."

The second recommendation was that Congress should decide whether it wanted to hear from the Rocky Flats Grand Jury.

Hopefully, our Citizens' Investigation would make Congress answer yes to both of those important questions.

I spent a lot of time thinking about the difficulties of what we were about to undertake. And then the difficulty of finding a way to talk about it without Wes ending up in prison. These were smart people with a lot to lose; how were we going to prove the cover-up when they had everything locked up in the Grand Jury vault?

I looked at Wes. Well, maybe not everything.

I wanted to talk with the other Grand Jurors. They were still represented by Jonathon Turley. After they'd lost their bid for congressional immunity, he'd filed a petition in the Denver Federal District Court asking the judge to give the Grand Jurors permission to speak. That was in 1996, and they were still waiting.

So even if Turley let me speak with his clients, I probably wasn't going to get much information. But Wes and I both wanted to at least let the other Grand Jurors know what we were doing. Since they have their own legal counsel, I'm not supposed to call them directly. So I called Professor Turley and left a message at his office.

Wes professed not to be concerned that he was under FBI investigation, but I soon noticed he didn't like to discuss on the phone what we were doing. He'd come down to Santa Fe when we needed to talk, or I'd meet him in Denver while we were doing more research. When we did speak on the phone, he was often cryptic. This made things difficult; his cowboy slang was often cryptic enough. And I'm sure my legalese was just as incomprehensible at times to him.

But *I* was concerned. I valued my law license and my liberty.

"It gives me the creeps to think the FBI might be investigating me," I said to Wes one day. "I haven't felt like this since the anti-war protests back in college."

Wes looked at me strangely. I could sense his discomfort: his own lawyer had been one of those peace activists. I knew he was sorely puzzled about my current lifestyle, too. Lawyers doing work for free was an unknown concept to him. I tried to explain that lots of lawyers do *pro bono* work, people just have to ask, like he did. But Wes hadn't seemed convinced. He just didn't care much for lawyers.

It made me smile, and I was reminded again of how different we were. We were going to have to trust each other to pull this off. But that might be a tough ride for both of us, I thought. Our politics and our backgrounds are as different as night and day.

Although we both downplayed the danger, we were well aware that some people with a lot of power had a lot to lose by what we were doing. We weren't sure what they might do to try to stop us. I found the prospect of being under FBI surveillance unsettling. We made jokes about it, but we were careful.

As the Citizens' Investigation progressed, we got some face to face interviews. I went to them with trepidation. Wes had to stay in the background, of course. I simply called folks up and explained that I was a lawyer interested in Rocky Flats and would like to interview them. Almost everyone was happy to oblige. A sense of history? Ego? A need to tell the story from their own perspective?

But I was always worried I was being set up. What kind of misinformation could they be feeding me? How was I going to tell the truth from the lies? Was someone waiting for me to slip and reveal some secret Grand Jury information so we'd end up in jail? Would someone accuse me and Wes of conspiracy to violate the law? Once we finish the investigation and give it to Congress, will that land us in jail? Was I going to ask the wrong guy the wrong question and tip off someone dangerous that we were poking around in some not so distant but very likely dirty history?

Dean, Wes' partner in their Kirkwell Cattle trail riding company, had a simple solution. Dean is a hard-drinking, tough-talking cowboy with a fierce temper and a gusty sense of humor. Rings on every finger, fringed cowboy jacket, pistol in his boot and hunting knife at his belt. The tourists he takes on horseback into the Colorado grasslands are never sure how much of Dean is cowboy bluff and how much they ought to be afraid of.

Don't worry about landing in jail, Dean announced. When the government breaks the law, you can, too. If you end up in jail, I'll come shoot you out.

He's only half joking.

Letter from Wes McKinley to his lawyer, 1997

Hi Caron:

Sure did enjoy visiting with you the other day. Your question-what would I say if allowed to talk?—I can answer. I've been writing cowboy poetry and cowboy stories for years, but writing this is something new for sure. And yes, I do realize this Citizens' Investigation is going to be a long and rocky trail to travel, and with some danger of me doing jail time. You are not the only lawyer who's warned me I could go to jail for talking about this; the government lawyers told us that often during the Grand Jury days. So did the judge.

I have lived all of my life right here on this little windblown ranch, working and enjoying the great outdoors most everyday. Being cooped up inside a jail cell is not something I want to think about much less experience.

But I have obligations to do my duty; we all do. I don't think I'm doing anything more than any other patriotic American would do under the circumstances.

Caron, I would start off by telling people who I am and how ordinary a person I am. My grandfather homesteaded at this very place where I now live. He came here with a fine mule, a good milch cow and a worn out wagon. The air was clear, the water was pure and a desirable woman soon joined him. He was a blessed man. Women, mules, and milch cows are just as good or

better today than they were then.* But the air and water are
killing us.

I learned in the Grand Jury room just how dangerous to the
people's health and the safety of our environment some of the
materials are that they used out at Rocky Flats.[42] This was not
just manure laden dust blowing out of the horse corral. We are
talking about just a small amount of plutonium getting in your
lungs and killing you. It's radioactive. It's what they use to make
the cores of nuclear weapons. It can damage your DNA, cause
birth defects in your kids. Pu, they call it. Think about how that
sounds.

You know how much Pu they had stored out there? More
than 14 tons. And a microscopic amount of it can kill you if you
breathe it.

Dr. Carl Johnson, the local health director, got fired after he
published studies showing increased cancer rates and increased
infant deaths around Rocky Flats.[43] That was back in 1982. The
cover-up of nuclear dangers had been going on for a long time
before the Grand Jury even got started.

You know how they handled all that deadly Pu-contaminated waste? They burned it. The contaminated ash is all over
the place. Pu ash sticks to dust and soil. It doesn't just contaminate Rocky Flats; it blows off-site, too. The Pu gets inhaled,
tracked into homes, washed into the streams, eaten by game.

They made Pu-contaminated liquid waste, and sprayed it on
the ground, dumped it in ditches and let it run off into the
streams that fill the drinking water reservoirs.

When radioactivity like Pu or strontium or americium or any
of the other dangerous stuff they make out there gets into your
body, it gets stored in your bones, in your tissues and organs, and
just keeps on causing damage. Plutonium stays radioactive and
dangerous for more than 24,000 years. Some of the other
radioisotopes are shorter lived; but they're all dangerous.

No wonder cancer rates are sky high. All of us can get cancer and DNA damage from radioactivity, but it's kids and the
already-ill and old people who're the most vulnerable. The very
ones we should be protecting.

And it's not just Pu that's a problem. One newspaper article

* CB Note: I had to register an objection to the attitudes implicit in this
categorization, but Wes just grinned.

in 1991 started out "Cancer-causing PCBs are dripping off a Rocky Flats building. . . ."

Government officials say there are at least 172 contaminated sites at Rocky Flats: landfills, ash and sludge pits and abandoned pipelines. That's just the ones they remember and will admit to.

They had so much contaminated waste they used to bury it around the grounds when they couldn't find some other way to get rid of it. I'm sure they don't even know where all of it is.

The Justice Department ended the Rocky Flats Grand Jury investigation saying there were no known off-site health effects from Rocky Flats. I want to make real sure no one believes that for a second.

I want to talk about how the FBI investigation of Rocky Flats Nuclear Weapons Plant started out as a cover-up. Never was intended to indict anyone. I want to tell how the Justice Department strong-armed us, told us things that weren't true. Lied to us and lied to Congress.

Do you really think the Grand Jury secrecy rules should stop me from saying that? In the United States of America?

I have spent a good part of the last 52 years enjoying the privilege of sharing the environment with my horses and dogs. The thought of doing jail time has been a real motivating factor in making me a student of the Grand Jury secrecy laws. You, Caron, my work-for-free-lawyer, tell me the Grand Jury secrecy rules are mostly for the protection of the members of the Grand Jury and innocent people accused by the government. but not indicted by the Grand Jury. Well, in this case the secrecy rules are being used to keep the Grand Jury from telling the truth about the contamination of the Denver Colorado area and the government's obstruction of justice in trying to cover it up. If the truth were told some government stud ducks and corporate big wheels would be exposed for the villains they are.

I became the foreman of Special Grand Jury 89-2. We swore an oath to uphold the laws of our country, to not be manipulated by the government lawyers, to insure no one is above the law, and see to it that justice was done.[44] The judge impressed upon us the importance of not being the prosecutor's agent. "Although you must work closely with the government attorneys you must not yield your powers nor forego your independence of spirit. . . . You must exercise your own judgment and if the facts suggest a different balance than that advocated by the government attorneys, then you must achieve the appropriate balance even in the face of their opposition or criticism. . . . The government attorneys cannot dominate or command your actions."

Those were the instructions the judge gave us. I swore to follow them and I am still trying to uphold the laws of America.

Sincerely,

Wesley P. McKinley

Lawyer's Notes

Wes and I arranged to meet in Denver. I needed to go through the court files, and he would go to the public library to see what they had in the archives.

Wes got us two hotel rooms. He'd spent a lot of time in hotels during the Grand Jury days and knew the best bargains on clean rooms. We met in the hotel parking lot, and went to the adjoining café to talk.

I knew Wes was shy and I was sure he'd be uncomfortable going in my room, or me going in his. I made a mental note to make sure our spouses met each other right away. Besides, I was curious about Jan. Wes spoke about her with such affection and respect. I'd thought they probably had a sort of traditional, patriarchal relationship until he told me Jan was the breadwinner right now, had been since the Grand Jury days. I was waiting until Wes was more comfortable with me to ask him about that. Sure didn't seem like the typical cowboy lifestyle.

The café was quiet. It was a little early for dinner, or supper as Wes called it, but we'd both made long drives that day and also wanted an early start on the research the next morning. We went to a table, ordered iced tea, and sat quietly for a minute. We were still a little uncomfortable with each other. We were so different in so many ways.

Wes didn't do small talk, and I'd never cared for it, so we started right in mapping our research strategy, talking quietly in the corner booth.

Since our last meeting, I'd read the three volumes of congressional testimony and the Wolpe Report, which contained the findings of the congressional subcommittee hearings about the Justice Department's handling of the Grand Jury investigation. Then, I read the Justice Department's official position on why the Wolpe Report was wrong.

One thing I noticed immediately was that the Wolpe Report didn't agree with the Justice Department's decision not to pursue the allegations of secret midnight plutonium burning in an aging incinerator with a 152-foot smokestack. The Wolpe Report hadn't provided detail, but you could sense their skepticism. The Justice Department, not surprisingly, decided that the Justice Department had done nothing wrong.

The secret midnight plutonium burning had been the most sensational charge in the search warrant. It got the headlines in many of the articles Wes brought me at our first meeting. It looked like Rockwell had been caught in the act. Maybe the Energy Department, too. The FBI had infrared videotapes of the secret midnight plutonium burning. Two whistleblowers had testified. Yet, the prosecutors had decided not to pursue the charges.

They told Congress the infrared expert had changed his position, and they could no longer rely on the videotaped infrared evidence of heat emissions from the 771 plutonium incinerator during the time the incinerator was supposed to be shut down. They said the whistleblowers weren't very reliable. And in formal documents filed with the court, the Justice Department had officially stated that the secret midnight plutonium burning had never happened.[45]

Yet, during the entire three months the 771 plutonium incinerator had supposedly been shut down, Rocky Flats had refused to allow the EPA or the State regulators to inspect it.[46]

That seemed like the place for this Citizens' Investigation to concentrate. If we could expose what had really happened with that one potential criminal charge, if we could find just one cover-up, then maybe Congress would start asking itself what else had been covered up at Rocky Flats.

"First we have to get copies of the documents," Wes noted.

I nodded. Getting the government to give up copies of its files was no easy feat, even though the law requires them to make disclosure. "If we can jump those hurdles, maybe we'll get somewhere."

The Denver research trip was a long three days of microfiche and tiny print on press clippings. We were both a little dizzy by the time we called it quits and headed back to our respective homes. We'd found a lot of good information, though. I'd gone to the courthouse and copied what seemed like hundreds of court papers from the files they'd let me see. Most of the files were off limits: Rule 6(e). But there were some awfully strange things in the files that hadn't been sealed. Wes found a lot of old newspaper clippings in the Western History Archives at the public library. We both left Denver feeling we'd made some headway into the massive research that lay before us.

Now we needed to get the infrared reports. I filed Freedom of Information Act requests. We needed to talk with Karen Pitts and Jacque Brever, the two whistleblowers in Building 771, to see what they thought about the Justice Department's statement that their testimony wasn't very reliable. I started asking around for their addresses. I called Jonathon Turley and left another message, still hoping to be able to talk with the other Grand Jurors.

I also decided to call Jon Lipsky, the FBI Special Agent who'd headed up the Rocky Flats investigation in 1989-1992. I'd read hundreds of pages of his congressional testimony. Edith Holleman and Bob Roach from the Wolpe congressional subcommittee staff had asked him a lot of questions. But not quite everything. I had a few more questions myself.

Why not? I asked myself. He works for the taxpayers, so, why not? The FBI routinely grants interviews for books and films. Of course, those usually made the Bureau look good, and I didn't think that would be the case here. But still, why not call him?

Finding Lipsky was surprisingly easy. I'd heard from some Denver environmentalists that he was back in Los Angeles, so I just called the LA FBI office and asked for him. It was that simple. Someone gave me his direct dial, and the next thing I knew a deep recorded voice was asking me to leave a message for Jon Lipsky.

I left my name and phone number and told him I was an attorney interested in learning more about Rocky Flats. I was a little worried about doing it. I had no little distrust of the FBI. Lipsky was one of the few who'd seemed honest and forthright in his congressional testimony. But he *was* an FBI agent, and I was investigating the Justice Department. I was nervous.

Lipsky didn't call me back. A few weeks later, I called again and reached him.

"I couldn't understand your phone message," he told me. "I would have called you right back. I couldn't understand how you spelled your last name so I didn't find you in the phone book. All I'd heard right was Santa Fe. I called directory assistance there, but I couldn't find your listing with the name spelled wrong. It was driving me crazy."

He was casual and friendly on the phone, but I felt concern run through me. I guess my nervousness had made my voice a little unintelligible on the phone message, but why had he tried so hard to track me down?

I tried to keep my voice neutral. We talked generally about the his-

tory of the case, and I told him some of the things I'd reviewed and a little of what I knew about the investigation and some of the nuclear issues
behind it.

I wanted him to understand that I was serious, and that I had the
background to understand this complicated story. I wanted him to talk to me.

I *didn't* want him to know I was investigating a potential cover-up by
his employers, and maybe involving him.

When I mentioned that I was trying to track down what had happened
with the FBI's investigation of possibly lethal criticality accidents[47] at
Rocky Flats, there was a sudden silence at the end of the line. After the
easy, conversational way we'd been discussing the generalities of Rocky
Flats, this change was almost palpable.

Lipsky's voice was still neutral when he spoke again, but I knew it
was the end of the conversation. "There are reports of elevated strontium
levels in the soils around the Plant," he said. "I'm sure you can get
copies. But I really can't talk to you about it until I get the green light
from my superiors."

I sensed I had touched on a subject that made him uncomfortable,
and it certainly piqued my curiosity. There were other radionuclides like
plutonium 239 and americium 241 which were known to be elevated at
Rocky Flats. But there was no reason for the strontium levels to be above
background.* Strontium is produced only in a chain reaction, and Rocky
Flats didn't do that kind of work. It didn't split atoms, it manufactured
triggers for bombs.

Strontium would only be present at Rocky Flats if there'd been a criticality accident, and although rumors persisted among workers and environmentalists, the Energy Department and Rockwell all strenuously
denied any criticalities,

It was also technically possible that Rocky Flats had been working
on a "black" project, one they'd kept off the books and briefed to only a
few members of Congress, one which *did* involve splitting atoms for an
intentional nuclear explosion. Or they could have been doing some
experiments with pure strontium, although there was no public information about that, either.

I tried to press Lipsky just a little about the elevated strontium levels. A criticality accident, especially an unacknowledged, covered up

---

* "Background" has been defined as the level of radiation resulting from natural causes
(natural background) together with man-made fallout from nuclear weapons testing.

one, would be awfully important to know about as Rocky Flats pressed forward with designing its clean-up plans. And important to the surrounding public, too.

But this wasn't just general conversation anymore, this was part of an old FBI investigation. Lipsky repeated that I'd have to get permission from his bosses at the FBI before he could talk about it.

Lipsky was more than willing to be interviewed. There was still information that hadn't been made public, he told me. That's why he'd tried so hard to get back to me when my phone message wasn't clear.

That made me feel a little better.

"But you'll have to clear it first with the media relations folks," he added. "I'm sure there won't be a problem. The criminal case is closed, it's been almost ten years, so I can't see any reason under Bureau policy to deny an interview."

He gave me the phone number of FBI media relations, and I called as soon as Lipsky hung up. After some back and forth, and a few days wait, I got a call from FBI headquarters in Washington. I explained that I was doing some research on Rocky Flats.

A few weeks later, I got a message on my voice mail that the interview had been approved.

I was ecstatic. I immediately called and left a message on Lipsky's voice mail that I was looking forward to speaking with him and that the interview had been green-lighted. I called Wes. First time I'd heard him excited. He'd always had a few more questions of Lipsky, he told me.

But the next day, I got a message that there'd be no interview after all.

When I called FBI headquarters, the media relations officer was apologetic. His superiors had decided there could be no interview because the case was still pending.

What case is still pending? I insisted.

I was aggravated, to say the least. The plea bargain had been approved years ago. Rockwell International had paid its fine. The case is closed. What is still pending???

He would give me no more information.

That was it. No interview. No explanations other than "the case is still pending," when it obviously wasn't.

I wrote to the FBI's media relations office. I waited several months, but heard nothing. I wrote again. Then I wrote to Louie Freeh, the Director of the FBI. I never got a direct answer from him, but a month later I got a letter from the Office of Public and Congressional Affairs, answering also for Freeh, still insisting that "due to a number of issues related to this matter that remain outstanding, we cannot. . . ."

I wrote Tom Udall, my Congressman.[48] I decided to file more Freedom of Information Act requests while I was waiting to hear from him. I didn't know what it was that the FBI didn't want me to find out, but its resistance so many years after the case had been settled made me even more suspicious that there was something still hidden that Congress hadn't found out about.

I really needed to talk to Lipsky. And so far the FBI wasn't letting me.

I kept looking for Karen Pitts and Jacque Brever. The two whistle-blowers would be incredibly important. And I asked Wes to tell me more about Special Agent Jon Lipsky.

E-mail from Wes

Can't make it down for a while. Here's what I remember about Lipsky. Got Matt to send this by e-mail for me. Guess he learned how in school. Over.

Lipsky: Medium tall, strong build, ordinary brown hair, standard issue part on the left side, standard issue suit, standard issue features. The best way to describe Special FBI Agent Jon Lipsky is to say he was a standard looking type of guy.

The Grand Jury saw Agent Lipsky on several occasions. Lipsky's answers to questions were straightforward, concise and comprehensive. He quoted facts and gave assessments in an informative manner. His body language revealed no insights into what his emotions might say, given the chance.

In the last session the Grand Jury had where the prosecutors were present, they had called Lipsky in as a witness. The prosecutors were trying to get us to go along with their plea bargain. Norton asked a couple of non-essential questions. Then Norton asked me, as the foreman, if the witness could be excused.

Usually, that's just a formality and the prosecutors do whatever they want. But, instead of excusing the witness, I asked the Grand Jury members if they had any question they wished to ask Lipsky.

Several did and Lipsky efficiently answered all or almost all of the questions. Peck, being a lawyer as well as a Grand Juror, usually had the most questions. Peck asked, do you still believe the allegations of the search warrant are accurate?

Before Lipsky could begin to answer, Norton abruptly said,

"I forbid the witness to answer the question."

Lipsky's gaze shifted, poker faced, from Grand Juror Peck to Norton. Norton and Peck then engaged in an interesting little lowbrow pissing match.

I have often wondered where and when the term pissing match gained such prominence. Is it because when we were boys we endeavored to see who could pee the highest mark on the side of the barn wall?

The arguments as to whether Lipsky should or should not answer Peck's question soon began to wear on the nerves of the Grand Jury. It soon became evident that there would be no clear-cut winner in this little brawl. Neither Norton nor Peck was capable of making a mark on the old barn wall.

I therefore said that if there were no more questions to be asked the witness could be excused. There were none. Lipsky arose from the witness stand, nodded farewell to the Grand Jury members and exited the room.

That was the last time I saw Agent Lipsky.

CHAPTER SIX

Citizens' Investigation Analysis: How the Justice Department Stonewalled Congress, 1992

I finally finished annotating the three volumes of testimony from the congressional hearings about the Justice Department's handling of the Rocky Flats Grand Jury investigation. That made me really understand how much I needed to talk with Special Agent Lipsky.

———————

Many environmental and anti-nuke activists had been enraged by the plea bargain back in 1992.[49] An informed and committed activist community had been studying Rocky Flats for years, and trying to do something about it. Quaker groups and Catholic groups, nuns and lay people; hippies; scientists; nuclear workers. The citizens had held demonstrations and teach-ins, seminars and protests. They'd written scholarly papers, done original field research. Non-government scientists had performed studies showing that Rocky Flats was contaminating the nearby neighborhoods, contrary to the Energy Department's repeated assurances to a worried public.

There'd been civil disobedience and peaceful protest. Some nuns had been regularly arrested for praying on the grounds at Rocky Flats.[50] Almost 10,000 people had attended one of the protest rallies outside Rocky Flats in 1979.

Some activists wanted to close down the weapons plant, some just wanted to make it safer. But they were all worried about what went on behind those barbed wire fences. Many had hoped the Grand Jury investigation would bring the secret dangers at Rocky Flats to light. But after the plea bargain was announced, some felt the Justice Department was hiding something terrible. They were worried that the Justice Department's actions would make it easier for the Energy Department to re-start bomb production at Rocky Flats.

There was nothing the activists could do about it, though. All the evidence was sealed in the Grand Jury vault, and no one was allowed to talk about it.

The Justice Department pretty much does what it wants, deferred to on policy grounds by even the US Supreme Court. Only Congress has the power to oversee the actions of the Justice Department.

So the activists complained to Congress.[51] There, partly because of politics, partly because the Justice Department's reputation for interfering with environmental prosecutions was getting a much-needed airing in other congressional subcommittees,[52] the environmentalists found a sympathetic ear.

Congressman Howard Wolpe, Democrat, Michigan, Chair of the Subcommittee on Investigations and Oversight, Committee on Science, Space and Technology, had a reputation for integrity and honesty that was rare in Washington.[53] Congressman Wolpe decided to take on the Justice Department over Rocky Flats. Not that he knew in advance what he'd find; just that he was sure that the Justice Department would fight any investigation tooth and nail.

He was right.

The Justice Department's position was that Congress had no right to interview FBI agents or Justice Department prosecutors, despite the constitutional mandate for congressional oversight as part of the checks and balances of the American system.[54]

The Wolpe subcommittee battled back and forth with Justice for a while. But the Wolpe subcommittee was particularly vulnerable to stalling. Chairman Wolpe was retiring in September at the end of that session of Congress. The Presidential elections were right around the corner. If the Justice Department stalled long enough, they could outlast the subcommittee Chairman and effectively scuttle the investigation.

The delay tactics were obvious. The congressional subcommittee would ask for documents and witness interviews and the Justice Department would stall, then raise objections, then simply ignore the requests. The back and forth between the Congress and the Justice Department lasted several months that summer of 1992. Finally, the subcommittee got tired of fruitlessly requesting cooperation from Justice, and issued subpoenas to US Attorney Michael Norton, Assistant US Attorney Ken Fimberg, Justice Department prosecutor Peter Murtha, and FBI Special Agent Jon Lipsky.

That definitely upped the ante. Now the witnesses faced contempt charges personally if they didn't testify. In September, with just two months left for the investigation, the Justice Department finally allowed the testimony to go forward in Congress.

Special Agent Jon Lipsky testified first.[55] His testimony made it obvious that something had gone very wrong with the Justice Department's Grand Jury investigation of Rocky Flats. Lipsky was complimentary of lead prosecutor Fimberg and US Attorney Norton for their dedication to the job and willingness to take the risk of such a complicated and politically loaded case. But it didn't soften the blow.

Lipsky testified that there was plenty of evidence of illegal midnight plutonium burning. The Justice Department's official representation to the court that the incinerator had not been operated during the shutdown, a statement Rockwell required in order to settle the case, was not true, he said.

Some of Lipsky's testimony supported the rumors that the case had been a political cover-up. Lipsky didn't say that. But he did tell Congress that he'd never agreed that no individuals should be prosecuted. He disagreed with the plea bargain with the Rockwell corporation; he thought there was enough evidence to support indictments against individuals. Lipsky also revealed that, contrary to the Justice Department's public statements, Fimberg had privately agreed with him that they already had enough evidence to indict some high-level individuals, but he'd been "outvoted" by Justice Department headquarters in Washington, DC.

Edith Holleman, staff attorney for the subcommittee, asked Lipsky about a quote from Fimberg in *The New York Times* that no Rockwell officials were indicted because there was only evidence against mid-level managers. Lipsky said that wasn't true; they were "the number one, two, and three level managers, and they were probably the most powerful out there."[56]

Lipsky told Congress that in June of 1991, he'd gotten instructions from Murtha and Fimberg to stop looking for more evidence against Rockwell and Energy Department officials because the case was going to be settled, Rockwell International would pay a fine, and there would be no individual criminal charges.

Lipsky had been investigating the bonus process and the cozy relationship between the Energy Department and its defense contractor. The Government Accounting Office, the investigative arm of Congress, had already done a lot of research on the issue of improper bonuses. In a report issued 24 October 1989, the GAO found that Rockwell received $27 million in bonuses during 1986-1988 in addition to its annual fee of

$6.7 million and the approximately $450 million in operating costs. The report noted that during those three years, three different inspections by Energy Department officials from Washington had found a total of 230 environmental and safety violations.[57]

Lipsky's investigation into those suspicious practices was dropped after the word came down that the case was going to be settled.

Lipsky testified that the United States Attorney General himself had issued special handling instructions for the Rocky Flats criminal investigation.[58] Midway through the investigation, Justice Department prosecutor Peter Murtha had told Lipsky that he'd received orders changing a major legal tool they'd been using for the investigation.

The "responsible corporate officer" doctrine was designed to hold high-level corporate officers responsible for corporate crimes that they knew about and didn't stop, even if they hadn't participated directly in the crime itself. According to Lipsky, Thornburgh's instructions had gutted the case against individual Rockwell and Energy Department officials. There'd been evidence that several high-level Rockwell and Energy Department officials had known that crimes were being committed at Rocky Flats but had done nothing to stop them. Under the "responsible corporate officer" doctrine in the environmental statutes, they could be indicted for that. Without that doctrine, it would be difficult to find enough evidence against them.

Congress had been working for several years to make corporate America more responsive to environmental laws.[59] Because of the nature of corporate structures, the people actually running the company rarely had their hands on the valve that dumped the toxic waste into the river. Seldom did they personally light the incinerator illegally burning waste. The persons with the power to decide whether a company complied with environmental laws were usually so far removed from the actual operations of the company that enforcement of those laws rarely involved them personally. The little guys did the bad deeds, and the big guys claimed they didn't know anything about it.

Hardly anyone was ever prosecuted and environmental pollution was increasing dramatically.

Congress had tried to change all that by amending the major federal environmental statutes to include "responsible corporate officer" provisions. To encourage the boss not to look the other way while environmental crimes are being committed. It would apply to government officials as well.

Apparently, however, Attorney General Thornburgh had decided to interpret what Congress really meant. Thornburgh instructed the prose-cutors that they had to use a more difficult standard in the Rocky Flats case. The Justice Department called it "responsible corporate officer *plus.*" The high-level executives had to have direct personal involvement in the actual crime. According to Thornburgh's instructions, it wasn't enough for Energy Department and Rockwell officials to be in charge of activities which broke the law, and knowingly fail to do something about the criminal activity.

This was exactly the opposite of what Congress intended in the amendments to the environmental statutes.

Lipsky thought Thornburgh had a conflict of interest being involved in the Rocky Flats raid: newspapers reported that he owned Rockwell stock. He could have stayed out of the raid altogether, but instead he got a special exemption from President Bush to be involved. Ironically, earlier in the year of the raid, Thornburgh had authored and signed a personal foreword to the Justice Department Ethics Handbook: "We must not allow even the appearance of impropriety in the performance of our duties."[60]

Colorado US Attorney Michael Norton was also subpoenaed to tes-tify to Congress. But on October 2nd, 1992, Norton wrote to Chairman Wolpe, refusing to appear. Norton had a previous engagement.[61]

Wolpe responded with a scathing letter, and threatened to hold the US Attorney for the District of Colorado in contempt of Congress unless he appeared the following Monday.[62] Over the weekend, Congress and the Justice Department held hurried meetings, trying to defuse the explosive situation.

Congress won. Norton would testify and would answer all questions except those involving confidential informants and Grand Jury secret information.

When US Attorney Norton finally testified, he said that he believed there was not enough evidence to warrant criminal prosecution against individuals. He went even further: "In fact, I had serious doubts about the possibility of success against the corporation itself."[63] And he repeated that the 771 incinerator was not used at all during the Energy Department ordered shutdown:

> *I want to add that it has been brought to my attention in the last perhaps day that Special Agent Lipsky may have testified to the*

contrary about this issue, that being that the incinerator was in fact used during the period of shutdown. I have verified my understanding with both Mr. Murtha and Mr. Fimberg, and following that verification my answer would remain the same, that to my knowledge the incinerator was not used during the period of shutdown.

Most surprising of all, Norton swore that he had consulted with Lipsky about the plea bargain. "All were in agreement." He denied that the decision not to indict individuals was Rockwell's requirement for settlement. He insisted there just wasn't enough evidence.

Assistant US Attorney Ken Fimberg, the Harvard law school graduate, the star prosecutor, also seemed to directly contradict his good friend Special Agent Lipsky about major issues. He insisted there was not enough evidence to indict individuals. He called the cases against Rockwell individuals "marginal," "questionable," with serious "fairness issues" because of Energy Department involvement. And he said there was no basis for any criminal charges against Energy Department officials, either.[64]

Lipsky had a lot more to say. But the Wolpe subcommittee had run out of time. Congress was ending its session, elections were right around the corner. Edith Holleman had to start writing the subcommittee's report before they were even finished with the interviews. Some of the documents they'd subpoenaed from the Justice Department and the Energy Department didn't come until after the report was already finished. Some of them never came at all.[65] And only subcommittee staff had been available to do the last round of questioning; the Members of Congress were doing last minute campaigning.

The Wolpe Report was published on January 4th, 1993. Among other things, it found that the Justice Department had "bargained away the truth" about what had really happened at Rocky Flats. The report was quickly attacked by the Justice Department as unfair and inaccurate.[66]

Within three days of publication of the Wolpe Report, the FBI transferred Jon Lipsky out of Denver.

CHAPTER SEVEN

Citizens' Investigation Analysis: Wes McKinley's Congressional Campaign, 1996

Looking through Wes' boxes of clippings and documents from his 1996 congressional campaign was interesting. After the Grand Jury's press conference on the courthouse steps, he'd returned to ranching and running trail rides into the stark open spaces of the Commanche National Grasslands. But Wes just couldn't forget the Justice Department's deception. The gag order that stopped him from revealing it seemed totally wrong.

———————

Adrienne Anderson, an environmental health and safety advocate, firmly believed that FBI Special Agent Jon Lipsky was an FBI plant to mislead activists. For years, she had been organizing workers, farmers and students while raising two small children in urban Denver. Her students loved her fiery activism and total lack of awe for the big guns she constantly challenged. At Anderson's invitation, Wes frequently spoke to her environmental ethics class, and she and Wes had become friends.

One summer, Anderson went on one of Wes' Kirkwell Cattle Company trail rides. Late in the night, after the other riders had wandered off to their bedrolls, she and Wes sat talking around the campfire.

She and a coalition of workers, ranchers, and students were fighting a plan to dump the contaminated groundwater from Lowry Landfill, a government owned waste dump, into the Denver public sewers. Then spray the water on the parks and spread the sludge on the Colorado wheat fields as fertilizer.

There were reports of radioactive contamination in the Lowry groundwater, along with the usual hazardous wastes. But the EPA and other environmental officials were denying the existence of any plutonium contamination.

99

Anderson and one of her students had uncovered evidence of pluto-nium from Rocky Flats in the sewage sludge being spread on the wheat fields. If there was plutonium in the sewer sludge, it most probably came from Rocky Flats.

Anderson and her coalition of activists were gearing up for a legal battle. The government and the nuclear industry have a solution to the nuclear waste problem, Anderson told Wes, her voice heavy with sarcasm. They want to recycle radioactive metal into spoons, bed springs, baby carriages. That's their way of getting rid of some of the waste. Recycle radioactive metal for household use; dump radioactive water and sludge on the Colorado wheat fields.[67]

Wes could only shake his head, and wish that he could help. He now understood that the problem he was fighting was a lot bigger than just Rocky Flats. There was too much nuclear waste and no safe method of storing or disposing of it. It was piled up at the weapons plants and the nuclear power plants, and in landfills around the countryside.

Wes kept attending environmental meetings. He started speaking at some of the nuclear safety meetings, always careful not to break the Grand Jury secrecy oath, but trying desperately to impart a sense of urgency to these citizens that would keep them working to halt nuclear weapons production. Always hoping the government he'd grown up believing in would step in and do something about the Justice Department's obstruction of justice at Rocky Flats.

Wes was awarded the 1993 Cavallo Award, given by a private foun-dation to citizens demonstrating moral courage. He was told he could invite some friends to the ceremony in Denver. Wes remembered Alex, the barefoot bearded peace activist he'd seen so often, standing quietly with his sign on the courthouse steps.[68] Wes tried to track him down to invite him to the ceremony. But one of the activists said Alex was in the hospital, and was not expected to survive.

So Wes was especially gratified at the awards ceremony when he saw Alex standing in the small crowd that had assembled. Alex was weak, but still smiling his peaceful smile.

And someone had given him a pair of shoes for the occasion.

Wes tipped his hat, and Alex smiled peacefully back. He died shortly afterwards.

The Sierra Club, too, thought the Grand Jury's courage in trying to speak out about the Justice Department's actions was an admirable demonstration of citizenship. In 1993, along with 21 other local and national groups, they awarded Wes, as Grand Jury foreman, a citizenship award.[*]

One day in 1995, Wes started down an even more unlikely path. Some activists had invited Wes to dinner before they went to yet another environmental meeting. Wes had come a little late, and stepped into the living room with the rest of the group, nodding to a few familiar faces. He stood awkwardly in the low ceilinged room while one of the women explained in detail how the room had been feng shui'd. The others were listening intently.

Wes looked up at the crystal hanging just above his cowboy hat. He moved slightly to get out from under it, shifting uncomfortably but saying nothing as the woman continued explaining its healing properties.

There's some mighty strange folks in this world, he thought as the group sat down to dinner. They just don't do stuff like this back in Walsh. He was used to eating beans, but he'd never heard of millet and quinoa. Not even a speck of bacon to flavor the stuff, he thought sadly, looking around in vain for some Tabasco sauce.

A TV was on soundlessly in the background as they waited for a news broadcast. A New Mexico Senator was addressing his assembled colleagues on the floor of Congress. Someone turned up the volume.

The Senator was saying something about his pet nuclear weapons lab. The group started scoffing; they all believed it to be an outright lie. One of them, an activist lawyer, muttered in passing that Members of Congress can say anything. They've got complete immunity so they can say any damn thing they please on the floor of Congress.

The room fell silent. Then the activists all turned to stare at Wes, and suddenly, plans were being made for Wes to run for Congress.

An odd assortment of nuclear safety activists and housewives, cowboys and peace protesters trickled in to the ranch to volunteer on Wes' congressional campaign. Wes had a campaign strategy based on his lack of political party affiliation and his lack of funds: he would ride the entire 1,200 miles around his District. Wes was not a Democrat; he was an independent.

---

[*] US Attorney Mike Norton was reported to have said that this was ". . . like Butch Cassidy getting a ... Friend of the Bank Award." Norton's statement is attributed to him by Jason Saltzman of Greenpeace in an article in *The Denver Post*, "Flats grand jury likely to be charged, lawyer says," 21 May 1993.

He wouldn't be riding a donkey, he'd be riding Marvin the Mule.

Bryan Abas volunteered to be Wes' campaign manager. He was the writer for *Westword* who had first broken the story about the leaked Grand Jury Report. He'd come to admire Wes' integrity, and wanted to help with the campaign.

Abas had sent Congress copies of the Grand Jury Report and the court reporter's transcript which he'd used to write his article. He'd offered to testify, if it was helpful.[69] But he'd never been contacted. He still wanted to help.

Greg Lopez, an award winning journalist for *The Rocky Mountain News*, called out to the campaign headquarters at the ranch one day. He wanted to write a series of articles about Wes' campaign. The volunteers were elated. With no money for advertising, this was critical to any hope for victory.

Lopez fit in well on the ranch. He knew how to handle a horse, and he and Wes spent some time together working the cattle, and became friends. Lopez's first article about Wes' campaign was a good one. He made it clear that Wes was running for Congress so he could talk about Rocky Flats.[70]

Campaign donations started coming in and Wes and the volunteers made plans for the campaign. Almost immediately, though, the problems began. Hang up calls started at the ranch. Some of the volunteers were afraid they were being followed. Wes got calls from lawyers advising him that congressional immunity was not such a clear cut matter, that if he talked about what had gone on in the Grand Jury room, even to Congress as a Congressman, he could still end up in prison.[71]

Wes lost an oil and gas well servicing contract that had been a major source of income for the family. The McKinleys tried to live a normal life around the ranch, even as the whole family mobilized to help with the campaign. Tamra walked gleefully into bars with a petition to get her daddy on the ballot. She'd never have been allowed in there otherwise. Toni sang at fundraisers. Jan took over just about everyone's chores. Dean, Wes' partner, handled the Kirkwell Cattle Company trail riding business on his own. The ranchers from the nearby community rolled out to help.

The McKinley family was limping a little financially because of the loss of that oil well contract. Wes was never sure whether the contract had been pulled because of the campaign, or if the timing was just a coincidence. Jan was supporting the family on her teacher's salary, working fulltime and studying for her master's so she could bring home more money.

Wes occasionally thought about how someone had intentionally contaminated that tall Grand Jury witness with deadly plutonium.

Jacqueline Brever. He remembered her perfectly. He thought about it every once in a while, but he hadn't really worried about his own safety, although some of his friends who'd seen the Silkwood movie were worried for him. Wes just laughed them off and ignored it. He never went to the movies.

But he did worry every once in a while about whether he was doing the right thing. Was it fair? Was he putting the volunteers and his family in danger just to stand on his principles? Was this the way things were supposed to work in the United States of America?

He pushed those thoughts from his mind and kept on with the campaign. Then one day, shortly after that first article about Wes' campaign had been published, the reporter, Greg Lopez, was killed in a one-car accident in the early morning hours outside Denver.

Many campaign volunteers were sure Greg Lopez had been murdered; when the suspect in the crash committed suicide shortly after the accident, some were sure of it.

Wes' journal April, 1995: Lopez was a fun guy to be around. He rode horses with Dean and me and helped sort Charles' cattle. He enjoyed shooting pistols and appreciated Dean's brand of whiskey. Lopez had an intimate feeling for the outdoors and seemed to be on speaking terms with our environment.

Lopez's article was a great morale booster to my fledgling campaign and his continuing support looked to be a great help.

It's hard to believe he's dead. I had to reread the newspaper article several times. Lopez had been forced off the road and he had died in the wreck. I was plenty nervous and hoped they found the hit and run driver soon. I thought the true story may be revealed when and if he was caught.

A few days later I read where the police had found the driver of the car that ran Lopez to his death. They found him, shortly after he committed suicide.

The truth of Lopez's death was now sealed.

Early the next morning I called a guy who is in the gun business. I'm not really worried that the DOJ would go that far to silence me. If their shooting ability is anywhere near the same as their ability to prosecute Rockwell's environmental crimes, I am confident they will get nowhere.

But I became very careful about walking outside to do the chores and I constantly watched behind and all around when riding the canyon trails. I stayed away from riding through any area that would make for an easy ambush and I became proficient at identifying tracks.

I have always been a fair shot. I started diligently practicing. I had not been concerned when the FBI started investigating me. This was entirely different.

After the initial shock and sadness wore off, the small all-volunteer band of cowboys, activists and housewives started trying to pick up the pieces of the campaign. They'd been counting on Greg's status as an award winning reporter and his upcoming series of news articles to get Wes in front of the voting public. No matter what the reason for the crash, the campaign seemed doomed.

The volunteers started bickering about whether it was time to just give up. There wasn't even enough money for Wes to travel the district campaigning. There was definitely no money for advertising. Maybe they could have a bake sale. What if Greg's death wasn't an accident . . .who's next?

The volunteers dispersed, squabbling with little enthusiasm. Some started taking down tables, packing up campaign flyers.

Wes half-heartedly picked up the mail Tam had brought in, and headed for his usual tree stump by the side of the barn.

He listlessly flipped through letters, sitting on the stump and leaning back against the wooden planking, twirling a straw between his teeth, looking grim. Tam came over and joined him as she often did, saying nothing but leaning back against the barn on her own small tree stump.

Abruptly, Wes' boots clattered to the ground and he sat up straighter, staring off into the hills, holding a lavender envelope with spidery formal handwriting addressed to *Mr. Wesley McKinley.*

Tam waited patiently, twirling her piece of straw in a perfect copy of Wes.

Wes started reading the handwritten letter aloud, but as though to himself. Tam was alert and listening. It was written with an old fashioned formality by a Mrs. Emily Stroh.

Mrs. Stroh and her knitting group wanted to help with Wes' campaign. We live on our pensions and don't have much money, she wrote. But we've all agreed to save our egg money.

Instead of going into town once a month for sodas, they'd decided to send the money to Wes.

We know it's not much, Mr. McKinley, Wes read to Tam, who stared at him impassively. We know the odds are against you. But we each have to do what we can.

Tam reached over and pulled out a twenty dollar bill Wes hadn't seen in the envelope, and silently handed it to him.

As he often did when he needed to think, Wes saddled up and rode off alone into the countryside. His face was thoughtful in the gathering dusk.

Just as he was turning back to head home, he heard hoof beats approaching. He quickly took cover behind a rocky crag, then saw it was Jan, looking for him as she cantered along.

He realized then from his suspicious response that Greg's death had gotten to him more than he'd thought. He tried to shake it off.

Wes and Jan moved closer together without speaking, as they had so many times in their lives together. Watching the light settle, saying nothing much. They reached out simultaneously, without even looking at each other, and briefly touched hands as their side by side paints swished their tails together companionably.

Jan turned to Wes and handed him an envelope she pulled from her saddlebag.

He opened it, and then stiffened. It was a check for $30,000.

It was Jan's inheritance. Her Dad had died earlier that year. This was more money than she would ever be able to accumulate in her entire life on her teacher's salary.

Jan's voice was calm.

It's not enough to finish the campaign, I know, Wes, but we can at least try.

In the early morning light of the ranch kitchen the next morning, Jan started the coffee. She asked Tam to find Wes for breakfast. He's probably feeding the horses, she tossed out over her shoulder as Tam headed outside.

The slim young woman returned shaking her head slowly.

Dad isn't out there and Marvin the Mule is gone, too.

Some campaign volunteers straggled in, sleepy eyed and dis-spirited, ready to head home. The phone rang. They waited before answering to see who it was, as they often had in the past. The usual corny cowboy greeting they'd heard so many times was gone.

Instead, they heard the familiar refrain Wes had been picking out on his guitar throughout the campaign. Wes' voice was singing the now-completed lyrics. "You gotta do what you can."

One of the volunteers finally answered the phone.

Jan looked down at the caned seat of her usual chair at the kitchen table near the coffeepot. She saw a single rose from the garden. She picked it up slowly and brought it to her smiling face.

Wes had taken Marvin the Mule and set out again on the campaign trail. He wasn't going to give up. He rode off alone on a country road, the magnificent Colorado countryside looking deserted and stretching out forever around him.

A rattling cloud of dust grew larger as it approached, and a battered old pick up truck pulled along side him. Wes straightened his spine, cocked back his cowboy hat, and got ready to start his campaign spiel.

The small brown mule had a bumper sticker on its flank: McKinley for Congress, in red white and blue.

The friendly old couple in the pick up didn't see many strangers and a nice chat seemed in order. The elderly driver leaned out of the window, smiling.

McKinley's a strange name for a mule, young man.

Wes laughed.

Well, his name's really Marvin the Mule. I'm McKinley.

Wes dismounted and limped over to the truck to shake hands, raising his voice a little so the elderly couple could hear.

Actually, though, *The Greeley Tribune* endorsed Marvin the Mule for Congress just last month. He's doing better than I am.

The old lady leaned forward from the passenger seat.

What made you decide to run? Seems like awful hot and dusty work.

Wes brightened. That was exactly the question he wanted to hear.

Later, Tam and some of the other campaign volunteers caught up with Wes, hauling the buckboard and spare horses. They continued on the campaign trail, as planned.

Wes' journal May, 1995: We came off the hill, crossed the bridge and as we pulled even with Mrs. Carnes place we saw three women standing outside waving. We pulled in. The three ladies, Mrs. Carnes, her daughter, and the home health lady who comes out each day to take care of Mrs. Carnes. Mrs. Carnes is 92 years old and came to this country as a baby in a covered wagon. Her bed was a drawer in a dresser. She was very happy today to see a covered wagon and horses and a fine Mule in her yard. We all introduced ourselves. We talked a little politics. They'd never heard of Rocky Flats. But they could appreciate a hard working cowboy.

Maybe they'll vote for me anyway, I thought as we rode off.

If old Mrs. Carnes can even make it to the polling place.

We had covered over 30 miles today and we all were experiencing the first signs of trail founder. Johnny Duvall and family hosted a very good barbecue and some of his family and friends came over and we visited politics. I was very weary by the time we got to the sleeping bags.

The big wind blew last night. The sleeping bags flapped and shook. But in the morning I felt rested and ready for another day on the trail. Johnny's wife fixed us a fine breakfast and he made a list of folks I could call who would be interested in helping me on my way across the county.

Some of the folks knew about Rocky Flats and one of them recognized me. Told me to watch my back.

I can't tell if I'm getting votes or not but many of the people I've been speaking with seem to agree that we need to make sure that the government is obeying the law, too.

The wind had a chill to it and after the lunch break I returned a call to the Gannett news service from the cell phone on the wagon. My traveling companions of this week would leave me and I would start on the trail by myself. Does anyone really want to know about what happened at Rocky Flats? Some seem interested, no one seems surprised that the government lies to them. That's maybe the most depressing thing I've run into. No one much seems surprised about it at all.

Maybe I'm the only one didn't know it was like that.

Wes lost the 1996 election. He got 4% of the vote. He continued the speaking engagements, trying to keep the public interested in Rocky Flats, hoping they would ask the right questions, and do their own investigations, demand answers from their elected officials. But he was a lone voice shouting in the wind. People soon forgot about the Rocky Flats Grand Jury investigation, forgot about the headlines, forgot about the danger.

CHAPTER EIGHT

The Citizens' Investigation Continues— Some Small Successes, 1997-2000

Wes and I kept meeting, trying to figure out a way around the impasse. But how were we going to find out what had really happened with the secret midnight plutonium burning charge if the key people wouldn't talk with us? We were still waiting for responses to our FOIA request for copies of the infrared reports. The EPA and the Energy Department had already said they couldn't find copies of any such documents. The Justice Department was our last chance.

Somehow, that didn't inspire much hope.

One summer afternoon, Wes and I were working in my kitchen making green chili sauced cowboy steaks for dinner. Wes was chopping jalapeños. It looked like way too many jalapeños to me, but I said nothing.

My friend Arjun Makhijani was coming to Santa Fe and I'd asked Wes to come down and meet him. Arjun—Dr. Makhijani—had been a friend and colleague for several years. An engineer and physicist from India, he had come to the US for graduate school in the 60s and stayed. He'd specialized in nuclear fusion at Berkeley. Now, he heads up the Institute for Energy and Environmental Research, a Washington DC area non-profit organization working on global problems of nuclear safety and other environmental issues.

Arjun was an essential part of the scientific foundation of the nuclear safety movement. For years, as "Dr. Egghead," he wrote a column about nuclear issues in the newsletter published by IEER. Now, Dr. Egghead is a nickname the activists he helps have affectionately started using for my intelligent and compassionate friend.

Arjun and I had worked together in Santa Fe on the lawsuit Concerned Citizens for Nuclear Safety had filed against the Energy Department about Clean Air Act violations at Los Alamos National Laboratory.[72] He was my mentor in all things nuclear, always available to explain the intricacies of the weapons labs, the regulatory nightmares, the nuclear science behind the weapons and the nuclear disarmament policy that motivated him.

I respected his science, his integrity and his dedication to making nuclear safety and abolition of nuclear weapons foremost on the global political agenda.

I wanted the cowboy to meet the Indian. Arjun and Wes could both stay at the house for a few days and get to know each other. Arjun would arrive later that afternoon.

Somewhere along the way since I'd last seen him, Wes had turned into an organic rancher. He'd gone with me to the health food store on an earlier trip, raised his eyebrows at the price of the beef I told him was organic, tipped his hat back and started thinking. I saw him start thinking, but I didn't know what he was thinking about.

Next time he was in Santa Fe I found out. He'd called the beef company I'd thought was organic. Gotten their brochures. They weren't really organic at all. They still used pesticides on the grain they fed the beef. And pesticides are what I'd been trying to avoid. Next thing I knew, Wes was bringing down some of his own beef.

"We never use pesticides," he told me while I was thanking him.

"Can't afford 'em. We raise our grain right near the house, and we've never used pesticides at all. These beeves have been given no growth hormones, no antibiotics, nothing except grass and then finished off on organic milo. Can't afford any of those fancy chemicals that ruin the beef taste anyway."

He was right. It was great tasting beef. Next thing I knew, he was checking into selling his organic beef retail.

Wes was an entreprenuring kind of guy. Sometime back, he'd invented a bag holder. A plastic gizmo that holds opens your plastic garbage bag. You just stick it into a counter drawer while you're working in the kitchen.

"Got ripped off by my lawyer on that one," he advised me solemnly.

The knife was flashing while he diced those jalapeños.

I was sure he was teasing me. I wasn't getting paid for doing the Citizens' Investigation. But then I guessed there were other ways to rip him off than with money, so I looked at him closely to see if he was trying to tell me something.

I couldn't tell. So I had to ask.

"You trying to tell me something, Wes?" I asked carefully.

He looked surprised, then started grinning. Flipped the diced peppers in with way too many onions.

"Nothing about you. Just thought you might want to know why I don't have a lot of affection for your profession. And that was *before* Rocky Flats," he added, laughing.

Wes and Arjun hit it off immediately.

Wes' journal summer, 1998: I had helped with the supper preparations, chopped several jalapeños and onions. Caron and I talked about the investigation while we were at it.

The beef, real beef and chemical free, was thawed and ready to throw on the fire and be cooked, cowboy style. (Cowboy style is you eat it and like it just the way the cook serves it.) All that was needed in order to start the final cooking stage was the arrival of the Indian.

I had heard about Arjun. He is well spoken of and highly regarded by my anti-nuclear activist friends in Santa Fe.

The Indian arrived and I was surprised to find myself not surprised. He was totally normal. I had kinda thought he would be.

I cooked the steaks to perfection (my standard) and they were served with the various side dishes, all delicious. Arjun liked the steaks. Said he truly enjoyed the flavor of good red meat.

He called himself the only beef eating Hindu in a land of Christian vegetarians.

During supper and afterwards there was lively discussion. On matters of nuclear stuff and other important subjects, Arjun was interesting and informative. I enjoyed his sharing of knowledge. Caron and Georges wore out, leaving Arjun and myself. Into the dark part of the night we kept drinking and discussing nuclear happenings during our childhoods and the effects of this on our bodies. This was most informative but not uplifting. We must have touched on cowboy lore a time or two because Arjun expressed an interest in the cowboy lifestyle.

We compared the books we read. Arjun reads for the information and I read for entertainment. We both silently thought the other needs help in their selection of reading material.

Since Arjun was interested in cowboy lore I told him I would send him some cowboy manuals. As soon as I got home I sent him some of my extra copies of Louis L'Amour's best selling, easy reading, western fiction.

Arjun sent me his nuclear newsletter. I am enjoying reading it. I doubt if the Indian learns to ride a horse and shoot a gun from reading Louis L'Amour and the saga of the Sacketts but I hope his interest is sparked enough to come out for a western experience this summer.

We never slashed our wrist and sealed in blood, but we did promise to go on a week of western adventures in the Commanche National Grasslands of southeast Colorado this summer.

We'd also done some work that night. We had some things we needed to talk about with Arjun. He, Wes and I had lounged around before dinner on the front portal. New Mexico has such clear air, such starry skies. It was dry and pleasant, and we were looking forward to a satisfying dinner.

Arjun started explaining a physics term to Wes at some point in the discussion. Wes interrupted and finished the explanation for Arjun. Then grinned and said he'd taught physics for a while and understood the terms.

Not many folks know about Wes' college degree, or the fact that, in his head, he can tote up the prices on the groceries as the clerk is running them through the cash register, and get the total, to the penny, faster than the cash register.

And once he reads something, he can spit it back to you nearly verbatim. Even stuff from years back. Even boring, technical information. Pretty much a photographic memory.

Very useful in this Citizens' Investigation.

There was no ego from either Arjun or Wes. Most folks probably would have been taken aback by the stereotype-busting image of the cowboy physics teacher. Arjun just nodded and they kept on talking.

We were discussing a question I'd asked Arjun. Why was the Energy Department willing to leave so much plutonium and other contaminants in the soil at Rocky Flats, even though they knew kids were probably going to be playing there?

The question made Arjun thoughtful and sad, and he paused a while before he gave us the historical answer.

"In 1996, the Energy Department and the regulators adopted the original Rocky Flats Clean-up Agreement. This set the level for how much plutonium could remain in the soil at 651 pico curies per gram of soil (pCi/g). Because of public pressure, the government funded an oversight panel of citizens and experts. The oversight panel rejected the 651 pCi/g level as not clean enough, so then the Energy Department eventually agreed to an independent scientific review. As a result of that independent study, the citizens' oversight panel recommended that the soil action level or clean-up levels should be set at 35 pCi/g for plutonium, a much stricter standard than what the government was proposing."

Arjun looked thoughtful again.

"As you know, instead of accepting this level, the government agencies started all over again. Now they've decided that the plutonium in surface soil clean-up level be set at 50 pCi/g. That's better than 651 and it's not a lot higher than 35. But in exchange for getting this better surface soil clean-up, the agencies intend to leave even more contaminants in the subsurface soils."

Wes interjected here. "But there's burrowing prairie dogs out there. And other animals that dig it up and leave it to the winds to toss around. There's wind and water erosion. . . ." His voice trailed off.

Arjun nodded sympathetically. "IEER worked with LeRoy Moore from the Rocky Mountain Peace and Justice Center and we both recommended a much more protective clean-up level.[73] But, of course, that's not what the government decided."

"But why?" I asked, then answered my own question. "There's probably no little concern at the Energy Department about political fallout. The sloppy practices of the past have made the price of cleaning up the nuclear weapons complex astronomical. And of course, there's that multi-million dollar bonus the Energy Department agreed to give its corporate defense contractor if it can get the clean-up done before 2006. The less they clean it up, the faster the clean-up goes."[74]

Wes looked at me, and I knew he was thinking about the discussion we'd started while waiting for Arjun to arrive for dinner.

Part of the Rocky Flats mission had been to re-cycle the plutonium from old bombs into new triggers for new bombs. And extract plutonium from the contaminated waste they created while they were at it. And re-cycle a lot of contaminated waste that had been generated off-site, too.

The bonuses offered by the Energy Department— in the millions of dollars—were for producing bomb triggers, not for complying with environmental laws. So Rockwell's financial interest lay in making as many bomb triggers as possible as fast as possible—regardless, apparently, of the contamination problems it created in the process.

For that matter, the more a process cost, the more money Rockwell made, since they were on a cost plus fee basis.[75] Rockwell had no incentive to do things the less expensive way, and in fact, all its incentive was to do the opposite. Nuclear defense contractors make money from everything, even their mistakes. They just add the cost of fixing them to their bills, plus their percentage.

Wes rarely got visibly upset. He'd been on the Rocky Flats trail for over a decade and it seemed to have settled in on him. But now he looked so mad I was glad I was on his side.

"We learned about this in the Grand Jury room. Our own government signs contracts that give these defense contractors lots of reason to break the law. 'Hurry up the bomb production and you get a bonus. Oh, if you get caught breaking the law, we'll pay your fine. We'll intervene with the regulators and have them go easy on us. We'll just say no to external regulation and tell Congress we're regulating ourselves.' It's awfully bad business.

"The Government Accounting Office has been writing critical reports about the problem for Congress for more than ten years.[76] But no matter what anyone does, the Energy Department keeps giving these sweetheart contracts to their buddies in the nuclear industry.

"Taxpayers not only pay those contractors billions of dollars to make nuclear weapons we don't even need anymore, we also pay their fines if they happen to get caught when they're breaking the law, we pay to clean up the damage they cause breaking the law, and we pay for attorneys to defend them from prosecution for breaking the law, even if they're found guilty."

We'd researched it. The same government agency that had created the nuclear waste problem during the 1980s, in part because of these sweetheart deals with defense contractors, had helped cover up the extent of that problem. Now it was in charge of pricing how much it was going to cost—politically and financially—to clean it up. Obviously, the less that was known about the past contamination problems—the better the cover-up had worked—the cheaper it would be to clean up the mess.

If citizens can ever get the government to face the reality of decades of unaccounted for nuclear waste, of all the lies about what had been produced and where the waste had been hidden, all the mistakes, all the spills, all the dumping, the government could never proceed with the plans to allow kids to play in what was really a nuclear waste dump.

———————————

I finally found Karen Pitts. I was really excited to finally get a chance to talk with an eye witness to the secret midnight plutonium burning. But after first agreeing to meet, she changed her mind. Karen Pitts seems to have learned a lesson about being forthright concerning Rocky Flats. She declined the interview, writing that ". . . my husband, Mark, who is employed at Rocky Flats as a Technical Supervisor [for clean up activities] could quite possibly be dismissed for my negative actions towards the plant site. Morally, I cannot place him or any other member of my family in a position of risk."[77]

I was having no luck finding Jacque Brever. She seemed to have just disappeared. Without her—or someone else on the inside of Building 771—we'd never find out what we needed to know about the midnight plutonium burning. I knew I had to give Wes the bad news.

Wes had invited me and the nuclear safety activists I volunteered with at Concerned Citizens for Nuclear Safety up to his ranch for a free trail ride. I was grateful for his generosity; activists worked hard and were rarely thanked for their time and efforts. We were riding into Picture Canyon near Wes' ranch in southeastern Colorado. I was straggling behind the rest of the riders, thinking more about the Citizens' Investigation than about learning how to stay seated on my horse.

It was blowing dust and hot that summer, but the ride to Picture Canyon was one of Wes' favorites. I was enough of a novice on a horse that I was looking more at the saddlehorn I was clutching than at the breathtaking scenery.

It was dry, much like Santa Fe, and studded with piñon and juniper and huge gullies we had to pick our way around. We were quiet for a while as Wes watched his gentlest horse negotiate the loose rock with me trying hard to let the horse control the choices.

I think Wes was enjoying my discomfort, because every once in a while I'd look up and he'd be grinning. But I didn't mind. I knew I looked the fool. But Wes was charming and humorous about it, and I soon relaxed and trusted his knowledge of this strange exotic countryside.

"We're at a dead end, Wes," I muttered through clenched teeth. I was talking about the Citizens' Investigation, not the canyon, and I was sure Wes understood. "The FBI won't let us talk to Lipsky. Karen Pitts won't talk with us and we can't find Jacque Brever. Jonathon Turley still hasn't called me back about whether I can talk with the other Grand Jurors, although I've called him three times. The government won't respond to our FOIA request for copies of the infrared reports. We've put together as much as we can from stuff that's been made public, but it's just not enough."

We were interrupted by a shout. It was Dean, Wes' partner. It was time to set up camp. One of Dean's favorite tricks is to mess with the trail riders he and Wes guide on overnight riding expeditions. A few hours into the trail ride, Dean had reined up next to one of the older volunteers who was already having enough trouble sitting her horse, and whispered urgently, gesturing at Margaret, the tall thin woman driving the chuck wagon.

"She's on furlough from jail for knifing her boyfriend over another woman," was Dean's whispered message. "Please don't offer Margaret any liquor when we stop for the night," he urged, "because that's what gets her riled up and waving the knife."

Dean chuckled madly as he left the woman struggling to stay on her horse, and now looking worriedly at Margaret. The message was passed quickly to the rest, and everyone stayed clear of Margaret and the chuck wagon.

Later, of course, Margaret, who'd never been in jail and doesn't drink anyway, tried to explain that Dean was just joking. Some folks believed Dean, some folks Margaret, but no one was real sure about anything after that. And as we were setting up camp, it was clear that the ones who believed Dean were in the majority.

Wes and I couldn't find any time that night to talk alone. But the next morning after we'd saddled up, we picked up the conversation as though there'd not been dinner, cowboy tales, campfire songs, worry about Margaret and a lot of bourbon in between.

"So I guess we can just drop the investigation into the secret midnight plutonium burning, right?" I asked testily.

Maybe it was the increasing physical discomfort that was making me short tempered. Also, all that congressional testimony was difficult to read. The thick, bound volumes were physically hard to handle, pages were always ripping out. There must be something else I could spend my time on.

Wes pulled his hat brim down a little farther before answering. "I don't think you should drop it yet," he said. "There was just something fishy about the whole way they handled it. The prosecutors just stopped mentioning the midnight burning," Wes continued. "No more evidence, no more witnesses about it, nothing. Later, they told us there hadn't really been any secret midnight burning. They said the FBI had made a mistake."

I was ready for him. "Well, that's what the prosecutors told Congress, too. That's why they decided to drop it. They said the infrared expert had changed his mind, so they didn't have a case anymore. They said Karen Pitts and Jacque Brever weren't very reliable sources, that they couldn't even remember whether the plutonium burning they were talking about had been during the shutdown or not.

"If all their evidence fell apart, dropping those charges might have been the appropriate thing for a prosecutor to do," I got out through clenched teeth. I was sore from yesterday in the saddle.

Wes nodded, then pulled his hat down even lower over his eyes.

"That's what the prosecutors said," he acknowledged. "That's what they told us and the newspapers, too. But why is it up to the prosecutors to decide who to believe? I thought that was up to the Grand Jury. And if the Grand Jury wants to hear more about a subject, isn't it up to them, not the prosecutors?"

He was right, according to the law. The Grand Jury decides the credibility of witnesses, not the prosecutors. And the instructions from Judge Finesilver said that the Grand Jury can decide what it wants to investigate, and can even have the clerk subpoena witnesses if the prosecutors won't. But given the way the Justice Department had been limiting Grand Jury powers in the last several decades, despite the constitutional emphasis on them,[78] I doubted that was how the system really worked anymore, despite the instructions from the judge.

The canyon walls started rising on both sides of us as the horses moved gently down what had become a sandy path. I was able to concentrate again. The rest of the group was far up ahead with Dean. Wes was still muttering.

"Well, I don't agree with the prosecutors. Something smells about the whole thing. Keep looking and you're bound to find something."

So I kept looking.

It bothered me that Ken Fimberg had called his two main witnesses "not very reliable sources" when he testified to the Wolpe congressional subcommittee. Jacque Brever and Karen Pitts had basically risked their lives to help Ken Fimberg's investigation. They'd been harassed and threatened and assaulted as a result of their cooperation. They'd lost their jobs and their friends. Jacque Brever had almost lost her life.

Who did Ken Fimberg think he was, calling them "not very reliable sources?" And if Fimberg just meant they were wrong, why didn't he say so? Calling them "not very reliable sources" is quite a different thing from saying he thinks they were wrong.

As a trial lawyer, I knew that Jacque Brever and Karen Pitts had been the main witnesses in the investigation. I knew that because they testified right after Special Agent Lipsky and another FBI agent had laid out the big picture for the Grand Jury about what the investigation was going to show. And as a lawyer I knew that Fimberg or Murtha or one of the prosecutors had talked with Jacque Brever and Karen Pitts before they went on the witness stand, so they knew what the two were going to say. Their testimony hadn't been any surprise.

If the two chem operators had not been reliable sources, why would the prosecution have put them on the witness stand in the starring roles?

It just didn't make sense.

I'd represented whistleblowers in the past and it really offended me that Fimberg had called his two main witnesses "not very reliable sources." I decided to find out whether Pitts and Brever had been wrong, or lying, or not very reliable. Or whether the prosecutors were the ones who weren't very reliable.

My husband Georges is Swiss, so when we visited Europe in the summer of 2000, I made a side trip to Holland. Ken Fimberg, the former lead prosecutor for the Rocky Flats Grand Jury investigation, had gone to work at The Hague as an attorney for the International War Crimes Tribunal for the former Yugoslavia.[79] He made time for an interview with me between his appointments.

He'd changed his name to Ken Scott. I thought it was interesting that he'd gone to such lengths to distance himself from his past. First changing his name, then leaving the Justice Department and moving almost half way around the world. Had the Rocky Flats case figured into all this?

Ken Fimberg/Scott advised me that the decision to change his name in 1995 had nothing to with the Rocky Flats case. Neither had the decision to leave the Justice Department and come to Europe to live and work. They were both personal decisions, he insisted. He'd just felt that his career in the Justice Department wasn't going anywhere very interesting. And when his adopted father and his mother had divorced, the name Fimberg didn't seem appropriate anymore.

Ken Fimberg/Scott and I sat at a small table in a café across from his office in The Hague. He looked over his shoulder often, although none of the diplomat-looking types hurrying by even gave us a second glance.

He was the worrying sort, I decided, noting the nails bitten to stubs and the frequent furtive eye movements. He wasn't anxious to talk, and said he didn't remember much of the details. That he didn't want to remember them. He asked me if I'd read the background news articles and the court files, and nodded quietly when I said I had.

Fimberg was surprised when I asked him why he'd called Jacque Brever and Karen Pitts, the two Rockwell whistleblowers, his main Grand Jury witnesses, "not very reliable sources."

He protested that he was sure he hadn't said that. When shown the copy of the congressional hearing transcript, he looked chagrinned. "I never meant they weren't reliable," he said, red faced. "Just that we couldn't corroborate what they said."

That's a lot different than saying they weren't reliable. What Fimberg actually said had attacked the women's credibility and reputations; what he says he *meant* would have just indicated that the investigation hadn't found any witness or document to support what the two women had said.

Perhaps, in the unpleasantness of being cross-examined by congressional attorneys, instead of being the one doing the cross-examining, he'd just mis-spoken. I'd never know. I had many questions. But Ken Fimberg wanted me to rely on the public documents. He just didn't remember a lot of details, even ones I was sure he would have, and he said he really didn't enjoy talking about the whole thing anyway. It had been a very difficult time, Fimberg told me.

It still bothered me that the Justice Department had leaked the fact that they were dropping the midnight plutonium burning charge at the beginning of the Grand Jury investigation. Why would the investigation want to ease up any pressure on Rockwell and the Energy Department? That's just not the way it's done.

"That's going to be a big hurdle," I told Wes when I got back from Europe. "We've got to see if we can corroborate what Karen Pitts and Jacque Brever said. But the FBI won't let us talk with Lipsky, so those infrared reports are our last shot."

We'd been going over the Fimberg/Scott interview during a lunch break at a small Vietnamese restaurant Wes had directed us to on the edge of a Denver suburb. It was the first time we'd seen each other since my trip to The Hague and we had a lot to catch up on.

"I finally got the radiation survey reports from right after the FBI raid,"[80] I told Wes. "The cesium levels were not above background. And the reports never even mentioned strontium."

We were too perplexed to even talk about it. What had Lipsky been talking about when he'd mentioned a report showing elevated strontium levels? Maybe he'd been mistaken? Or remembered wrong?

I thought back to the worried sound in his voice when I'd asked about the FBI investigation of a possible criticality accident at the Plant. I remembered the details he'd recalled while testifying to the Wolpe congressional subcommittee.

Chairman Wolpe had commended Special Agent Lipsky on the amount of detail he was able to remember.[81] When Lipsky had been a cop driving a black and white in Las Vegas before he joined the FBI, he'd started memorizing license plate numbers as a type of memory training. I doubted seriously that Lipsky was mistaken or mis-remembering. But I had to try to verify what he'd said. Maybe I was the one who'd been mistaken or mis-remembered. I really needed to talk with Lipsky.

"Wes! I found her!" I was almost yelling into the phone. I couldn't believe it; we'd finally gotten a break. I'd found Jacque Brever's phone number and address. She lived far, far away from Rocky Flats.

But would she be willing to talk with me? After all these years of hiding, would she really want to go back to those awful memories?

"Only one way to find out," Wes said practically, but I could tell he was excited, too. "When you going to call her?"

I called the next day, Sunday. I woke her, and she almost hung up when I told her why I was calling. Almost hung up, but didn't. She was too polite. But she did tell me quite clearly that she didn't want to talk about Rocky Flats.

"Who'd believe me anyway?" she asked, quickly angry. "They didn't believe me before."

I didn't blame her for not wanting to get involved. Those memories must have been awful.

"You know, it's interesting," she said. "The phone company made a mistake publishing my phone number. Tomorrow it's being changed to an unlisted number the way it was supposed to have been from the beginning. If you'd called tomorrow, you wouldn't have reached me."

I said nothing on the other end of the phone, thinking how lucky I'd been, after so much time spent searching for her. Wondering if she would let me have that new phone number, I decided to tell her about the Citizens' Investigation. I didn't want her to know about Wes yet. No telling what she might do with that information. So I skirted around the issue of who was doing the investigation.

"We've formed a Citizens' Investigation to look into what happened during the Rocky Flats Grand Jury investigation," I started out. "There are plans now to turn Rocky Flats into a wildlife refuge, and allow kids to play there."

"What??" Jacque exclaimed, in obvious disbelief.

I repeated myself.

"That is about the dumbest idea I've ever heard," she said. "Don't they have any idea how contaminated that place is?"

"Well, the government says it's going to clean it up first and . . ."

"Yeah, right," she cut me off. She didn't want to talk any more, excused herself, and hung up.

She hadn't given me her new phone number.

I wrote her a note, giving her my card, and asked her to call if she ever changed her mind. But I'd given up hope of getting Jacque Brever to talk with me about Rocky Flats.

The FBI was still refusing to let me interview Lipsky. No FBI response to Congressman Tom Udall's letter yet; surprisingly rude treatment of a Member of Congress. Mr. Udall's office sent another letter to the FBI, requesting a response. I'd just have to wait.

I was frustrated. I really need to find out what Lipsky had meant by elevated strontium levels. I needed to know a lot of other things as well. I decided to do some more background research into the levels of contamination in the soil and water, while I was waiting to be allowed to speak with the man who already knew about it. It turns out that I had a piece of luck there. The scientist who'd headed up one of the clean-up studies was Dr. John Till.[82] He was a Rear Admiral in the nuclear Navy (reserve). A physicist and outdoor enthusiast.

I'd met Till while working as a volunteer attorney for Concerned Citizens for Nuclear Safety. In 1994, the citizens' group sued Los Alamos National Laboratory, center of the nation's nuclear weapons program. We'd proved that the radioactive air emissions from the lab violated the Clean Air Act. As part of our settlement, we won the right to require Los Alamos National Laboratory to undergo the nation's first independent environmental compliance audit of a nuclear weapons lab. John Till and his team had done the audit. Arjun Makhijani and his team had monitored the audit on behalf of the citizens' group. Over severe opposition from the Lab, they'd announced that Los Alamos National Laboratory was in violations of the law. The lab was then required to come into compliance.

Till had often been willing to answer questions from the public, so I called him. I told him about the newspaper articles detailing suspicions of criticality accidents at Rocky Flats. The regulators had discovered strontium in the landfill and the water at the Plant. Had he heard of elevated strontium levels?

"There's nothing in what we reviewed, and we reviewed a lot of data, to support any idea that there was a criticality event at the Plant," he told me.

While working on the clean-up studies at Rocky Flats, Till and his team had done some investigating into the criticality issue, although the work they'd done had all been a review of the old sampling and monitoring data. They'd done no field tests or radiological measurements themselves.

"I've read that conclusion, too, John," I told him. "But I've got a problem. I've learned from a very reliable source that there were official reports of elevated strontium levels in the soils."

Till was hesitant in his response. He obviously didn't believe there was any elevated strontium, but he also knew me well enough to know I wouldn't be wasting his time.

I know he thought I'd been talking with a whistleblower, as I had many times during the lawsuit against Los Alamos. I didn't say more about the source of the information, and he didn't ask. He agreed to ask his team again whether they'd specifically looked for elevated strontium. But he sounded confident that there'd been no criticality accident at Rocky Flats.

"Elevated strontium from a criticality would mean elevated cesium, too. But we've reviewed that data and there wasn't any elevated cesium. Also, a criticality would leave evidence off-site. It would be hard to cover up. I'd say you need to have your guy prove what he's saying. Let him send you the report, or at least give you the reference number."

"I wish he could, John. I really wish he could. I'm going to try to get the original data myself. And I'll FOIA the report and see what I get."

"You get me the original data and I'll review it," he told me as we said goodbye. "In the meantime, I'll send you what I've got, but I'm sure there was no evidence of any elevated strontium at the Plant."

John Till sent me almost ten pounds of documents.[83] As I hefted them into the office, I reviewed my decision to ask him for help. He was a data driven man, and there was a lot of data here. It was going to take me a while to get that question about the elevated strontium levels answered.

During many phone calls, I'd gotten to know Edith Holleman, the congressional staff attorney who'd written the Wolpe Report. She'd been helpful and forthcoming during my first call, so I'd started calling her regularly. We discussed the case and the progress of the Citizens' Investigation. She was intrigued with what we were doing, and helpful.

Most of my FOIA requests had remained unanswered for over a year. But who knows what documents Edith Holleman might still have in the subcommittee files? When I asked her if she still had any of the documents, she'd laughed.

There's at least ten boxes, she told me. I never throw stuff like that away. Come look through them any time you've got a week to spend in a dusty old basement.

I didn't know much about Edith personally, but she'd mentioned one day that after a difficult hearing, some co-workers had given her a tee shirt with an image of a cobra on it.

"I treasure it," she'd laughed.

So I was expecting a large, tough looking woman when I flew into DC to review her boxes of old Wolpe subcommittee files.

Edith Holleman must weigh all of 100 pounds. She has huge blue eyes and an elfin face, a steel trap mind and a passion for justice. Her disarming grin and pixie haircut were also a bit of a surprise. She'd been an investigative reporter before going to law school. She'd been a staff attorney for the Democrats in the House of Representatives for years.

She remembered a lot from the congressional hearings about the Justice Department's handling of the Rocky Flats Grand Jury investigation. She'd first heard about the Rocky Flats Grand Jury from some environmental activists in March of 1992, shortly after the plea bargain had been announced but before it was approved by the judge. Many of the environmental groups were unhappy with the plea. They felt there needed to be individual accountability or there'd just be business as usual at Rocky Flats.

Some of them had more specific concerns.

"Some of the local citizens told us the Grand Jury wanted to indict some Rockwell and Energy Department people but the prosecutors had stopped them. They told us the Grand Jury had written a report but the prosecutors didn't want it published. We were obviously interested."

She and Bob Roach, an investigator then in law school, boned up on the criminal investigation, and the week the plea bargain was finally approved by Judge Finesilver, they were in Denver getting interviews with anyone who would talk with them.

"The US Attorney's Office didn't want to talk with us. Neither did the FBI. We finally did get some interviews arranged, but it was difficult."

I'd already read the three volumes of transcripts containing thousands of pages of questions from Members of Congress and their staff directed to the FBI agent and the three prosecutors.

"We didn't get to follow up on a lot of leads, Caron," Edith told me when I met her in Washington. "There's more out there we just didn't get to. I sure hope you can find it."

It was one of the best confirmations we'd gotten so far. And it motivated us for a long time, even when we seemed to be getting nowhere.

She gave me seven banker boxes full of files to review. That was motivating, too. Sixty-nine pounds of paper. It would take Wes and me another three months of reading and annotating to what we already knew. But we'd circumvented at least part of the Freedom of Information Act roadblock.

There were copies of many of the documents I'd been requesting—unsuccessfully—through the Freedom of Information Act. Copies of the Energy Department Safety Team Report on the midnight burning charge, the one the Energy Department couldn't seem to find. Copies of correspondence between the US Attorney and Rockwell concerning the plea bargain. Debarment information. Copies of Sanchini's notebooks seized by the FBI.

And copies of Jacque Brever's FBI interviews. I went to them first, hoping to get the story on the midnight plutonium burning, wanting to understand why the prosecutors had called her a not very unreliable source.

I should have known better. Even when responding to a congressional subpoena, the Justice Department had felt it had the power to withhold information. The last six pages of Jacque Brever's FBI interview were totally blacked out.

Wes and I met next at a sushi restaurant in Santa Fe. He was always up for trying new foods, and they don't have a Japanese restaurant in Walsh, he told me. Just one little smoky café that served up burgers and chili.

It was interesting watching him try to fold those long blue jeaned legs onto the tatami mat on the floor in one of the curtained rooms. He couldn't do it, so we sat at a table. He couldn't manage the chopsticks, either, with those raw knuckled hands. But he loved the sushi.

"I talked with Mike Norton," I announced.

Wes sat up straighter. I really had his attention now.

Former US Attorney Norton wasn't even listed in the phone book as a lawyer. But I'd tracked him down through the local bar association. A few days later, I drove to his office in the Denver Tech Center with more than a little curiosity.

Norton had been making statements in the press for years about the Rocky Flats investigation. He'd milked the media attention something fierce when the investigation had started out. He was heavy into politics then, and had wanted to run for Governor. After the Rocky Flats plea bargain and the congressional investigation, he wasn't even listed as an attorney.

What was going on?

Norton and I had met in his crowded conference room. It really was a law office and he really was practicing law. Things started out normally with coffee offers and pleasantries, but Norton wasted little time before stunning me into silence.

If I had it to do over again, Norton announced, I would have simply let the Grand Jury's term expire and *then* I would have announced the plea bargain. I never should have let the Grand Jury know I was going to settle the case. I should have just let them meet, do whatever they wanted to do inside the Grand Jury room, and then sent them home. Then I'd do what I had to do to settle the case.

I just stared at him for a while, but he was oblivious. After the interview was over, I spent several hours trying to understand how a United States Attorney could have that kind of attitude towards the constitutionally protected function of the Grand Jury.

Wes didn't have much to say for a while. He moved a piece of leftover ginger around the plate with one end of a chopstick. He'd eaten the wasabi with no problem. He'd been after me for a while to taste one of his homemade recipes of pickled jalapeños, so I knew the hot Japanese horseradish was nothing to him.

He looked troubled.

"I knew Norton was a fool," he said shaking his head. "But I never thought he'd be taking that fine trait to the pulpit. We didn't actually meet Norton until the end, when things started really falling apart. Before then, his Assistant Fimberg was running the case. We liked ole Fimberg."

Wes shook his head again, as though physically banishing the thought of Mike Norton from his mind.

"Peck gave Fimberg a hard time, but the rest of the Grand Jurors thought he was really a good guy and knew what he was doing. All the Grand Jurors were still paying attention for the first year. The Justice Department hadn't started dragging things out and repeating themselves, like they did later. Back then, we didn't know why they were doing that.

"Now I know they were stalling while they worked out their deal with the Energy Department and Rockwell. They were using the threat of Grand Jury indictments to open up Rockwell's wallet a little farther. So they needed the Grand Jury to be in session, looking like we were doing something.

"But in the beginning, we didn't know that. We were sure we were involved in something historic and we were going to see that justice was done."

———

Peter Murtha was Fimberg's co-trial counsel. Murtha had been sent down from the Justice Department's Environmental and Natural Resources Division in Washington, DC to help with the case. He was much more conservative than Fimberg. Murtha reported back to headquarters in Washington about everything.[84]

Letter from Wes

Peter Murtha is a government employee from Washington DC. After Grand Jury 89-2 made national news and the antics of the US Attorneys were questioned, Murtha is said to have stated the Grand Jury had ruined his career and if he ever saw me on the street he would attack me. Here's a little Peter Murtha story:

Murtha was questioning the Grand Jury witness from the Colorado Department of Health when Ken Peck asked the witness a question. Grand Jurors are allowed to ask any questions they want, but Murtha told the witness not to answer the question. Peck reminded the witness that he had to answer any question asked by a Grand Jurist and he asked the question again.

In a loud voice, Murtha instructed the witness to not answer the question. The witness indicated he had sufficient knowledge about the subject in question and would be willing to answer it. Murtha, his neck veins pulsating, screamed at him to not answer the question.

Peck and Murtha then entered into an entertaining little lawyer brawl about whether or not the witness had to answer his question. I stood up and told them to quit arguing and since the witness was a knowledgeable man and wanted to provide the answer to Peck's question, he could go ahead and answer it.

The judge's instructions had told us we could ask witnesses what we wanted, and we weren't supposed to be controlled by the prosecutors. We were independent from them.

Murtha, the top of his balding pate turning a violet red, savagely threw his notebook against the wall. The papers drifted erratically about the room. He kicked the podium, knocking it over. He stormed out the door. He failed in his attempt to tear the hinges and latch off the door as he crashed it closed.

The Grand Jury basked in the deep silence that settled over the room following Murtha's spectacular departure. I told the witness to now please go ahead and answer Mr. Peck's question.

Fimberg had been seated at the table behind the podium. He stood up. He looked around the room. His gaze came to rest on the debris Murtha had created. He sat down. Peck and the witness went on with their question and answer exchange.

Fimberg's color was not good. While Peck was extracting the desired information from the witness, Fimberg got down on his hands and knees and crawled on the floor, picking up the papers strewn about. He got all the papers collected, then stood up again. Fumbling, he reached down and rightened the podium and took refuge behind it. His color had gotten worse.

Peck got all of his questions answered and told me he had no more questions. I asked the other Grand Jurists if they had any questions. They did not. I told Fimberg we had no more questions and he can now question the witness. He was still in a state of shock and said he had no questions. I excused the witness, then called for a recess.

Wes and I were working in the office one day, running through the list of notes we'd developed from reading the transcripts of the Wolpe congressional subcommittee testimony. Maybe it was the passage of time, maybe I'd learned some things since I read it the first time, but I was surprised at what jumped out at me on this second go round, and I was frustrated that I hadn't noticed the significance of it before.

Jon Lipsky had testified that he'd wanted to press charges against Energy Department and Rockwell officials for lying to the government. But the Justice Department lawyers had told him they couldn't, because the statements had only been made to the public, not directly to a government agency.

Wes scoffed at that. "So it's legal for them to lie to the public?" he jeered.

I hadn't yet had the chance to research the Justice Department's interpretation of the statute. But on this second reading of Lipsky's testimony, that statement of the law really struck me as wrong. I went online and in five minutes, right in the US Attorney's Manual that's on the Justice Department website, I found the section that instructs prosecutors that a criminal false statement doesn't have to be made directly to a government agency.

I swiveled the laptop around so Wes could read the excerpt from the US Attorney's Manual, and sat there while he read the rather simple language.

> To prove a violation of 18 U.S.C. 1001, the government must show that the defendant knowingly and willfully made a false statement regarding a material fact that is within the jurisdiction of a federal agency or department. <u>Items Not Required to Be Proved</u> The courts have concluded that 18 U.S.C. 1001 does not require any proof of the following:*** 2.that the false statement be made or submitted directly to the federal government. *United States v. Uni Oil Co.*, 646 F.2d 946, 954-55 (5th Cir. 1981), *cert. denied*, 455 U.S. 908 (1982)

"Lipsky was onto some serious charges. Lying to the government is one of the few crimes that could have caused Rockwell to lose its right to bid on future government contracts," I said. "Debarment."[85]

I stopped to look at Wes; he was following me.

"Breaking environmental laws usually just means a fine,"[86] I continued, "but lying to the government could have meant an end to Rockwell's multi-billion dollar business."

Getting the prosecutors to drop the false statements and the secret midnight plutonium burning charges was obviously a mainstay of Rockwell's litigation strategy. Starting the first month of the Grand Jury investigation, Rockwell wrote persistently to US Attorney Norton and to his superiors in Washington complaining about the midnight plutonium burning charge, and insisting that it was untrue and that the Justice Department should withdraw it and apologize.

If these lying and fraud charges were dropped, the beleaguered defense contractor could then insist that the Justice Department follow its usual policy of punishing environmental crimes with a monetary fine and an agreement to come into compliance in the future, no matter how much damage had been done, no matter how long the violations had been occurring. Rockwell would be able to argue that this policy required that the Justice Department drop criminal prosecution of individuals and possible jail sentences for some of its high-level executives. Debarment would not be a concern.

Energy Department officials obviously would also be protected by a settlement. The case would be over.

Wes was reluctant at first, but I convinced him we needed to check out the story he'd been told about the two men who'd died investigating illegal dumping from Rocky Flats in an abandoned mine.

"Even if you don't care for the guy himself, we need to see if there's any truth to his story," I said again as we were driving up from Denver. Wes shrugged good-naturedly. He still didn't think there was anything to the dead body tales.

I went alone to the Sheriff's Department. We thought it best that Wes stay in the background.

"There was never any murder investigation," Detective Sergeant Ted Schoudt informed me politely after I'd explained what I wanted.[87] "That death you're asking about is classified as a suicide, not a homicide. Always was. Don't know where you got that information, ma'am."

"What about the friend who went looking for him and then disappeared?" I got a quizzical stare.

"You were right, Wes," I told him after the interview. "So that's one less reason to be worried. But what about Greg Lopez's death? Was it really an accident that he got run off the road?"

Wes looked a little sheepish. "I was a mite concerned about that for a long time, like I told in my journal, Caron. But then there was a long investigation, and later it turned out there really *was* an accident. I think I was worried about that for nothing, too."

We laughed. There were enough real concerns about chasing down the facts of this investigation.

Sitting around a breakfast meeting one day, my friend Lee Lysne asked the question at the heart of this Citizens' Investigation, the one that really requires answering. Why would the Justice Department have approved the FBI raid to begin with if they were just going to do a cover-up? Why not just ignore the problems, as had been done for decades, and as was happening at the rest of the weapons plants around the country?

Lee was the former Executive Director of Concerned Citizens for Nuclear Safety. She and Wes had gotten to know each other on the trail ride Wes had hosted for the nuclear safety group, and we all tried to get together whenever Wes was in town. Lee had a lot of communications savvy, having been a field producer at MacNeill/Lehrer before going into the nuclear safety world.

I'd been thinking about that motive issue a lot over the past several weeks. There were many possible answers, and maybe more than just one. Maybe the bigwigs in Washington had one reason for doing the raid while the prosecutors and FBI agents in Denver had a different one. With as much power as the Justice Department and the Energy Department wield, with all the secrecy they're so fond of, a few folks in the right place can do a lot of bad things and get away with it.

We'd never know for sure, but it made for some interesting over-coffee conversation as we reviewed the context of the FBI raid and criminal investigation at Rocky Flats.

By the time the search warrant had been executed on Rocky Flats, on June 6th, 1989, the problems of the Energy Department and Rockwell International had become very public. So, too, was the fact that the State of Colorado, the EPA, and even the Sierra Club were closing in fast on the aging weapons plant with their own agendas. After 1987, it wouldn't have been possible to stop *someone* from going after Rockwell and the Energy Department in court. It was just a question of who would do it first.

• In February, 1989, four months before the FBI raid, the Sierra Club filed a lawsuit to close the Building 771 plutonium incinerator because of allegations of illegal waste incineration. This was a different stance than the position the Justice Department took later in the criminal case, which was just to seek criminal fines, and not a shutdown. The incinerator was a critical part of the weapons work at Rocky Flats;[88]

• Colorado Governor Roy Romer had threatened to close down Rocky Flats for illegal waste storage;

• The Colorado Department of Health had forced the Energy Department and Rockwell to enter into a compliance agreement with which the weapons builders were afraid they couldn't comply; the State had published a Notice of Intent to Deny a Permit to Rocky Flats;

• The EPA was moving in on the contaminated groundwater problem. In 1985, the EPA had determined that Rockwell's groundwater monitoring system was inadequate. In 1987, the EPA had formed a task force which found that Rocky Flat's certifications of compliance with groundwater regulations were false when made. Rockwell's own consultants had advised them in 1985 that they couldn't comply with groundwater regulations. The Energy Department had fought off EPA regulation of its weapons plants for years, contending it had no jurisdiction under the Atomic Energy Act. The Energy Department's position was that only the Energy Department could regulate the Energy Department. The EPA was starting to take the offensive in this bureaucratic turf war;

• In 1988, the Energy Department released a study of the environmental problems at all of its nuclear weapons sites. On a scale of 1-10 with 10 being the worst, Rocky Flats rated a 9. And the groundwater contamination at Rocky Flats was the single greatest environmental hazard at any of the Energy Department nuclear facilities.[89]

"Here's what could have happened," I told my friends. "Once the Sierra Club lawsuit got started, damage control would have become increasingly harder for the Energy Department and Rockwell. Parties to lawsuits have the right to demand evidence, and get it. They can take folks' depositions, and ask them questions under penalty of perjury. They can demand to see the waste storage documents and a court will probably order Rockwell and the Energy Department to comply.

"Litigators know that the best strategy is to try to take control of the investigation itself, and then try to control the results. Once criminal charges were filed, and the search warrant executed, the Justice Department got control of most of the documents and evidence.[90] Almost all of that evidence is now sealed as Grand Jury information to which no one—except the Justice Department—can have access. The Justice Department simply hauled off over a million documents, put them under lock and key, and pretty much sealed the Plant."

I was on a roll now, strolling around the dining room talking. I'm sure the others were humoring me; it was too early in the morning for this kind of stuff, but I'd been thinking about it a lot.

"And the raid gave the Justice Department almost exclusive access to all the witnesses. A civil case can't be allowed to interfere with the criminal case, so frequently, the civil case gets put on hold until the criminal case is finished."[91]

Lee and Wes seemed to still be listening so I kept on.

"But the best part for the Justice Department was the Grand Jury. Although a Grand Jury can request to interview witnesses and can ask questions, can ask for documents and can even hire expert witnesses, usually they follow the lead of the prosecutors. In this case, US Attorney Norton or his designee, Assistant US Attorney Ken Fimberg. There's an old courthouse joke: Grand Juries are usually so compliant that a good prosecutor can get them to indict a ham sandwich.

"Through Norton, Fimberg, and Peter Murtha, Justice Department headquarters had control of who testified, where the investigation went, and where it didn't. It controlled what the Grand Jury got to hear, and it controlled what the Grand Jury got to say."

"And usually no one finds out anything about this, because of Grand Jury secrecy rules," Lee said quietly, looking at Wes across the dining room table.

"That's right," I said. "And now that a Grand Jury has considered the issue, anytime someone complains about a problem at Rocky Flats, the government can point to the broad ranging search warrant and say, 'Well, we presented everything to the Grand Jury, and there just wasn't enough evidence to support those claims. We showed the Grand Jury over a million documents; they met for over two and a half years. More than 185 witnesses testified and 1,200 more were interviewed. We did a thorough and complete investigation. But the Grand Jury didn't find enough evidence to indict anyone. And now I can't say anymore, 'cause of the Grand Jury secrecy rule.'

"Here," I said, handing them the sentencing memorandum the Justice Department used to persuade Judge Finesilver to accept the plea bargain with Rockwell. "Look at this. You can almost see that strategy at work."

The UNITED STATES wishes to publicly thank and commend the Special Grand Jury for its extraordinary attention, patience and vigilance over many months of active service. The difficult investigation—leading to these charges and this disposition—would not have been possible without the Grand Jury. It has rendered to the UNITED STATES, and to the citizens of Colorado, an invaluable service.

At first blush, it looks like a polite and harmless enough tribute to 23 Colorado citizens who had, indeed, spent almost three years of their lives investigating Rocky Flats. But on March 24th, 1992, when the Justice Department filed this sentencing memorandum with the court, the Justice Department knew that the Grand Jury actually *opposed* the disposition—the plea bargain—and wanted to indict three Energy Department officials and five high-level Rockwell employees, not settle for a fine from the corporation.[92]

The Justice Department undoubtedly assumed that the Grand Jury's opposition to its plea bargain would be forever sealed behind the oath of secrecy and the threat of prison sentences for any violation.

"This isn't the first time the Justice Department has used the courts and the legal system to cover up what went on at Rocky Flats," I said quietly. I watched the puzzled looks on their faces. Wes started to nod as I explained.

A while back, I'd decided to investigate whether the Justice Department had ever previously covered up criminal activity at Rocky Flats. I went to the court files and didn't have far to look.

Back in 1975, some adjoining landowners had sued the Energy Department, Rockwell, and Dow Chemical,* which had operated the Plant before Rockwell.[93] The lawsuit charged that the Energy Department and its defense contractors had contaminated the adjoining property so that its value was diminished. Thousands of acres of prime real estate were involved.[94]

The lawsuit was complicated and expensive and drawn out. The landowners had spent a large amount of money on expert witnesses to

---

* Dow Chemical has a reputation similar to Rockwell's for its indifference to the environmental disasters associated with its profit making enterprises. See, Chandana Mathur and Ward Morehouse, "Twice Poisoned Bhopal: Notes on the Continuing Aftermath of the World's Worst Industrial Disaster," *International Labor and Working-Class History*, No. 62, Fall 2002, pp. 69-75.

prove their contention that the land off-site had been contaminated. They wanted millions of dollars in compensation.

Most of the court file had been sealed, but what was still open to the public was fascinating. The Energy Department, represented by the Justice Department and the US Attorney's Office, had put out a settlement offer to the landowners with some very strange terms.

The US government, acting on behalf of the American people and the citizens of Colorado, insisted as a term of settlement that the landowners must retrieve every piece of information they'd received from the US government concerning contamination from the Plant. In addition, the landowners were required to give the government all the other evidence they'd gathered, everything they'd used to prove off-site contamination.

In order to get the over $9 million dollar settlement, the landowners had to turn over all this evidence to the Justice Department. Then the court sealed the evidence which had already been placed in the court file from public view.

And, most amazing of all, the judge then held a little evidentiary trial and made findings of fact about whether there had been any off-site contamination.

Only this wasn't the usual kind of trial. In the trial required by the US government and its defense contractors as a condition of settlement, only the defense contractors and the Energy Department presented evidence. The landowners' lawyers remained mute. The court then decided that the land was not too contaminated for development, and approved the monies for the landowners.

Boxes of evidence of off-site contamination that the landowners' lawyers had amassed over the years of litigation were not presented to the judge and would be kept secret from the public.

In addition to the money, the plaintiffs also got approval from the local government entities so they could develop their property adjoining Rocky Flats.

There were still some hints in the court file about some of the evidence which got sealed away from public view. Increased cancer rates outside Denver. Admissions by the government of off-site radionuclide contamination. Problems with the filtration system for the plutonium incinerator.

Dr. Carl Johnson, the former public health director for Jefferson County where Rocky Flats was located, had been outraged by the terms of the settlement. "Rocky Flats bought the suit off," he charged. "I prepared a rebuttal to the information presented at the trial, but it never saw the light of day."[95]

The Justice Department had manipulated the legal system to keep information from the public about the extent to which the Energy Department and its defense contractors had contaminated the neighborhoods near Rocky Flats.

Just like they did seven years later during the Grand Jury investigation, refusing to sign the Grand Jury's indictments, sealing their report from public view, and hiding the evidence away forever in a Grand Jury vault. In fact, the Energy Department, represented by the Justice Department, has succeeded in having many of the major lawsuits involving public health issues in Colorado sealed from public view.

We now had evidence that the Justice Department had a pattern of manipulating the judicial system to cover up evidence of contamination from Rocky Flats.[96]

My mother came to Santa Fe again to help with the Citizens' Investigation.

"Aren't you afraid that by concentrating on the midnight plutonium burning, you're going to give the impression that no other crimes were committed at the Plant?" she asked.

It was a good point. We certainly didn't want to give that impression. That wasn't the only criminal conduct the Justice Department had ignored in its desire to get the case settled.

I searched in the piles of paper lining the office table, and handed her the investigation summary we were starting to prepare, detailing the evidence we'd found of serious Rockwell, Energy Department and Justice Department criminal conduct.[*]

"So when the US Attorney said the plea bargain charged the most serious crimes, he was wrong,"[97] she said a while later, handing it back to me and looking upset. "Or lying."

Although my mother had been helping with the Citizens' Investigation almost from the start, she was still having a hard time accepting all the lies. I'd heard her muttering under her breath while she was reading through some of the material. She was almost 79 years old, had been in the WACs in World War II. She had grown up believing the

------

[*] See, the website at www.Ambushedgrandjury.com

government worked for the people and that its officials had pride in public service. She was deeply shocked at the corruption this investigation had revealed.

"You know we need to include this chapter," Wes reminded me, handing me a stack of papers in his barely legible handwriting. The computer I'd lent him was temporarily down. I'd read the smudged pages earlier, and it was a subject I didn't want to address but I knew we had to.

"Well, Wes," I said looking him in the eye with a worried feeling. "This is the stuff the Justice Department could use to try to send you to prison."

I watched to see if I'd gotten his attention. This was where I needed to be really careful that he understood his personal risk. This wasn't about the Citizens' Investigation, about Rocky Flats, about what a bad idea it was to turn a former nuclear weapons plant into a playground.

This was about the FBI coming after Wes McKinley claiming he'd violated the Grand Jury secrecy rules. This was about the possibility of arrest, a criminal trial, a conviction, a jail sentence. His reputation. Even his credit rating. Slim, Tam and Toni having to drive to prison to see their dad. Jan spending the next who-knows-how-long without her husband, single-handedly raising the three adopted children still at home. The grandkids. Wes locked up behind bars.

It was enough to make me real worried and I saw I had his attention, too.

He swung his boots off the desk and sat up and looked at me. We both just sat there silently for a while.

"We're going to have to get you independent legal advice if you're still determined to talk about what went on in the Grand Jury Room, Wes," I started. "I can't advise you on that, as I've told you before."

He nodded, almost impatiently, but said nothing.

I was determined that he was going to hear my lawyer spiel whether he wanted to or not.

"We've been over this before. You need to have expert legal advice from a criminal lawyer. So if you're still set on spilling those beans, it's time for you to go do that."

He tried to talk me out of it, as I knew he would. Wes just didn't like lawyers, and the idea of having to meet with another one, talk about the same old stuff all over again, didn't sit well with my cowboy friend.

"You've already told me you don't think the Grand Jury secrecy rules were meant to protect prosecutors from breaking the law," he began.

"Look, Wes, that's not the issue." I didn't want to get distracted. "You haven't broken the law yet," I reminded him. "So far we've done the Citizens' Investigation legally, with information that's been made public by others. Mostly by the Justice Department, actually.[98] But if we use your journals, you're taking a risk, Wes. You're making some big enemies if you do this."

His jaw was set, but he managed a laugh that was midway between a snort and a chuckle.

"What we're gonna expose about the cover-up will make us plenty of enemies as it is, Caron. What's a few more folks shooting at you when you're already facing off a posse of sharpshooters with just a shotgun? You're not saying I should let them get away with it?" Wes continued incredulously.

"This isn't about them and it isn't about me. This is about how the government works. It's no use going half way and showing how you can't trust the government to do nuclear stuff because they lie, if you don't go the rest of the way and show that you can't trust the government to enforce the laws, either, because they lie. It's the same issue, it's the same problem. If people aren't held accountable for what they do, the system won't work.

"And I have to be accountable for what I do, too. Or what I don't do. Maybe this is just a little bit of accountability, but it's better than nothing."

CHAPTER NINE

Flashbacks from Wes' Journals: Inside the Grand Jury Chambers, 1989-1992

I know some folks think I'm violating my Rule 6(e) Grand Jury secrecy oath by doing this. But we don't think the Rule or the Constitution or the law was meant to protect illegal acts of the Justice Department. So here's what happened inside the Grand Jury Chambers.

The Grand Jury kept hearing evidence all through December 1990. After that, it seemed like the prosecutors were stalling us. During the first year and a half, we heard a lot of evidence.

Most of what we heard is out in the public record now: Rockwell was mixing concrete with radioactive and hazardous waste to solidify it for what was supposed to be temporary storage. Despite their high tech training and their multi-million dollar contract, they couldn't seem to figure out how to make concrete set right.

I did that last year when I was fixing the barn. But it seems to have been beyond the abilities of Rockwell and the Energy Department. The big blocks of contaminated concrete started melting outside and the contamination soaked into the ground. They didn't fix it. They didn't put adequate covering over it. I think they tried to hide the problem, but they got caught.

The price of cleaning up from the pondcrete/saltcrete disaster alone is estimated at over $100 million. But Rockwell didn't lose a penny for doing such a bad-assed job. In fact, because of their sweetheart deals with the Energy Department, they got paid all their costs plus a percentage on top of that. They actually made a profit off their incompetence.

So that was one of the crimes we heard about.

Then there were the spray fields. The FBI pictures of that made us all so pissed we could hardly sit still. The spray fields weren't supposed to be used to dispose of contaminated water; only water from the sewage treatment plant, after it had been treated. But Rockwell was letting radioactive and hazardous waste into the sewage treatment plant, and then was spraying it all over the fields. The water still had the radioactive and hazardous waste in it.

There was so much contaminated water that the ground couldn't soak it up, so it ran into Walnut Creek and Woman Creek, which run off-site down to the drinking water reservoirs for the Cities of Broomfield and Westminster. Rockwell knew it was happening, but they kept doing it anyway. The Energy Department knew about it and let them do it.

The run-off contaminated the drinking water reservoirs and seeped into the ground and contaminated the groundwater, too. Rocky Flats sits on a cap of impermeable rock. So the contamination seeps down, then it travels across the top of the rock cap, then it comes out at the creeks.

Then there was the fact that Rocky Flats didn't have a permit to be a waste dump, but they were using it for that anyway. And the fact that it wasn't permitted wasn't just a technical violation; it meant they didn't have the necessary safeguards in place and no one was inspecting it to make sure it was handled safely.

Then there were the lies to the government. The false groundwater certification. The safety problems putting the workers in danger. The lies to the citizens around Denver, the Governor, the regulators and who knows what else.

That's why Special Grand Jury 89-2 wanted to write a public report so the country would know about Rocky Flats. We didn't get to do the kind of report we had wanted to. We needed help from the prosecutors, and they wouldn't help us. We needed to hear from some more witnesses, but the prosecutors refused to bring them in. We needed time, and we needed some questions answered, and we needed to see some more documents and we needed their legal help.

But they wouldn't help us. If the Justice Department had been interested in doing justice, a whole lot more would have come out in our Grand Jury Report.

Around January of 1991, things started getting strange inside the Grand Jury room. The prosecutors started repeating themselves, slowly reading us stuff we'd already heard. There were days when we sat and listened to stuff and had no idea why.

It was boring. Folks soon started falling asleep, doodling, playing with paper airplanes. I couldn't figure it out. The prosecutors had been doing really well until then.[*]

In May, 1991, tired of all the delay and worried that our term would expire before we could get our work done, I told Fimberg we were ready to draft some indictments against Energy Department folks. He exploded and insisted that we were not going to write any indictments against anyone in the Energy Department.

It's not legally possible to indict anyone at the Energy Department, he insisted, after he'd calmed down.

I remember looking at him strangely as he left the Grand Jury room. That loss of temper wasn't like Fimberg, and what he'd said didn't make a lot of sense. The search warrant was full of charges against Energy Department employees. And who ever heard of not being able to indict a government employee for committing a crime?

I remember thinking that boy must be real weak headed if he thinks this Grand Jury is going along with that idea. I let him go without too much response. No use arguing with him now.

We heard more months of boring repetitive testimony. They kept bringing back a witness who kept repeating himself, said nothing the first time, and after two or three times of the same stuff, it was three times nothing still equals nothing.

So many witnesses remember so little. One seems to have been out playing golf on every date there was proof that Rockwell had been doing something illegal.

We are all getting really bored. Jim holds up a design he drew for T-Shirts (I survived Rocky Flats). Connie holds up her design (I survived Rocky Flats but cannot recall).

After dinner it is so dull no one is paying attention. Mostly bullshit today. The witness talks so soft and low you could not understand or hear anything if you wanted to. Anyway, they're repeating themselves again.

I asked the prosecutors for help writing our Grand Jury Report. And I told them again we were ready to draft our indictments. Fimberg told me he'd put aside some time to help us out. He told me that many times. I thought there must have been a reason for all the stalling. I didn't know it was an evil reason until much, much later.

I had been noticing over the last several months that the boxes of

---

[*] CB Note: we now know that settlement talks had started around this time. The prosecutors may have been stalling to keep the Grand Jury in session to pressure Rockwell with the possibility of indictment.

exhibits and notes we were using had been messed with. Someone was getting into our stuff.

Finally, in July, 1991, with the Grand Jury bored to tears, time flying way and nothing happening, almost two years of investigation, seven months of Justice Department stalling, I told Fimberg we were going to write our report and indictments whether they helped us or not.

The Justice Department cancelled the August Grand Jury session. In September, we told Fimberg no more Rockwell witnesses, we are ready to write our report and indictments. No sessions had been scheduled for October.

Shortly afterward, everything really went crazy.

Wes' journal Nov. 12: The attorneys told us we were through. Just got up after presenting two insignificant witnesses and said the case was over and walked out.

We sat around looking at each other for a while, angry, worried, confused. Several Grand Jurors wanted to just go home. He said we were through, they argued.

But we hadn't written our report, hadn't done anything with all the information we'd been gathering for the last two years. After a bit of visiting among ourselves, we decided to do what we'd been sworn to do whether the prosecutors would help us or not.

We were on our own.

Wes' journal Nov. 13: I arrive at the courthouse, go to Laura's temple of command, receive the vault key, gather the paperwork and meet the rest of the folks in the Grand Jury room. Coffee, morning pleasantries, and nearly ten in the morning and still no government boys. Government late was an accepted condition but this went a little beyond even that. We concluded we have really been abandoned.

Without the prosecutors to help us, we decided to ask the judge for help. That's what his instructions, way back in the beginning, had said to do. We requested the judge to meet with us and clear up some questions we had regarding indictments, Grand Jury Report and presentments.[*] We needed some legal answers.

---

[*] According to Judge Finesilver's printed instructions to the Grand Jury: ". . .[a] presentment is an accusation initiated by the Grand Jury itself without any formal charge or written indictment having been submitted by the government. You have the power to make a presentment, even over the active opposition of the government attorneys. . . ."

I conducted the Grand Jury session. A few of the folks wanted to go home and call it quits. After much discussion and some heated moments it was agreed we would meet next month (Dec). It would be a very important meeting. We would hold our second Christmas party. Grand Jury 89-2 would be the only Grand Jury in recorded history to be impaneled long enough to hold two Christmas parties. We parted for our homes with a solemn promise to meet next month.

The judge had ignored us. I asked Laura why we had no response and she told me the judge could not respond to our letter because we had not dated it. She handed it back to me and I wrote a date on it, any old date, it didn't matter, and handed it back to her.

The judge responded with a letter telling us how good our questions were and the court would have to take some time and think about the good questions. The letter also told us to have a nice holiday and to await word from the court as to when we would meet again.

We never did get word from Judge Finesilver, and no one ever called us back into session.

Wes' journal Dec. 9: I talked to Steve [Deputy Clerk]. I asked him to call the Grand Jury members and remind them to be in attendance tomorrow. I drove to Denver.

Wes' journal Dec. 10: I waited in the foyer of the courthouse. Soon I was joined by Paul, later Peck showed up. We waited, the three of us. Ten in the morning and still we waited. Just then [another Justice Department attorney] strolled by. He stopped, grinned, and commented, Looks like you guys are about to be history.

Stunned, we asked him what he meant and he told us our term was up after this week. Pleased with himself for this last stab to the heart, he sauntered on down the hall.

I rushed down to Laura's desk and asked her why she had not called anyone to remind them we were to meet today. She told me the judge would not authorize our meeting. I talked to Clerk Manspeaker. He said any time there is a quorum while the Grand Jury is lawfully impaneled, that we are entitled to meet.

We then awoke to the truth of what was being done to manipulate us. Peck and Paul went to Peck's office to call the rest of the Grand Jury members. I went to the clerk's office to see about getting our term extended. Clerk Manspeaker said he would personally deliver our request for extension to the judge.

Wes' journal Dec. 11: Spent the day in the courthouse to make sure we got our extension. I wanted to be conspicuous so they'd have a hard time pretending we didn't exist. I strolled the hallways of the courthouse, I sat in the foyer, I stretched on the hard oak hallway bench and took a noon day nap. It was a long day, and still no word from the judge as to our extension. We got commitments from the Grand Jury members they would be in attendance tomorrow.

Wes' journal Dec. 12: This morning I went to Clerk Manspeaker's office. He was smiling. Yes, the judge had granted us our extension. We had a quorum.

Starting time of nine o'clock, just a short few minutes before, and I was making preparation to start the meeting. I was making assignments for the various aspects of the report, the presentments, and indictments when the government lawyers all stalked in.

This was the first time we had seen Norton since the first meeting in August 1989. Norton told us there would be no report, no indictments, and we were to do nothing. There was nothing we could do. The case was over, we were to go home, and it would be inappropriate if we were to ever meet again. Fimberg then waved a piece of paper and told how his feelings had been hurt. He felt we did not trust him. He said he had our extension right here in his hand and that he had promised us he would not let the Grand Jury's term expire until we were finished, why did we have to go to the judge ourselves for an extension?

Later, when I told Manspeaker about Fimberg telling us this he banged his fist on the table and said, that son of a bitch. I lobbied the judge hard for that extension. Fimberg didn't have anything to do with it.

Norton and Fimberg put some information up on the overhead projector and Fimberg read it into the record. It was a draft indictment of Rockwell corporation. Nothing about Energy or Rockwell people. They said they were giving us an overview of the case. I asked for a copy of it, but Norton said no, and they left the room.

I wondered why Norton wouldn't let us have a copy of the overview he'd just showed us. I went to Manspeaker's office and asked him for a copy of the day's transcript, and he said he'd have it to us the next day. Fimberg had read the information from the overview so it was in the written transcript from the court reporter.

Wes' journal Dec. 13: The transcript was ready that morning and we used it to prepare our report, presentments and indictments. We worked all morning. Without an over abundance of enthusiasm, yet we did make good progress. At noon, after solemn promises to meet next month we departed for the Armadillo restaurant for our second annual historic Grand Jury 89-2 Christmas party. At its best a subdued Christmas party. I extracted yet one more promise to meet next year, next month, January 1992. We adjourned.

Wes' journal Jan. 23: Judge Finesilver came lumbering in today and visited with us. He was very cordial and pleasant. The judge must have finally realized we would persist in seeking a visit with him.

Finesilver immediately recognized me and tried to establish a good ole boy, fellow cowboy relationship. He rambled a little about his summers of working on a ranch while in college. It appeared to me to be a meaningless discourse. The judge acted rather pissed at Peck. I got the impression they were personally acquainted.

The judge then talked about the legal questions we had asked. But he didn't ever really answer the questions. He told us the indictments and the Grand Jury Report are done under the direction of the US Attorney. He omitted saying anything at all about presentments.

I reminded the judge that we wanted to know what a presentment was. This pissed the judge off. I now had the same low status as Peck. The judge shook a fat finger at me and said presentments were an old fashioned term and they were no longer used. I read to the judge his own instructions to us that mentioned the presentments. The judge, his fat finger still activated, told me the instructions he had given us were an old set and I could rest assured the next Grand Jury would see a new set of instructions.[99]

The judge's discussion over, he gathered his black robe about himself and marched out. Manspeaker followed the judge out.

A few years after the Grand Jury was dismissed, Clerk Manspeaker told me he had walked out of the Grand Jury talking to himself that day. When I asked what he meant he said it was the most incredible thing he had ever heard, the way the judge talked to us.[*]

When the judge and Manspeaker had left the room, the Grand Jury members looked at one another and said, What did he say? The general consensus was there could be found no meaning to what had been said.[100]

Left on our own, we discussed the evidence we'd heard over the last two years. We didn't have much trouble coming to our conclusions. I remember waving around a copy of a *Reader's Digest* I'd found in my hotel room. Some poor rancher had been fined and prosecuted because he'd repaired a broken river levee without a permit. He'd been trying to keep the overflowing river from flooding his property. But he got prosecuted anyway because he broke the law.

If the Justice Department could prosecute a rancher who'd been trying to help protect his property in an emergency, it sure as heck wasn't right for them to let Rockwell and Energy Department folks off the hook for serious crimes Rockwell had made millions from.

But it wasn't just the fact that government employees shouldn't be treated any differently than the rest of us citizens. There was a bigger reason for what we did.

We all felt that holding individuals accountable was the only way anything would ever change in the nuclear industry. There was so much money involved, slapping a fine would be just another cost of doing business, anyway.

It wasn't only Rockwell as a company that needed to be held accountable. A very simple premise was underlying our decisions. If you hold individuals accountable for what they do, you can change the system, break the cycle. If people know they might go to jail, maybe they won't agree to break the law, even a little bit.

Sort of the way you raise children, I said at one point.

It's the only way to keep a system with that much power in check.

---

[*] CB Note: We now know that Justice Department headquarters had vetoed the issuance of a Special Grand Jury Report by the time Judge Finesilver finally met with the Grand Jury. He did not tell them this. Also, Finesilver had the power to overrule this Justice Department decision, and order the prosecutors to assist the Grand Jury in writing a report, or to help them himself. He did neither.

The presentment charging five Rockwell and three Energy Department folks with crimes would tell the public about the criminal activity we had investigated. Norton had already told us he wouldn't sign the indictments we wrote saying the same thing. We wrote the indictments anyway.

The Grand Jury wrote our Report of the activities at Rocky Flats using our notebooks and the boxes of documents we'd been working with over the past two years. We used our Report to let the public know about the terrible things the government had been doing at Rocky Flats for the past several decades, without mentioning names, like the law required. Our indictments told about the Energy Department and Rockwell officials who had committed those crimes.

We worried about why the government lawyers wouldn't help us, but we kept going anyway. We can't let a few bad folks stand in the way of justice, I said at some point. The judge gave us instructions not to be swayed by anyone, including the prosecutors. The law calls for this report to be public. We've got to follow the rule of law, I said. I remember feeling sad as I glanced at Fimberg's empty chair.

Each of us took a section for the report and worked it up, using our notes and the boxes of evidence. We assembled our notes, and Peck then did most of the writing, seeing as how he knew how to do it. But we all decided what to put in it.

We gave it to the judge's secretary to be typed. We finished the draft report, presentments and indictment, and put them all in the locked vault. There were still some finishing touches which would be done later at Peck's office.

Finally it was finished, and we made arrangements to present it all to the judge in open court, just as he'd told us it should be done back in 1989.

Wes' journal Jan. 24: By our invitation, Mr. Norton came in this morning. We wanted to give him the indictments, like the judge had instructed us in the beginning. He wanted to make a peace offering, told us how good a job we had done, and that we were through. I handed him our indictments and asked him to sign them. He looked surprised, then sort of curled his lip.

I suppose you've got the statute numbers and the days of violation and the facts? he sneered. He was surprised when he looked and saw that we had all that. He didn't know we'd gotten it from the court reporter's transcript where Fimberg had read the government's overview. We just changed it as we needed to.

The rest of the members and I had already planned that when we were through handing Norton our indictments, we would ask him to leave. We didn't want another lecture. So, when I handed Norton our indictments, and he started to lecture us again, I excused him from our Grand Jury session. Jere got up and held the door of the Grand Jury chambers open for him. Norton looked at the smiling faces of the rest of the Grand Jurors, and stomped out.

Wes' journal Feb. 19: I took the presentments, report and indictment down to Manspeaker's office to be placed in the vault.

Wes' journal Mar. 11: Left for Denver this morning. Tomorrow is to be the last session for the Grand Jury. We are going to give the judge our report, presentments and indictment in open court and then we will be through.

When I got to the hotel they told me the news. The judge's secretary had called them and left a message for me. Grand Jury had been cancelled. This was hard to figure because the courts had not scheduled the meeting. I had called the meeting and here the courts had cancelled it. I got the session rescheduled for March 24.

Wes' journal Mar. 24: Last week I called the court secretary and told her I was getting my old pickup—The Grey Ghost—serviced and I went to the county courthouse and brought the tags up to date and was coming to Denver to hand the Grand Jury Report, presentments, and indictments to the presiding judge, Judge Finesilver.

The judge's instructions, handed to us over two years ago, instructed the foreman, me, to hand the findings to the judge in open court after we had completed our investigation. I was going to do so on this date. I could tell from the displeasure in the secretary's voice that my call had not improved her day.

I called the session to order, and started to say this was our last session and the judge would receive our findings this afternoon. Before I could get started on my speech there was a knock on the door.

The court clerk came in. Mr. Foreman, he said. The US

Attorneys have requested one last meeting with you.

I was stunned. I did not want to meet with the attorneys. Over the last three months, abandoned by the attorneys and the judge, we had worked on our own. We had completed the report, the presentments and the indictments. There was no need to meet with the US Attorneys. But the majority wanted to meet with the attorneys.

We filed out of our familiar Grand Jury room for the last time. The clerk led us deep into the bowels of the federal courthouse to another room. This was the first time we would meet anywhere but in our regular Grand Jury room. He opened the door. We, single file, walked into the dark room. The door clanged shut.

Ambushed.

The windows were covered in heavy black cloth so that it was technically a "sealed courtroom," but we were in a courtroom for regular juries, not like our Grand Jury room. Judge's bench to one side, the jury section where in regular court trial jury members would be seated, oak pews for spectators.

And seated in the judge's chair was US. Attorney Norton, his assistants Murtha and Fimberg at each side.

Lambs to the slaughter, we sat down in the spectators' section.

Norton said, As you know we did not want you to do a Grand Jury Report. But since you have worked so hard and are persistent in your efforts to write a report, we have decided to help you.

He nodded to Fimberg.

Fimberg got up and came down to us and handed each of us a sheaf of papers. My heart skipped a beat then stopped. It was a copy of a rough draft of our Grand Jury Report. My hand written notes were scrawled all over it.

It was the rough draft we had revised for the finished report I had in my briefcase ready to hand to the judge.

The papers all handed out, Fimberg scurried back under the protective wing of Norton. Deep in shock, my heart not beating, I sat silent.

Norton began. As we looked over this report, we realized it contained some good material. We also found many parts that will fail the test for a legal Grand Jury Report. Now that you have an extension, you have three more months 'till the end of your extended term and over the course of these three remaining months we, working together,[*] can write another report that will pass the requirements for a Grand Jury Report.[101]

For the next two hours, he went over our draft report, pointing out the parts he said needed revision. He finished just as there was knock on the door.

The attorneys' ambush had been choreographed very well.

We will now pick up the copies of the report you have and adjourn for lunch, he said.

I jumped to my feet. No, I said. You will not get my copy of the draft report. This report was locked in the Grand Jury vault when we adjourned the last session. Only the foreman, or in case of his death, the foreman's replacement, has the authority to remove this from the Grand Jury vault. Someone has committed a serious breach of security. As soon as this court session is over, I am taking this down to the court clerk's office and I am going to find out who stole this from the Grand Jury vault.

Norton was calm. No one stole this from your vault. It was hand delivered to me by a Grand Jury member.

If this was true there had been no breach of security. Any Grand Jurist had the right to take our work and show it to the US Attorneys. But I was sure Norton lied about receiving this report from a Grand Jurist.

Norton said, If you will let me have your copy of the report I will meet with you in the court clerk's office when we finish for the day to discuss this.[102]

I had no choice. I held up my copy.

Norton nodded to Fimberg. A sad man, Fimberg came over and collected my report.

There was a second knock on the door.

Norton said, It is past lunch break. We knew there would be a lot of work to be completed so we have ordered a lunch to be brought in. We will now take a short lunch break in order to allow you to eat. You will remain locked in here while we leave to take a break in my office. We will be back in thirty minutes.

They trooped out. An unknown, never before seen, fright-

---

[*] CB Note: The prosecutor's attempts to convince the Grand Jury to let them help write the Grand Jury Report were in December 1991 and February, 1992, when the prosecutors already knew no Grand Jury Report would be allowed by the Justice Department. Any Grand Jury Report that was written was going to be sealed.

ened person brought in a large box and set it on the first pew, turned and rushed from the courtroom.

We were all weary. The completion of the indictments, presentments and Grand Jury Report had consumed the last of our energies. I knew if we allowed the US Attorneys to lead us in the writing of a report it would end up saying what they wanted it to say.

I looked around. Together the three prosecutors were a powerful force. Some of the Jurists were ready to throw in with Norton. Silently I opened the box and handed out the sandwiches. The last one, mine, I left laying in the box. I was not hungry and the grease seeping through the waxed paper was unappetizing. I would have preferred sardines packed in mustard anyway.

After much discussion, we agreed the Grand Jury Report met the guidelines the judge had given us nearly three years earlier. We had completed it on our own, the judge's instructions told us we could put in the report what we wanted as long as we didn't identify any individuals.

The report would stand as written. We would hand it in unaltered by the US Attorneys.

There was a knock on the door. For the first time in two and a half years the US Attorneys had returned from a lunch break on time.

I went to the door and returned their knock. While they filed in, I collected the greasy sandwich wrappers. Some with half eaten sandwiches, some with uneaten sandwiches. The eating instinct was weak in the Grand Jury today.

The attorneys assumed their earlier position on the judge's dais. Norton said, We will now begin the joint effort of rewriting the report.

I stood up, taking advantage of my high heeled cowboy boots to stretch myself to my full height.

No, I said. We will not rewrite the report. We are going to hand in all of our documents as they now exist. You are through, Mr. Norton, we will hear no more from you.

Norton was dethroned. He shriveled. Recovering quickly, he reached down and pulled some papers from his briefcase. He held them up. He looked directly at me. His face red, his lips pulled back, he said, Mr. Foreman, here is an indictment against Rockwell International. It charges the company with violations of criminal environmental laws. I am giving it to you to vote on and you had better sign it.

I tried to ignore the papers he was holding out. While I do not profess to be a very good poker player, I do often join in a poker game with the other cowboys in the bunk house on the ranch. I knew that at the right time, a properly executed bluff can often win a sweet pot. I prayed this was the time.

I said, Mr. Norton, in one hour it will be two o-clock. This morning before I came to the courthouse I called the Denver newspapers and told them the foreman of Special Grand Jury 89-2 was following the judge's instructions and today at two o-clock he is going to, in open court, go into Judge Finesilver's court-room and hand in the Grand Jury findings.

Norton said, It will not be possible for you to go to Judge Finesilver's courtroom. He is presiding in a court case today.

If Norton could keep us from handing in the documents in open court, they'd be invalid, all our work for nothing.

I don't care if he is in court today, I replied. The reporters are probably here by now and I am sure they will enjoy seeing us interrupt the honorable Judge Finesilver's court to hand him our findings. In one hour we are going to Finesilver's court.

If Norton was a poker player I hoped at least he was a poor one.

When the attorneys finally left us alone to make our deci-sion about whether to hand up the government's indictment, Fimberg was the last to pass through the door. Just before the locked door clicked shut, he stepped back into the courtroom.

It makes no difference, he said, whether or not you sign the indictment against Rockwell. The case is settled, it is all done, your decision will make no difference on what happens at Rocky Flats.

Fimberg looked like a man with a sordid burden laying on his soul. He looked inward summoning strength. But please, he said, I beg you, for my sake, for your own sakes, please sign the indictment.

I looked at the papers Norton, the US Attorney, a political appointee by President Bush, had handed me before leaving.

Norton wanted us to hand up an indictment charging the company, Rockwell International, with environmental crimes. No individuals—from either the Energy Department or Rockwell—were to be charged, just the corporation.

Fimberg's pleading eyes sought out each of the other 15 members of the Grand jury present at this session. My eyes locked with Fimberg's. Swiftly he broke eye contact.

My heart was heavy. Fimberg had several people who would support him. They would back him in any action. Norton knew when he handed me the indictment that I had, by law, to conduct Grand Jury deliberations and have the Grand Jury vote on it. If I didn't, he could invalidate everything we did.

In order for the government's indictment against Rockwell Corporation to be valid, the vote had to be twelve in favor of it. There were several people in the Grand Jury who felt that by handing in the indictment against the corporation as a True Bill we would have something to show for our efforts. If twelve or more people voted in favor of a True Bill on Norton's indictment, the company Rockwell would be charged with environmental crimes, it would pay a fine and no one would be held accountable.

If there aren't twelve votes in favor of the indictment, it is Not A True Bill and Rockwell is not charged.

The Grand Jury had written an indictment charging Rockwell, as well as individuals at the Energy Department and top level Rockwell employees, with violations of environmental crimes. Norton had refused to sign *ours*.

If we signed Norton's indictment, our whole point about holding individuals accountable, including government officials, would be down the drain. But the Grand Jury was tired, we all wanted to be through with this arduous task. Some members wanted something for their two and a half years of being the conscience of the country. Agreeing to indict just the corporation might be better than nothing, some of them felt.

For the next hour I had my work cut out for me, but this was not my first rodeo. I opened the floor for deliberations.

One hour later, my boots soggy with the sweat that had formed at the top of my bald head and coursed downward to collect in them, I called for the vote *against* the indictment drafted by the US Attorneys.

My heart raced. As foreman I cast the first vote. I counted the votes against. It did not take long. I counted them again. It still didn't take long. There were not enough votes to kill the government's proposed indictment against the corporation.

Beaten, I had to complete my duty as foreman. My voice slightly trembling and weak, I called for the vote *in favor* of the government's indictment.

The hands went up. I counted them. Not enough. In a millisecond the truth hit me. Some of the Grand Jurists had refrained from voting.

There were not enough votes in favor of the government's indictment, either.

I must not be accused of closing the vote too quick. I directed my gaze in turn at each of the Jurists who had not voted. They stared at the floor. While unwilling to vote against the indictment, they nonetheless had refused to vote in favor of it, either.

The US Attorneys had lost this round.

Now, I was faced with another problem. How do you close the vote of a Grand Jury? I resorted to the method used at the horse sales I had attended over the years.

I shouted, Going once, going twice. I paused, looked around and lacking a gavel I slammed my hand down on top of the court-room railing. I nearly forgot myself and said SOLD, but stopped in time and managed to croak out, The vote is closed.

I crossed over to the lawyers' table in the courtroom and with great ceremony laid the indictment down and reached into my pocket to get a pen with which to sign the indictment Not A True Bill.

I had no pen. Humbled, I asked the nearest Jurist if I could borrow his pen. I signed the indictment Not A True Bill and recorded the voting record underneath my signature.

We sat in silence, toying with our thoughts. No one seemed inclined to visit with his neighbor. Soon there was a knock at the door.

The courtroom clock stood at two o-clock.

Norton was not a poker player.

The judge, Sherman Finesilver, the US Attorneys and their court reporter, and the court clerk came in. This time the judge sat in the judge's chair.

This was turning out to be a good day for me. Not so for the judge. He looked the Grand Jury over. This was the third time the Grand Jury had seen the judge. We had lost our respect for him during the second meeting. I sensed he knew this. He said, I understand you want to meet with me.

Yes, your honor, I said. I walked up to his bench and handed him our Grand Jury findings.

These are the indictments drawn up by the Grand Jury, signed A True Bill, I said. I handed him our signed indictments.

These are the presentments drawn up by the Grand Jury and signed by the members. I handed him the presentments.

This is the report the Grand Jury has compiled. It is signed by the Grand Jury members. I handed him our report.

This is an indictment given to us an hour ago by the US Attorney Mike Norton. The Grand Jury has signed it Not A True Bill.

I handed the judge the government's indictment against the corporation that we had rejected.

The judge took the sheaf of papers. He then gave us a little speech on patriotism. It fell short. He asked me if we had completed our duty. I told him we had. The judge then asked the Grand Jury who was in favor of ending our term.

I raised my hand hoping the rest of the Grand Jurists would do the same.

The judge looked over the Grand Jury and pronounced the majority in favor of ending our term.

I could see Fimberg, his eyes pleading, shaking his head from side to side. He wanted the Grand Jury to continue to meet. To the very end, the US Attorneys had hoped to get the Grand Jury to give their stamp of approval to the indictment against the company without the individuals.

Fimberg's efforts were in vain. The judge dismissed us.

It was done.

CHAPTER TEN

The Citizens' Investigation Continues, 2001

Phone Message from John Till

Caron, John Till here. I checked into that strontium issue. The team and I feel certain there were no criticality incidents at Rocky Flats. They did do some criticality experiments, but those were microsecond things, they would not have disbursed strontium to the environment in levels that would have been picked up by a monitoring survey and called elevated as your information source says.

I'm sending you some more reports. . . .

I wasn't finished with the strontium issue. There was too much evidence of some kind of strontium release to the environment to just drop it. I wasn't sure Till had the original data and newspaper clippings; so much seems to get covered up at Rocky Flats. And I had some other areas of concern that I wanted to discuss with him.

August 13th, 2001
Dr. John Till
417 Till Road
Neeses, South Carolina 29107

Dear John,

It was nice to see you the other day in Santa Fe. Hoping for a repeat soon, with a little more time.

I'm taking you up on your offer to help with the Citizens' Investigation of the 1989 Rocky Flats criminal investigation. I know you said your team was sure there hadn't been a criticality at Rocky Flats. I know you said my inside source needed to give me the proof of the elevated strontium levels. But he's not inside anymore, so he can't, and I can't just drop it. You once told me I was persistent. This strontium issue is important if it's true, so I guess I'm still being persistent.

Strontium was found in the landfill and seeping into the groundwater in the early 1980s, according to some court records and old newspaper articles I just found. Did you have access to these? I'm enclosing them in case you hadn't seen them.

Is there some other reason that Rockwell might have been using strontium? Maybe pure strontium, without cesium? Some medical experiment? Some "special" project, off the books, totally classified? We know the government admitted in some court documents that there were "special projects" being conducted, but we don't know what radioisotopes were used.

An unknown, unreported project using strontium could result in unknown, unaccounted for waste that needs to be considered when devising a clean-up plan, especially if they're going to allow public access at Rocky Flats.

I'm still trying to get my hands on the original data my inside source saw. FOIA pending; you know that song and dance. I'll let you know.

I've got some other concerns that involve the clean-up plan and the studies you and your team have done at Rocky Flats. I'm wondering if you would look at the attached FBI interview sheets and give us your opinion.

One of these guys had worked at Rocky Flats for over eight and a half years.[103] He quit because of concerns about health and safety. His repeated complaints about falsified laboratory data were ignored, and there were many instances of unsafe practices which went unremedied.

What he and others reported is outright fraud and probably criminal. Specifically, he told the EPA investigators involved in the 1989 FBI raid that the weekly water samples from the Great Western Reservoir which were intended to sample for radioactive contamination from the Plant were not taken from Great Western Reservoir at all. Instead, they were a mixture of treated tap water and water from Denver which did not originate from that drinking water reservoir.

This worker also revealed that samples taken to measure radioactivity levels were allowed to decay before they were analyzed and reported; that proper preservation measures were ignored. This was a matter of routine. When lab results for radioactivity levels were high, workers were directed to re-run the analyses, even though the sample was decayed, and would read lower. The lower result was recorded.

Samples were often diluted, and the dilution ratio was done by guesswork. There were many problems with the equipment used to detect whether contamination was running off-site in the streams that run from the Plant into the drinking water reservoirs. Sometimes the equipment was allowed to remain broken for months at a time. Often, it was improperly placed so that it didn't measure the water flow at all. So when high levels of radioactivity were found in the Plant's holding ponds, they tossed out the information and didn't notify the regulators, saying that the contamination never reached the reservoirs because there was no water flow from the Plant downstream. But they relied on equipment they knew was broken to say that.

This man also worked on the analysis of stack exhaust to determine levels of radionuclides released to the environment. This was a filter analysis; the filters were dissolved in acid and then the solution was sampled. When a high count was obtained, they were directed to re-run the analysis. By that time, however, the radionuclides would have leached into the side of the container and the sample would read lower than what was actually in the solution. If it was still high, they would conclude there was something wrong with the sample, and disregard the results.

It wasn't only a few people who reported this kind of deception, John. And I found the same type of deceptive practices here in Santa Fe by a different private nuclear contractor. It seems to have gone on for such a long time, and the deception seems so pervasive.

Some of our current concerns are that because the sampling was unreliable, and often falsified, the reports which were generated by the regulatory agencies and the Plant, which relied on this data, may have been unreliable, too.

To what extent could the falsified or erroneous data have impacted your studies and to what extent could it affect the decision-making process on how and to what extent the Plant should be cleaned up? Or on what future uses, such as recreational access, should be made of it?

Were you aware of the on-site dumping which is documented in the attached FBI interviews? If not, does it impact your studies and how could it affect the on-going plans for clean-up and future use?

I'm hoping to be able to call you and interview you about this, rather than asking you to write anything since I know you are so busy and I'm asking such a big favor of you. I'm sure you

can understand my concern about the amount of on-site dumping and the falsified data.

  And thanks for all the new reading material.

  Sincerely,

  Caron Balkany

John Till made time for me as soon as I called.

  "No, we hadn't heard about the reports of falsified lab data and monitoring reports," he answered slowly. "If no one tells us about them, we'd
not be likely to see them."

  "These were from the 1989 FBI investigation," I answered. "The
Energy Department didn't give them to you? Or the Justice Department?"

  I wasn't surprised when he repeated that he hadn't seen them.

  "But it's not just intentional falsification that we should look at," Till
continued. "There's also a lot that hasn't been monitored or measured
because of the way Rocky Flats technicians set up and managed their
equipment. They didn't look at all the problem areas. So, when they
report that they didn't find problems, it's not always very meaningful."

  In addition to falsified and incomplete data, there was a problem
with erroneous and deficient data as well. The Special Assignment
Environmental teams convened by Admiral Watkins after the raid had
discovered inaccurate data, deficient and illegal monitoring of plutonium
emissions, and non-complying monitoring equipment for measuring
radioactive air emissions at Rocky Flats. The Plant hadn't even measured some of the more common radionuclides at all until very recently.[104]

  There's nothing we can do about it now anyway, I thought to myself.
We'll never know the real extent of the contamination from Rocky Flats
because so much data was either falsified or deficient.

  Data falsification wasn't unique to Rocky Flats. When our friend
Arjun Makhijani had first met Wes during our jalapeño steak dinner in
Santa Fe, he'd told us a story about discovering data fraud at a uranium
processing facility—The Feed Materials Operation—in Fernald, Ohio.
Arjun had been there reviewing stack emissions data as an expert physi-
cist and nuclear engineer on behalf of local citizens.

  "The falsification of data and incompetence was astounding," Arjun
had told us. "The scientists working at Fernald had entered zeros in the
records of uranium stack emissions when they hadn't even made any
measurements. It wasn't an occasional thing. They did it under the direction of their supervisor, and they did it consistently from 1969-1982.

They had no idea what amounts of uranium were actually being released from some of the stacks, but they entered zeros.

"They didn't calibrate their flow meters. Sometimes the samplers weren't operating properly. They knew that much of their data on stack emissions was invalid because of these problems, but they used the data to make their calculations until we caught them at it in the late 1980s.

"The scientists knew their scrubber system[*] often wasn't working properly, so they entered estimates of the releases to the environment. But there is documentary evidence that they knew the efficiency was really less than that. In fact, on occasion, it was pretty close to zero."

Arjun had finished his story with a sad shake of his head. It's not pleasant for a scientist to see other scientists behave so unprofessionally.

I was thinking about Arjun's supper table story as I called John Till. He was a reputable scientist and here he was, having to rely on data from a company that had been proven to have falsified official records and effluent release data.

"If there'd been independent oversight of Rocky Flats, we wouldn't have the problem with contamination that exists there today," Till advised me. "This isn't unique to Rocky Flats.

"Any facility that creates risk to the public should never be in charge of determining how the problem should be solved, or certifying that the problem has been remedied. We know about the importance of independent auditing of financial institutions. Why do we accept anything less for public health issues?

"The big worry now," he continued, "is that there's nothing really to stop companies that run the plants or do the clean-up from making decisions that are not to the public's benefit. That's because there is little independent oversight.[105] The EPA isn't equipped to police the weapons plants. So nobody does."

"The EPA is too political to enforce the law against another branch of the government, anyway," I interjected. "It was the Sierra Club's citizens' suit that got the Building 771 plutonium incinerator closed down for good.[106] Not the Justice Department, not the State Health Department, not the EPA."

The lawsuit Concerned Citizens for Nuclear Safety had filed against the Energy Department was a citizens' suit like the Sierra Club's. We'd

---

[*] The scrubbers were used to cool down and clean incinerator exhaust before it's vented to the environment, just like at Rocky Flats.

first tried to get the EPA to agree to enforce the Clean Air Act at Los Alamos National Laboratory. Instead, the EPA kept making agreements with the Energy Department, giving them exceptions and exemptions. Not enforcing the laws Congress had clearly enacted for the public health.

In fact, one EPA lawyer had told me that the White House had developed an internal legal position called the Unitary Executive Policy, which meant the EPA wasn't allowed to take the Energy Department to court no matter how long or how badly it broke the law. All the EPA was able to do, he'd told me, was negotiate.

We'd pursued our lawsuit even more vigorously after that, and won. And Los Alamos had partially cleaned up its radioactive air emissions. But the Unitary Executive Policy was still out there.

———————

We finally got an EPA response to one of our Freedom of Information Act requests.[107] It was one of the few responses we'd received. Wes analyzed the documents and gave me the details.

"These papers say they were having problems with the incinerator filters at Rocky Flats in the early 1980s. They had problems with the amount of exhaust. The permit they got back in 1985 gave them permission to incinerate over 22,000 pounds of plutonium-contaminated trash a year. Then they got permission to up it to 336,000 pounds per year, 'essentially around the clock' incineration," Wes said.

"More than at any other weapons complex in the entire country," he added. "Since 1970, they burned more than *345 tons* of plutonium-contaminated trash. And that doesn't include the more than 10 years the incinerator had been operating before then. And some years they burned it 24 hours a day," he continued. "This says the HEPA filters were supposedly 99% efficient. So, assuming that's true, and assuming the filters were always in place and operating properly—which we know isn't true—what's the effect of incinerating 336,000 pounds of plutonium-contaminated waste a year in a process which allows 1% of the exhaust to escape?

"Rocky Flats is in a very windy area. Denver and much of its suburbs are directly downwind. What does 1% of that plutonium-contaminated exhaust do to people?

"Would you live there if you knew they were doing that?" he asked. Wes got up, shaking his head.

"If folks knew how much plutonium-contaminated waste was incinerated on a regular basis at Rocky Flats, not just during those few months of the shutdown, but regularly, Congress might have focused on the *real* problems with the Energy Department and its defense contractors. It's not possible to make nuclear weapons without creating tons of nuclear waste. It's not possible to make nuclear weapons without sacrificing the health of the neighboring citizens and the workers. There's no safe way to make the bombs, there's no safe way to dispose of the waste, to transport the stuff, or store it. There's no way to hide it from terrorists and other criminals.

"And the worst part of all is that we don't need any more nuclear weapons. We've got enough to blow up the planet twenty times over.

"The real problem with the Energy Department and its nuclear contractors is that they're all slurping at the public trough. We don't need more bombs, but there's so much money to be made. . . ."

He headed for the front door, as he always did when he got worked up. He closed it quietly, but I knew it had been an effort for him not to slam it. When he came back inside a while later he was calmer, and just continued talking.

"All those tons of plutonium-contaminated waste, for all those years. And the Colorado health department didn't even know about the plutonium burning until 1987.[108] So who do you think was watching out for the public safety all that time?"

He crossed his arms and stared at me.

CHAPTER ELEVEN

Jacque Brever,
2001

Jacque Brever called me occasionally. I knew she wanted to help us, but without getting too involved. She was still scared, and her feelings that the Grand Jury hadn't believed her remained very painful for her. But she felt that talking was good for her.

After she'd left Denver, Jacque told me, she'd gone into hiding.

"I remember walking out of the Grand Jury room and thinking, 'I didn't communicate to them what I wanted to tell them. They couldn't understand me because I wasn't well enough educated to know how to speak. I'm never going to let that happen again.' I felt so stupid, why couldn't they understand what I was saying?"

So she'd gone to college. While she'd been hiding, afraid to even sleep in her own bed, the only place she went besides to get groceries for herself and Jessica had been to school. She got a bachelor's degree with a minor in chemistry. Then she went on and got a master's degree in environmental policy. She'd even applied for scholarships, and won them.

Jacque interrupted her story to laugh gleefully. She was almost chortling. "They were Energy Department sponsored scholarships!"

It got me laughing, too. There was a fine irony to it.

"I decided I wanted to be part of the solution, after being part of the problem for so long," she explained when I asked her why the Energy Department and why environmental policy work. "I developed environmental educational programs for kids in high school as part of my thesis. I wanted to learn to communicate about the environmental issues that were important to me. I never wanted to feel as frustrated as I'd felt after I testified to the Grand Jury.

"Even though I went to school on an Energy Department scholarship, with a requirement that I get a job in the Energy Department after I graduated, I just can't get hired by them. I must be on some kind of Energy

Department blacklist. I know they're hiring all the time, but I can't even get anyone to acknowledge they've received the resume I sent in."

I shook my head. How surprising.

"In the beginning, when I first ran away, I had flashbacks almost every year about when those guys contaminated me with plutonium," she continued. "I got panicky, and I'd think they were after me again. Every September 14th since it happened back in 1989 I spent huddled in my house with the curtains drawn, afraid to even sleep in my own bed. At first I just couldn't control it. All I could do was go to school, go get groceries, and come home and lock the doors. I lived that way for five years.

"One day I had to take a chemistry test on the September 14th anniversary. I'd been so busy studying I didn't realize what date it was. But in the middle of the test, I just freaked out. I ran out of the room, didn't know where I was, didn't know how to get home even though I only lived a block and a half away.

"A psychology professor found me sort of wandering around the campus, freaked out. I started some therapy, and slowly started to get better.

"I retook the chemistry test. That's my minor. I got an A. It wasn't the test that had freaked me out, it was the date. It was September 14th. It was that damn anniversary.

"Now, I celebrate September 14th," she finished. "Now, it's a symbol to me that I'm mostly over what happened at Rocky Flats. I still have post-traumatic stress disorder; the government classifies me as totally disabled. I have reactive airway disease from the plutonium inhalations; I've had two tumors removed from my breast. . . ."

Her voice trailed off.

"But you're also working fulltime, you're not on disability, you've supported yourself and your daughter all these years. And you're not a victim. You didn't let them turn you into a victim," I reminded her.

"No, you're right," she said slowly. " I didn't let them turn me into a victim."

I could almost hear her thinking on the other end of the line.

"I've spent so much of my life since then trying to forget about Rocky Flats, trying not to be bitter, not to be angry. Trying not to let it ruin my life. But now, to find out they're going to let kids play there. . . .

"If I don't help you guys with your Citizens' Investigation, when I know how dangerous that place is, then I've let them turn me into a victim after all," she said finally. Her voice was firm.

"Count me in."

Jacque agreed to come to Santa Fe. We'd be able to go over some of the paperwork she'd never seen. The FBI interviews. The Energy Department report on the midnight plutonium burn. She'd never even read the Wolpe Report, or the congressional testimony about the investigation. She'd spent a lot of money on therapy trying to put Rocky Flats out of her mind.

When I met her at the airport, I remembered Wes' first description of Jacque Brever. Tall. Tall enough not to look so scared of a bunch of government lawyers. But tall wasn't enough. Jacque'd had good reason to be scared.

We stopped off to get her some Mexican food. It had been a long time since she'd had any, having moved so far away.

"How did the Grand Jury react to your testimony?" I asked her after we'd ordered.

She was silent for a while, then looked sad. "Well, I think they didn't understand what I was saying. And I don't think they believed me," she said, looking down at her plate.

I saw the sadness in her eyes, even after all these years.

"Why do you think that, Jacque?" I asked as gently as I could. It was hard to bring up painful memories in someone who had been so traumatized. Yet this memory needed to see the light of day.

"Why would they have dropped the midnight plutonium burning charge if they'd believed me?" she answered, as though stating the obvious. "I wasn't able to communicate well back then. I was so uneducated. They just didn't believe me."

She looked away.

"Some of the ladies on the Grand Jury might have believed me. I remember going into the restroom during a break and three of them came in after I did. We were all quiet, because we're not supposed to talk about the case, but as I was leaving, a small dark-haired Grand Juror came up and put her hand on my arm. She told me, 'You're being very brave and courageous to do this. Here, take this, and it will keep you safe.'"

I was quiet, but looked at her expectantly. Jacque reached into her bag, opened her wallet, and pulled out a small religious medallion.

"I've kept it all these years. It meant so much to me that at least one person didn't think I was lying, didn't think I was so stupid I couldn't even communicate."

It lay in her hand, barely tarnished, the size of a nickel. The kindness behind it had helped keep Jacque Brever together all these years.

We talked the entire drive home to Santa Fe, and then late into the night, sitting on the portal under quilts to keep off a surprisingly cool wind for a summer evening. We watched the lights glitter over Los Alamos and Santa Fe.

I'd talked with Wes earlier, while she'd unpacked, and now seemed like the right time to tell her. I peered over at her in the dark, and could barely see her face in the flicker of the portal lights.

"Jacque, I need to tell you something. I'm not doing this Citizens' Investigation alone. I'm doing it with Wes McKinley."

I strained to see her reaction.

She had to think for a minute. Then her face lit up. "The Grand Jury foreman!" she said happily. "How is he? I've always admired they way he and the rest of the Grand Jury stood up to the Justice Department after the plea bargain."

Then it sunk in. "You mean he's part of this Citizens' Investigation?"

I nodded. "We couldn't tell you that at first, Jacque. Wes is taking a risk doing this, too. He's still under FBI investigation. But I called him earlier and asked him if it was OK to tell you, and he said yes. If you were willing to get involved again to help the Citizens' Investigation, after all you've been through, you could surely be trusted not to tell anyone what we we're doing.

"We don't want the Justice Department to try to stop us before we're finished with the investigation," I explained.

"I won't tell anyone," Jacque said quietly, and I knew she understood the value of that kind of promise.

I went inside and called Wes. I wanted him to tell her the next part himself.

Her eyes were a little wet after she'd finished talking with Wes. But she was happy, almost radiant. "He believed me. He told me he'd believed me way back then."

I nodded, watching that realization do its healing work on her tortured self-image.

"Then why did they drop the midnight burning charge if they believed me?" she asked me later.

"The Grand Jury didn't drop it; it was the Justice Department," I advised her, watching understanding settle in on her face. She had a fragile skin that showed color based on how she was feeling.

"And that's why you're here. To help me find out why the Justice Department did it."

She nodded, and early the next morning, we got to work.

"First things first," I announced as we sat down in the office across from the stacks of documents, newspaper articles and interview notes. Wes and I had been four years in this investigation, and the piles and boxes seemed to be growing and multiplying around me.

Jacque settled back and looked at me expectantly. I started in with no preliminaries.

"If Rockwell wanted to run the 771 plutonium incinerator secretly, so hardly anyone would know, could they do it?" I asked.

She thought about it for less than a minute.

"Sure," she answered. "A special run. Sometimes we fired up the incinerator just for a day to take care of something special they wanted to get rid of. The incinerator usually operated for several weeks at a time, when it ran, with lots of people operating all the different components and cleaning up after it. But you didn't have to do it that way.

"You could run that incinerator with only two people if they were good," she explained. "And you didn't have to leave a big trail showing what you'd done, either. That way fewer people would know you'd done it. It's called a special run.

"Now you're going to ask me whether that's what happened during the shutdown back in 1988. Whether it could have been a special run so hardly anyone would know about it."

She was getting into the spirit of being a Citizen Investigator. I nodded at her.

"Around the time of the midnight burn, Rockwell was having us de-contaminate areas of the building, because they'd gotten in trouble for so much contamination where we worked. And then we went into preparation for the semi-annual inventory as long as we were shut down anyway. But if someone wanted to do a special run, they could still do it and hardly anyone would know. They could do it on a weekend, or at night."

She started drawing a sketch of the burn box where the contaminated waste was fed—using gloveboxes—and then ignited.

"You're supposed to keep the temperature in the burn box below a certain level. It's real dangerous otherwise. But most of us ignored that rule. The higher the temperature in the burn box, the faster you'd get rid of your contaminated trash. And we were always trying to go as fast as we could.

"It was easy to do. You'd stuff as much of the contaminated trash into the burn box as you could, instead of going slowly and feeding the trash into the fire in small amounts. Then you'd hold the needle down on the control box graph so the high temperature alarms wouldn't sound. Also, the sprinklers wouldn't come on when so much heat went up the stack." She handed me the sketch. "You'd probably burn up the filters, but no one would be there to see it, and you'd get rid of your contaminated trash fast and easy."

I was hesitant to ask her, but I did.

"Did you do that kind of burn when you worked in Building 771?"

I tried to make the question gentle, but obviously I was asking her if she'd broken procedures and helped further contaminate the surrounding area with plutonium and other deadly materials.

She looked sad but she answered without hesitation.

"We did it all the time," she said softly. "We called it spiking. It was a sign that you really knew what you were doing if you could spike. Not all the chem ops were good enough."

She shook her head sadly, remembering who she'd been back then and some of the things she and the other Rockwell employees had done.

"Rockwell workers were always bypassing safety rules, looking for the fast way to get the work done. Rockwell was paid bonuses for speed, not for safety, and all of us knew it. Our own promotions and salaries were based on speed, too. I remember how we used to dump contaminated liquid waste in a pond outside Building 771, for instance," she said quietly. "It was an easy way to get rid of the stuff when the equipment was backed up. And it was almost always backed up. Or broken."

Her eyes fell.

"The pond wasn't lined," she said quietly.

"But if the pond wasn't lined, the contamination got into the groundwater," I objected. "From there it can get into the creeks. . . ."

Jacque nodded and finished my sentence.

"And from there into the drinking water reservoirs. I know," she continued sadly. "But we did it all the time. We called it feeding the ducks.[109] Lots of radioactive and hazardous liquid waste went into those leaking ponds, right up until the time of the raid. Maybe even after the raid. It was a fast way to get rid of the contaminated waste.

"Sometimes when the tanks were full and the system backed up— and that was often—we just ran garden hoses out of the tanks and over the hillside, and just let the contaminated water drain out onto the fields. We knew it was wrong and we knew it caused contamination, but somehow, that didn't stop us."

She was quiet and sad.

I repeated my initial question about the midnight plutonium burn.

"So if you wanted to burn plutonium-contaminated trash, if you wanted to do it when the incinerator was supposed to be shut down, and you didn't want to leave a big trail of evidence, or let a lot of people know, could you do it?"

She nodded. "Easily. Special run. Two people would know. And it would take two others to clean up the burn box afterwards. No paperwork necessary. A foreman could arrange the whole thing with no problem."

"So is that what happened the overtime Sunday the FBI caught on infrared videotape?" I couldn't stop at the supposition. We needed the facts, not the speculation.

"I don't know what happened that night. I only know that the incinerator had been operated. We found the burn box still hot and dirty when we came to work in the morning. And it took at least four hours until it cooled down enough for us to clean it up. It was really hot."

She sat back as though we were finished. She'd convinced me that Rockwell could have done a special run, and ordered the incinerator operated during the shutdown without a lot of other employees knowing about it. But I still had a point to pursue.

"I don't understand something, Jacque. With everything that went on after the raid, why didn't you ever go talk Ron Avery? He was your old boyfriend. He was the foreman who assigned you to the 771 shift. Why didn't you just ask him to verify what you were saying? For that matter, why didn't the FBI talk with him?"

Jacque looked at me strangely. She bent down to pet my dog for a few minutes before she answered.

"Ron Avery disappeared about a month before the raid. Friends said he just sold all his stuff and moved to Florida. But he was only a few months away from his twenty-year retirement, so it just doesn't make any sense. Why would he would throw that all away and leave town so suddenly?"

She looked sad. "I never thought about the connection before, but it's sure a strange coincidence, isn't it?" she asked staring at me.

I nodded, and said, "Well, I guess the FBI couldn't find him; maybe that's why they never interviewed him."

Jacque shook her head. "His ex-wife worked right there at the Plant. She'd have known where he was. So did a lot of his friends, I bet."

I'd already checked the list of FBI interviews.[110] No interview with either Ron or Debby Avery.

I'd also read the FBI interviews themselves. I'd gotten copies from Edith Holleman. No one had been asked about the whereabouts of Ron Avery, the foreman Jacque Brever and Karen Pitts had both testified had set up the overtime Sunday to clean up after the illegal midnight plutonium burn.

"I'm still angry at Lipsky and the rest of the FBI," Jacque blurted out. I could hear it in her voice. "They didn't protect me. They just used me. They let everyone know I was cooperating, and then they abandoned me. Even after someone tried to kill me, the FBI didn't do anything. Then my co-workers just harassed me until I couldn't stay there any more. I still hate the FBI for doing that to me."

"Here's the game plan," I announced a little later. "There was an official Energy Department report that said ' . . . by a preponderance of the evidence . . .' that the midnight plutonium burn probably hadn't happened.[111] Sounds like a lawyer wrote it, not a scientist," I smiled. "But we have to deal with it anyway. And Rockwell insisted it hadn't happened either.[112] Rockwell says the exhaust from the stack isn't much hotter when the incinerator is operating than when it's not. Since the incinerator exhaust is run through the caustic scrubber process, and then the wet cyclone, and then mixed in with room air from the rest of the building, Rockwell says it would have been cooled off before it left the incinerator stack. Listen, here's what the letter says: 'We believe this would increase the temperature of the chimney structure less than 1.5 degrees centigrade.'"

We sat there for a minute.

"So the infrared photographs of the incinerator stack could actually look the same when it was operating as when it wasn't. If they could really cool the incinerator exhaust down that much." Jacque said it slowly, reluctantly. But it was true.

I waved a sheaf of papers at her.

"The Justice Department has refused to give me the calculations that were run by the Energy Department about the temperature of the incinerator stack exhaust. And I've FOIA'd the Energy Department and the Justice Department for copies of those infrared reports for over a year. No one will give me copies. But I did find a copy of the June 19th Energy Department report in the files from the congressional investigation Edith Holleman let me copy.

"Rockwell got the report, of course, and then Rockwell sent it to the Justice Department on September 7th, using it to support their argument that the midnight burn charges were false."[113]

I waved the sheaf of paper again. "We have to analyze this Energy Department report and the Rockwell letter and see if there are any holes in either of them. And then we have to compare it with the transcripts of Lipsky's congressional testimony."

Jacque held out her hand.

"This Energy Department investigation is bullshit," Jacque announced the next morning. "They can't even read the oxygen logs."

She looked at me, but I said nothing, waiting for her to continue.

"You know the only equipment in Building 771 that uses liquid oxygen is the incinerator, right?" she asked.

I nodded.

"Well, the Energy Department report says that the oxygen logs show only evaporative loss of a few inches per day during the shutdown.[114] But Lipsky testified to Congress that the logs show much more than that. Plus, Lipsky's agents found the liquid oxygen delivery records showing that liquid oxygen deliveries had actually been made during the time the incinerator was supposed to have been shut down, not using any oxygen at all."

I laughed. "But didn't Rockwell claim that its employee read the gauge wrong because he was too short?"

We both smiled, remembering that bizarre testimony in the Wolpe transcripts.

Something else about the report concerned me, but I said nothing, wanting Jacque to draw her own conclusions.

She did, continuing.

"But that's not even the worst part. What's worse is that the whole Energy Department investigation was looking for evidence of a *normal* incinerator operation, one lasting the usual seven days to two weeks. No one made any investigation of what the evidence would be if the burn had been a special run, an illegal burn, not the usual one."

And of course, since the time period in question was during the Energy Department shutdown, it would not have been a normal, usual incinerator operation. They would have been very careful to use a special run so they could try to keep it secret. They hadn't known the FBI's Night Stalker would fly overhead with infrared cameras on board.

The Energy Department's failure to properly direct the investigation towards the obvious was stunning. And the FBI had done the same thing.

Jacque was excited, now, driving home her point. "The most important thing, though, is that there are parts of the report which actually support the midnight burning charges. The sampler readings from the incinerator are higher in December than in the months before or after December. It was high, like it was in February and March,[115] when we know the incinerator was being run. Here, let me read it to you," she said, holding the report up to the light streaming through the window. "'The data does seem to indicate higher activity in December 1988 than in November 1988 or January 1989 and is comparable to data in February and March 1989.'"

We looked at each other with satisfaction.

The next morning Jacque joined me for a walk with my dog. I wanted to keep testing her memory a little, to see how believable she would have been then, to try to understand why the US Attorneys would have said she wasn't reliable.

"How can you be sure that the midnight plutonium burning you cleaned up after was during the shutdown, Jacque? You worked the incinerator a lot. Maybe you had it confused with another time in February. That's what the prosecutors said, anyway."

She shook her head. "No, I'd been transferred to another building at the time of the shutdown. By that time, I hardly ever worked the incinerator anymore. I only worked the incinerator that Sunday because Ron offered me some overtime to do it. And there are lots of reasons I can remember the midnight burn was in December. I'd offered to baby-sit for a co-worker so he and his wife could go out for New Year's Eve. We'd been gossiping about buying Christmas presents while we were working. . . ."

She paused, looked away, and when she started talking again her voice was angry and closed down.

"But what difference does it make what I say? I'm not reliable, remember? That's what Ken Fimberg said. If I was reliable, they wouldn't have dropped the midnight plutonium burning charges, and that whole stupid plea bargain probably wouldn't have happened.

"So don't ask me anymore, because no one's going to believe a word I say anyway."

She started walking quickly back to the house.

I could see that bringing up these old memories was taking a toll on Jacque. She looked drawn, and she hadn't been sleeping well. And I knew she was starting to be afraid again.

I decided I'd been pushing her too hard. We still had no evidence to counter the assertion that the incinerator exhaust was not much hotter when the incinerator was running than when it was not. And if that were true, the infrared analyst's comparison between the night in December during the shutdown, and later in February when the incinerator was admittedly operating, would be useless. But Jacque was having a hard time with the painful memories. And it was time for her to get back to her job. We were tired, and decided to call it a day. Enough of the tiny text and contradictory details. We got Georges and went out for margaritas.

I didn't want to say anything to Jacque, but despite the help she'd given us in the Citizens' Investigation, that "not very reliable source" label that Ken Fimberg had hung on her was still a problem. Even though Fimberg acknowledged to me that he hadn't really meant to say that, we were still going to have trouble getting Congress to pay attention to Rocky Flats without something more than just her testimony. We still need to get those infrared reports, and so far the Justice Department hadn't answered my long standing FOIA request.

Without the infrared reports, or something else, we only had Jacque Brever's uncorroborated testimony. And as Jacque had often told me, the pain evident in her voice, they didn't believe her before, so why should they believe her now?

So when I finally got the Justice Department FOIA envelope in the mail, I tore it open eagerly.

More bad news. The Justice Department denied the request for the infrared reports. Rule 6(e) confidential Grand Jury materials, they said.

CHAPTER TWELVE

Special Agent Jon Lipsky, 2001

Shortly afterwards, out of the blue, I received a response from the FBI to my request for an interview with Special Agent Jon Lipsky.[116] It had taken intervention by New Mexico Congressman Tom Udall, but finally the Bureau was no longer stating that the FBI's Rocky Flats criminal investigation that had ended back in 1992 was still pending. They were considering granting my request.

At first I was excited. Then I heard the restrictions.

First, the FBI wanted to approve the questions in advance. I asked who had placed that restriction. Media relations from FBI headquarters refused to tell me. That got me suspicious right away.

I flatly refused to play that game. It would affect the credibility of the entire Citizens' Investigation. I didn't know if that was going to be the end of it, but I simply wasn't willing to accept that kind of restriction. Especially from someone who wouldn't acknowledge that they'd done it.

I did agree to tell the FBI what I wanted to interview Lipsky about: the FBI investigation of Rocky Flats, and the congressional inquiry into that investigation.

I was pleasantly surprised when the FBI agreed the next day that I needn't submit questions in advance. But then they added another restriction.

No questions concerning the congressional inquiry.

I couldn't believe it.

I'd been allowed to interview every other member of the original investigation team—former US Attorney Mike Norton, former Assistant US Attorney Ken Fimberg, "A Justice Department Prosecutor," EPA lead Agent Bill Smith. But the FBI was trying to hamstring the interview with Special Agent Jon Lipsky.

I refused the restricted interview. I wrote Congressman Tom Udall and thanked him for his efforts. I sent Agent Lipsky a copy of my letter declining the interview because of the restrictions imposed by the FBI. I had a feeling the Bureau wouldn't be telling Lipsky the whole story.

That was the end of that. No interview with Special Agent Jon Lipsky. All this time of waiting, and that was the end of that.

If an investigation of the government has to rely on the government's cooperation to succeed, you can count on it failing. As in the original Rocky Flats criminal investigation almost ten years ago, we needed to talk with the individuals involved. And the government wasn't going to let us do that.

All that waiting, and now I wasn't going to get an interview with Special Agent Jon Lipsky after all.

Things have a strange way of turning out, though, so different from what you'd ever expect. I got a surprising phone call the next week. The voice was controlled, but I could sense the emotion behind it.

"This is Jon Lipsky," he said. "I'd like to talk with you. . . ."

I was on the next flight to Los Angeles.

I called Wes from the hotel room in the morning before my meeting with Lipsky. I hadn't talked with Wes in a while, anyway, I told myself. But to be totally honest, it was more likely the idea that I was about to meet with an FBI agent who might be trying to set us up that made me want to talk with Wes. I didn't really feel like that about Jon Lipsky, but I knew better than to assume I'd be able to tell if he were really up to something. For all I knew, he was just fishing for information to find out what this lawyer from Santa Fe, New Mexico was poking around in.

Maybe it was just being in California. But the night before, I'd started worrying about what the Citizens' Investigation was doing and I hadn't slept well.

What if Lipsky's part of a set up? I wondered bleakly as I dialed Wes from memory. I hoped I'd be able to reach him before he left for his morning chores. Wes answered cheerfully and I quickly filled him in on my brief conversation with Special Agent Lipsky.

"Lipsky doesn't know you're involved in this investigation with me," I said. "That's the last thing we want circulating around the halls of the Justice Department. 'Gagged Rocky Flats Grand Jury Foreman Starts Citizens' Investigation of the Justice Department.'"

Wes laughed and started to say good-bye. But I also wanted to talk with him about what had kept me up most of the night.

"I want to talk with you about something else," I started. "The thing I'm worried most about is something we can't do anything about anyway. So I might as well stop worrying about it, I guess, huh?" I said trying to sound casual.

I didn't want to worry Wes, too, but I also didn't want to keep things from him.

Wes was quiet on the other end of the line, waiting for me to continue. He never did help any with things like, "Go on," or "Tell me more," or even "So?" He just waited until I was ready to keep on talking.

"Well," I said. "It's not really about Lipsky. It's about the whole thing. If any of these folks decide to get really peeved at us, they can sue us and tie us up in court for years, and maybe win and take everything we own. Even if they're wrong. Even if they ultimately lose, they can use up a lot of our lives worrying about it and dealing with the legal stuff, and it can cost a fortune.

"And, the Justice Department could get really peeved, too, and try to prosecute you.

"And me, too.

"But I guess that's nothing new is it?"

I paused again, but still he offered no conversational help.

"And then there's a possible attack on my law license, of course, and maybe public comments from them that make us look bad, even if they're not true.

"And then there's income tax investigations, and nosing around our private lives, and well, who knows, Wes. You just can't tell what they might do."

I was quiet then. There really wasn't much we could do about any of this, anyway.

Wes' voice was even toned when he finally said something.

"You want to change your mind, Caron, just let me know. I was doing this on my own before, and I'll just continue on my own. I got no interest in you feeling worried or doing anything you don't want to do."

I felt a little ashamed. But the only thing to do was keep on being frank about how I was feeling.

"Wes, I didn't tell you this to make you feel responsible for my worries. That's my responsibility. But I do want to be totally honest with you, and that's just how I'm feeling. You don't have to do anything about it; I just wanted you to know, see if you were feeling the same way, see if there's anything to those worries," I finished lamely.

Wes laughed then. "Sort of like the hunch you get when you're out riding and you think you hear something but the wind's blowing too hard to tell and you just have to go with your guts, is that it?" he asked.

"Yeah, that's it, just like what happens to me all the time when I'm out riding, Wes. All the time."

We laughed, and then there was a silence.

As much time as I'd spent with this man, as much as he had to trust me to be doing what we were doing, he never really told me much about himself. I remember asking him once how he felt about Fimberg. He looked at me like I was crazy and I never did get an answer. He'd tell me what he thought, but never how he felt.

Once, when I'd pushed, Wes had told me about his wife's worries that the Citizens' Investigation was going to end up with Wes and me in jail. And although he hadn't mentioned it, the financial pressure must have been hard, too. Jan was working full time and going to school, too. They were raising adopted and foster kids. I was sure the family could have made good use of the time Wes was spending investigating the government. Which is why Wes and I agreed that Jan had the final say about whether we sent this investigation to Congress, assuming we ever finished it.

"Good luck with your meeting with Agent Lipsky," he finally said as we hung up. "But don't forget, anytime you want out, you just tell me, and we part friends."

I started wondering what Special Agent Lipsky would be willing to talk about.

Lipsky had arranged to meet me in the lobby of my hotel in Los Angeles. I saw him coming across the room before he saw me. Big. Wearing tennis shoes and slacks and a casual shirt. I'd seen pictures and news footage of him from the time of the raid, of course, but he had no idea what I looked like.

He hadn't changed much in the decade since the Rocky Flats raid. Maybe his face didn't look quite so innocent. He looked worried, and at the same time resolute. I was nervous, afraid to scare him off. I'd wanted to talk with him so many times over these last several years of the Citizens' Investigation.

I stood up to catch his attention. We shook hands and I gestured over to the small table I'd chosen in the corner. I offered him the seat with the back to the wall and that made him smile.

"Old habit," he said as he put his briefcase down on the carpeted floor. "But thanks, I'm definitely more comfortable like this."

Jon Lipsky and I had only spoken a few times but I recognized the deep voice immediately.

"Is this OK, Jon?" I started. I glanced around the room. No one much here except a few waiters and some huddling businessmen at a small table far across the hall.

Lipsky arranged his briefcase before answering. He looked at me for a few minutes without talking. And then he still didn't answer me, choosing instead to pose his own question, something I found he often did.

"You mean talking to you, or talking to you here?" he asked.

We both smiled, and then sat quietly. I had read everything I could find about Jon Lipsky. All the newspaper articles, hundreds of pages of congressional testimony, the search warrant he'd help write. I felt I knew a lot about him, and realized with a start that he knew almost nothing about me. He sat across the table having tea with a person he'd only spoken with over the phone, someone he didn't have Bureau permission to talk with, a lawyer investigating a case he'd once worked on that had turned out to be dirty.

How uncomfortable this must be for him, I realized, as I offered him tea.

We eyed each other warily.

"OK, who goes first?" I finally asked.

He laughed.

"I will," he answered. "Because I have something to tell you that you don't know anything about."

That got my attention.

"It's not about the Rocky Flats investigation directly. But it's a lot of why I'm here," he started. "I know you've been trying for a long time to get an interview with me about Rocky Flats. And then, when the Bureau finally agreed, they put that restriction on the interview that you couldn't ask about the congressional investigation back in 1992."

I nodded.

Lipsky took a deep breath and unsnapped his briefcase. He slid a single piece of paper across the table towards me.

"That restriction was only part of what the Justice Department was up to," he said. The words came out in a jerky fashion. He was obviously holding back a lot of anger. "They sent me this memo just before you wrote and told them you weren't going along with their restricted interview."[117]

I took the paper from him slowly. He'd passed it across face down. I put on my glasses, turned the paper over, and read the few short sentences quickly.

I looked up at him with amazement. I couldn't believe the risk he was taking by giving me that FBI memo.

"They wanted me to lie," he said quietly. "They ordered me not to say anything prejudicial about the Denver US Attorney's Office. But a lot of what went bad with the Grand Jury investigation was *caused* by the Denver US Attorney's Office. And they know I know it. The Bureau was telling me to lie, and if you'd agreed to the interview with the restrictions the Bureau wanted to put on *you*, you'd never have known about the big restriction they put on *me*."

"If you'd agreed to go along with it," I said. There was a question in my voice. Would he have lied? Would he have followed those orders if I'd agreed to go forward with the interview?

"I wouldn't have gone along with it," he stated emphatically. "If you'd asked me a direct question, I would have told the truth, and then my handler would have terminated the interview and I'd have been hauled up to headquarters and all hell would have broken loose.

"This is the only time they've ever ordered me to lie about Rocky Flats," he continued as though to himself. "During the congressional investigation, they gave me some pretty strong hints, but never a direct order.

"I probably should have written to Congress years ago about what happened to the Rocky Flats investigation back in 1992. I tried to tell them during the congressional investigation, but the Justice Department instructed me that just about everything was secret Grand Jury information, under Rule 6(e), and that I couldn't tell it even to Congress," he said sadly.

I looked at him inquiringly, wanting to ask for an explanation, but not wanting to interrupt. He noticed.

"The Justice Department instructions to me about what was supposedly confidential Rule 6(e) material were much broader than any I've ever seen before or since. And the Department lawyer sat right next to me. I had to confer with him before I answered almost any of their questions. Congress never learned many, many important things which are not really secret because of the way the Justice Department manipulated Rule 6(e)," he explained.

"And after the congressional investigation was over, every time someone wanted to interview me, the Bureau refused. So then the Justice Department could just say whatever it wanted without contradiction. Spin it out to hide what really happened."

Jon Lipsky looked at me across the table, straight into my eyes.

"If I talk with you, if I help you with this Citizens' Investigation you told me about on the phone, you have to agree to give the information and all the research you've got to Congress. They need to look really closely at that legislation that will have kids playing at Rocky Flats."

I was afraid to say anything for a moment.

"Of course I can agree to that," I finally answered. "That's the purpose of the Citizens' Investigation anyway. And remember, Congressman Wolpe told you to contact Congress if you suffered any type of retaliation from your testimony back in 1992."[118]

Lipsky shrugged. "The Bureau has been retaliating against me since the Wolpe Report came out in January, 1993. But that's not the point. The point is the Rocky Flats National Wildlife Refuge Act. Rocky Flats is no place for recreation."

I nodded. "What's going to happen to you if you talk to me without Bureau approval?" I asked. I thought I knew, but I wanted to make sure he had thought this through carefully.

"I'm three years away from retirement. I guess the worst thing they can do is fire me. I'd probably lose my pension."

He has three daughters in high school, I thought to myself. I remembered Wes' three daughters, and the risk Wes was taking, too.

Lipsky was still thinking out loud. "I don't think they can trot out any criminal charges. I'm not going to break any laws."

I nodded to myself, wondering if he'd talked this over with his wife.

"The worst thing they can do is fire me," he repeated. "And I don't think they will."

I looked at him in surprise

"There's a lot of good people in the FBI," Lipsky said, noting my disbelief. "I don't think they'll let the bad ones get me. I'm ready to talk, even without Bureau approval."

Lipsky was continuing, as though to himself.

"I just can't let them shut me up anymore. This is too important. Kids playing at Rocky Flats?"

There was a long silence for a while. We were both thinking. When he started talking again, he seemed calmer.

"Did you read the *LA Times* articles about Rocky Flats?"[119] he asked.

I nodded. I'd read them many times.

"Well, there's a lot of things in there that just aren't true."

That didn't surprise me. I'd found some things in there myself that I knew were wrong. I didn't say anything to Lipsky yet, but apparently someone from the Justice Department had told the journalist that the document the prosecutors submitted to the Grand Jury for consideration right before the plea bargain was the sentencing memoranda, a document ultimately submitted to the court and made public.

In fact, it was an indictment against Rockwell Corporation—no individuals—and the US Attorney's Office had tried to get the Grand Jury to sign it. The Grand Jury had refused, wanting to hold the Rockwell and Energy Department officials accountable, too, not just the corporation which would then simply pay a fine it would probably write off as a cost of doing business.

It's unethical for a prosecutor to negotiate a plea without informing the defendants that the Grand Jury had already refused to indict them. And none of the prosecutors had told Rockwell that the Grand Jury had rejected the prosecutors' indictment against only the corporation.[120]

The Justice Department would not have wanted to admit that before the government attorneys had submitted the Justice Department's settlement with Rockwell to the court for approval, the Grand Jury had rejected it, returning the proposed indictment with *No True Bill* written across the top in Wes McKinley's angry scrawl.

But if I mentioned this to Lipsky, I'd have to tell him how I knew what had happened in the Grand Jury room. And until he proved himself to me, FBI Special Agent Jon Lipsky was not going to know that I was doing this Citizens' Investigation with the foreman of the Rocky Flats Grand Jury.

Lipsky looked at me for a while longer before he continued. Those pale blue eyes of his were clear, despite the lines of worry I could see around his mouth.

"I've kept quiet about it for almost ten years. I just didn't see what I could do that would matter. . . ."

He looked despondent.

"They were just using me. Using me so when they settled the case, they could say they'd done a complete investigation. 'We've done a thorough investigation headed by Special Agent Jon Lipsky, our expert on environmental cases. But we didn't find the type of criminal acts everyone suspected.'" His voice was heavy with irony.

"But to say there'd been a complete investigation? With the stranglehold the Justice Department put on us? The whole thing was a joke. A bad, bad joke."

I tried to keep any expression off my face. This is what I'd been suspecting for a while now. Was he going to be able to prove what he'd just said? I watched while he came to his own internal decision.

"And now that they've calmed down the public about Rocky Flats, they can encourage people to believe it's safe to let kids play there. And that's just crazy. It's dangerous for any of us, adults or kids. Rocky Flats is no place to play around. It's a closed down nuclear weapons plant, not a playground."

Lipsky leaned forward. "So let's get down to it," he said. "But remember, this is all going to Congress."

I nodded and picked up my pen.

More than two hours later we finally took a break. So many questions answered, so many issues he knew nothing about. Apparently the prosecutors and the Justice Department had tried to cut Jon Lipsky out of the picture almost from the beginning. But still, he was able to tell me a lot.

––––––––––––

Special Agent Jon Lipsky had been the first witness for the Wolpe congressional hearings. He'd been personally willing to answer questions, privately glad to have a chance to tell Congress what had really happened. But he'd been provided with a Justice Department lawyer, Roger Cubbage, and a Justice Department position: no testimony. Deputy Assistant Attorney General David Margolis was to represent Norton, Fimberg and Murtha during the investigation, and he took the same position.

Lipsky had protested. He had nothing to hide, didn't even want a lawyer, hadn't asked for one, and had no desire to be prosecuted for contempt of Congress.

Don't worry about their threats of contempt of Congress, Lipsky was told. The Justice Department decides who and whether to prosecute and *we're* not going to prosecute you. You do what we say, not what Congress says.

This Justice Department position worried Lipsky even more.

Finally, in September, 1992, the Justice Department had agreed to allow Norton, Fimberg, Murtha and Lipsky to testify. All of them met together before Lipsky was to start off the testimony. Margolis liked to take Polaroid photos, and snapped several of the uncomfortable FBI agent and the three attorneys lined up in his office. The meeting was brief. But it really worried Lipsky. The message was direct and unmistakable.

*We need to remember that we're here today because of opin-
ions that each of you has formed. Those opinions can change.
Even today, they can change. You're not stuck with how you felt
before. Even today, your opinion can change.*

Lipsky had understood the little speech. His differences with the
prosecutors about the handling of the case were well known. Lipsky felt
the Justice Department was telling him to change his opinion and toe the
party line.

And he knew there'd be fallout if he didn't.

On September 11th, 1993, Lipsky stood up before Congress, swore
to tell the truth, and began answering questions. He didn't get far. Justice
Department lawyers started right in with objections. When asked by
Chairman Wolpe, Lipsky answered that he would personally be willing
to answer the questions but had been instructed not to by the Justice
Department, both his employer and his legal counsel. A difficult position
to say the least.

He felt the pressure from his friends and colleagues, from his superiors, to toe the line. The Bureau had made arrangements for Lipsky to
meet the FBI Director, William Sessions, when Lipsky was in
Washington for the hearings. That normally would have felt like a privilege and an honor for a Special Agent.

But Sessions had been part of the opposition to Lipsky or any of the
other FBI agents testifying to Congress at all. So when Sessions shook his
hand and commented that he was sure Lipsky would make the FBI proud
of him at the hearings, it sounded to Lipsky like a message to keep his
mouth shut.

Instead, Lipsky decided that he was going to answer whatever questions his Justice Department lawyer would allow as fully and completely
as he could, even volunteer information if he could get away with it. And
try as hard as he could to get the truth out.

Lipsky testified for two days that September. Afterwards, he left
Washington DC relieved. But at the same time he was mad. Really mad.
He knew the Justice Department was going to get away with it. Something
they'd happily send Joe Blow to jail for, they were going to get away with.

I'd read his congressional testimony, but you can't tell from the cold
dry record what had really been going on behind the scenes. Now I

understood a little more about why the FBI hadn't wanted me to talk with Special Agent Jon Lipsky. He looked exhausted. It was an emotional issue and he was taking such a huge risk talking to me. But he wasn't finished.

"Remember those questions you asked me when we first were trying to arrange the interview? About the elevated strontium readings from the soil samples at Rocky Flats?"

I nodded. Those elevated readings had troubled me since he'd first told me about them. I'd brought some information about them with me that I was anxious to show him.

"Well, that's one part of the investigation that was never finished. And it was important. Here's what happened," he said and sat back in his chair, looking me straight in the eyes as he remembered back.

"I was in the administration building at Rocky Flats one day in 1990, still looking for evidence for the Grand Jury investigation. As I was walking by, one of the analysts, I never knew his name, pulled me aside and showed me some documents. I used to go in there every once in a while, just in case someone wanted to give us some information. Well, it seems that approach worked. This guy just sort of grabbed me when no one else was looking and showed me the documents.

"There were a lot of papers in a thick, three ring binder of data and color pictures," he continued, exhibiting that ability to recall details that Congressman Wolpe had commented on.

"Did the guy say anything?" I asked.

"Yeah, he said something." Lipsky's voice was almost challenging. He sat back, folding his arms across his chest. "He said, 'Wow, look at these elevated strontium readings. Wonder what that's from?'"

I was thinking hard. This was serious. Elevated strontium readings meant a criticality, or some type of experimental project using strontium that the public and the clean-up team didn't know about. If they didn't know about it, they wouldn't be checking to make sure it was cleaned up before opening the Plant for recreation.

"What happened to the studies?" I asked.

"I never saw them again, and I never saw that analyst again, either. I told the prosecutors about the elevated strontium readings. They just shrugged and said 'So what?' The prosecutors were heading towards settlement and didn't want to hear about any more incriminating evidence. They just wanted to make their deal. Any new evidence could screw it up. That's why they pulled us off the investigation so early in the game. They'd decided by 1990 that they were going to settle the case rather than take it to trial. And if there was too much evidence about criminal acts, they wouldn't have been able to settle."

I looked at him quizzically. That didn't make sense. Usually, the more ammo you have, the easier it is to force the other side into a settlement.

"Rockwell told us from the beginning that they weren't going to settle if we insisted on including criminal charges against any of their people," he explained patiently. "Rockwell insisted that we file charges only against the corporation, and even then they wouldn't settle if we filed charges that might expose them to any additional civil liability for causing off-site damage. They'd made it clear they would only agree to petty charges, technical waste storage type charges.[121]

"They didn't care that much about the money—that was a cost of doing business, and the fine ultimately wasn't even as much as their profits at Rocky Flats," he continued. "But filing charges against any of their people was a deal breaker for Rockwell. But for me, that was precisely the point. The only way you get a corporation to change its ways is to put some of its big wigs in jail. Financial losses just get passed on to their shareholders. But if the Justice Department was going to settle the case, they had to accept this bottom line from Rockwell. And someone at the Justice Department had decided, early in the game, that they were definitely going to settle the case."

Lipsky had made it real clear. This wasn't the kind of settlement you'd expect from someone representing the public good: the government doing a thorough investigation and then pummeling the Rockwell corporation and the Rockwell and Energy Department officials with the evidence until they agreed to an adequate fine, penalty, clean-up and restitution, or went to trial. This wasn't a situation where the government gathered all the evidence and facts in a detailed manner, informed the public, and pursued criminal charges against the guilty the way it would if Joe Blow were the criminal. Instead, this was a case of the government limiting the amount of evidence it received so it could settle the case and be done with it.

"So, despite the requirements of the US Attorney's Manual, the Rocky Flats Grand Jury investigation wasn't a complete investigation of the criminal acts of Rockwell or the Energy Department at the Plant?"[122]

I wanted to phrase the question precisely. Then, later, I'd try to figure out why the US government would want to waste taxpayers' dollars doing something like that.

Lipsky answered just as precisely. "They limited the types of crimes we could investigate, the time period we could investigate, the people

who could be investigated. They even limited how we could use the law.[123]
And they cut off the investigation before we'd even really gotten started."

I was looking at him intently, and he must have known I'd want examples and proof of everything he'd just said. He sighed and then started to detail it out for me.

"Ken Fimberg told us in the beginning that we couldn't investigate any violations of the Atomic Energy Act, for instance."

"But that's the main statute governing radioactive materials at weapons plants," I protested.

Lipsky shrugged with a see-what-I-mean look in his eyes.

"We didn't investigate any crimes involving purely radioactive materials. We were investigating only hazardous materials. If radioactive materials were there, too, fine. Otherwise, forget it."

I looked at him in amazement. Radioactive materials—plutonium in particular—were what had concerned the public the most, even though exposure to some of the hazardous materials from Rocky Flats could be dangerous, too.

"And we really weren't supposed to investigate any criminal actions after 1989," he continued, "even though there was evidence that EG&G, the new contractor, was doing some of the same things Rockwell had been doing. And only RCRA,* Clean Water Act and Clean Air Act violations. No false statement or fraud charges were going to be considered because that might interfere with settlement. Those crimes are too serious to be easily negotiated away."

"But those allegations were in the search warrant," I interrupted. Lipsky just looked at me, and continued.

"There was hardly any investigation into why the sewage treatment plant was spraying radioactive waste onto the grounds when it was only supposed to be treating and disposing of ordinary domestic sewage. We didn't investigate how much radioactive and hazardous waste had seeped into the groundwater or run off into the drinking water supplies in Standley Lake. Or the monitoring and data falsifications, lying to the regulators. We never did a thorough investigation of that, either."

I'd stopped protesting by now. The pattern was becoming clear. I was writing as fast as I could, looking up at him often and watching the complex play of emotions across his face. I assumed an FBI special agent

---

* The Resource Conservation and Recovery Act gave the EPA the authority to regulate hazardous waste from its generation to its disposal.

could do a poker face if he had to, but he wasn't doing it now. His face was alternately angry, sad and frustrated as he detailed the sabotage of an investigation he'd worked his heart out for.

"I didn't realize at the time what was actually happening," he said, as he sat back and drank some of the now cold tea I'd poured hours ago. "We were so busy, there was so much to do and so few people to do it. The Justice Department just gradually kept throwing roadblocks in our way. One day, headquarters just announced no more investigation of crimes by individuals. By that time it was clear there was no political will to do this investigation. I don't know what changed from the time we started the investigation until it got derailed. I don't know if the defense contractors put pressure on the Justice Department, or what. You know, it wasn't just Rockwell that was worried about this FBI raid. The other defense contractors had a lot at stake, too. Maybe it was something else. But all of a sudden, everything just changed. . . ."

I could sense how uncomfortable he was, but I was determined to push forward.

"Do you remember US Attorney Norton saying that he'd never discussed the settlement with Energy Department officials? He said he'd met with them to discuss some issues about indemnification of fines, but that he hadn't discussed the terms of the proposed settlement. Do you remember that?"[124]

Lipsky nodded. "I remember reading that in his congressional testimony. But I don't know one way or the other whether that's correct because I wouldn't have been involved."

I slid a copy of an internal Energy Department memo I'd found in the boxes of documents Edith Holleman had given me across the table to him, and watched while he read and then re-read it.[125]

Based on that March 28th, 1991 internal memo, Norton's congressional testimony was not correct. In fact, he had talked with the Energy Department's Deputy Secretary and the Energy Department's General Counsel about the confidential aspects of the case, including the outlines of the proposed indictment against Rockwell.

Worse, before the investigation into the conduct of the Energy Department's high-level officials had really started, before the top-level Energy Department officials had even been interviewed, US Attorney Mike Norton had told the Energy Department's top lawyer that Energy Department officials were not likely to be indicted.

Norton apparently didn't tell his investigation team what he'd done. And he told Congress, under oath, something different.

I waited to see Lipsky's response.

His face got red fast. He looked away from me, across the almost empty room where his eyes fixed on a watercolor slightly askew on the tapestried wall.

"Why were they lying to the investigation team?" he finally muttered, still not looking at me. "Why tell us we're going to be focusing on high-level Energy Department officials if they'd already decided not to charge them? And how could they tell the public and the judge that the decision not to prosecute had been based on what the investigation revealed? There really wasn't any investigation into what those high-level Energy Department people had done. We never got that far."

One of the main reasons I'd wanted to see Special Agent Jon Lipsky was to talk about some documents I'd found in the congressional storage boxes. The Justice Department and the Energy Department had probably thought those documents would never be seen by anyone on the outside.

"What were Rockwell's main demands when they first started talking settlement?" I asked him.

Lipsky answered without hesitation. "No indictments of any of their people, only the corporation; no Grand Jury Report; no debarment; no charges that could increase Rockwell's liability for money damages to surrounding property owners; and official public statements from the Justice Department that there'd been no midnight burning and no substantial off-site harm."[126]

"According to the Wolpe Report, Rockwell got virtually all these concessions," I noted.[127]

Lipsky nodded. A look of disgust passed briefly across his face before the usual professional, expressionless demeanor returned.

"But what interests me," I continued, "is *how* Rockwell got those concessions, and why the Justice Department insists that the plea bargain had nothing to do with them."

This time, the look of disgust stayed. "The Justice Department is always saying it settled the case based only on the facts and the law, and that's a bunch of bull," Lipsky muttered.

I passed him a Memorandum for the Record, signed by the Energy Department's Deputy Director, Office of Procurement, agreeing that if Rockwell pleaded guilty, it would not be debarred from further government contracts. It was signed the same day the Grand Jury was discharged. Despite the fact that Rockwell had been routinely criticized for its operation of the Energy Department's Hanford nuclear facility in the state of Washington, as well as for its operation of Rocky Flats, and despite his public condemnation of Rockwell, Energy Department Secretary Admiral Watkins had agreed.[128]

"It might be a coincidence," I said, thinking it most surely was not, "but it seems strange that Rockwell had been demanding no debarment almost since the beginning as a condition of settlement, and here, two days before the settlement is publicly announced, the Energy Department agrees. Yet, the Justice Department claims no connection."

I started to hand him another document. Lipsky finished reading the first one, turned it around and slid it back to me before he picked up the next one. Thorough guy, I thought.

"Didn't Rockwell also insist that the Justice Department not intervene* in Jim Stone's whistleblower lawsuit filed against Rockwell?" I asked.[129]

Lipsky stopped reading long enough to nod at me, then went back to the document I'd just handed him. A letter dated the same date as the plea bargain, where the Justice Department civil division agreed not to intervene in the Stone lawsuit. Again, just a coincidence?

"And then there's the plea bargain itself," I continued. "Only charges against the corporation. The prosecutors announced there wasn't enough evidence to indict any individuals, that there'd been no secret midnight plutonium burning, and that there'd been no real off-site harm from the charged conduct. Sounds to me like the Wolpe Report was right: Rockwell got virtually everything it asked for."

"And paid a fine that's less than its award fees at Rocky Flats, too," Lipsky added. "Rockwell still made money at Rocky Flats, and taxpayers got stuck with the bill for clean-up."

I looked at him closely before continuing. "And what about the Grand Jury Report? No Grand Jury Report was one of Rockwell's original demands, too. Just another coincidence?"

Lipsky deliberately turned the letter around and gave it back to me before answering. "Here's what I know. First, the prosecutors told Rockwell's lawyers that the Grand Jury was authorized to write a report, and was planning on doing it. We even filed a memo with the court giving the citations and advising the court, too, that there'd be a report. Then, when Rockwell kept insisting it didn't want a Grand Jury Report, the prosecutors said, don't worry, it won't be about Rockwell."

Lipsky shook his head. "I don't know how the prosecutors were going

---

* Join the case on behalf of the whistleblower.

to pull that one off, because Fimberg told me the Grand Jury was really angry at both Rockwell and the Energy Department and was going after both of them in its report."

I didn't say anything about how the prosecutors had tried to get the Grand Jury to let them re-write their report.

"Anyway, in November, 1991, the Justice Department changed positions and decided there couldn't be a Grand Jury Report after all. Again, it's just a coincidence, huh?"

Lipsky was clenching his jaw and staring at the wall behind me.

"The Criminal Division at headquarters just pulled the rug out from under us and the Grand Jury, too. Everyone knew the Justice Department had agreed that a Grand Jury Report was appropriate under the statute because of the type of case it was. And then they just said no."

He sounded so bitter. Yet another betrayal of years of hard work. Another betrayal by the government he'd sworn to defend.

"All of a sudden, just like that, they just ordered no Grand Jury Report. They said reports are only authorized when there's organized crime involved, like the mafia. But that's not what the law says. A Special Grand Jury like at Rocky Flats can write a report if there's 'ongoing criminal activity collectively undertaken.' It's not about organized crime. It has nothing to do with the mafia."

I shook my head in sympathy. The Justice Department excuse had been pretty lame.

We talked for a while longer, then stopped to stretch and walk around the lobby. It was still deserted. I could tell there was a lot more Lipsky wanted to talk about. But he had to get to work. We agreed to meet the next morning at 6 am. He'd stop off again on his way to the FBI office in Westwood.

The next morning I went first.

"I brought you some more documents to look at," I said, pushing a pile of environmental surveillance reports across the table towards him.

He started flipping through them quickly.

"Never saw these before," he said, looking up at me. "Why do you want me to look at them?"

I didn't answer right away and he looked back at the title page of the first report.

"These aren't the environmental surveillance reports I told you I saw during the investigation," he said as he kept flipping through the pages. "Those reports were much thicker, with color photos and graphs."

"These don't say anything about strontium, either," I said, looking at him. "You said you were concerned about the reports you saw because they showed elevated strontium, which might indicate a criticality accident and a bad public health problem. But the people at the Energy Department archives say these are the only environmental surveys at Rocky Flats from this time period."

I paused, until he looked up at me, finger still in place where he'd left off scanning the documents.

"The Energy Department says there was never any study done on strontium levels," I told him. "They've looked through their archives. And the analyst I talked with didn't know why there'd be any reason to do a study of strontium levels, anyway."[130]

Lipsky looked at me quietly. "I saw the studies, Caron," he said firmly.

I nodded. He had no reason to lie about it, and he had a phenomenal memory. But I had to be certain.

"Are you sure what you saw wasn't about elevated cesium levels? There's some information about cesium in those reports," I said pointing at the stack.

"No, it was strontium," he said with certainty, looking at me. I knew he knew the difference.

He wanted to know if I believed him. If I didn't, why go on?

I did believe him, and had reason to.

I pulled out a file and slid it across the table to him. Inside were two newspaper articles from the time of the FBI raid, talking about elevated strontium readings at Rocky Flats. Leo Duffy, Special Assistant to the Energy Department Secretary, had testified to Congress that because of rumors of criticality accidents at the Plant and the fact that local authorities had found indications of elevated strontium in the groundwater, the Energy Department had arranged for some independent studies.[131] There were strontium studies done in July 1989, and in August it was reported that the experts had determined there were no elevated strontium levels or evidence of criticality accidents at Rocky Flats.

Lipsky read and then re-read the articles. He looked up puzzled.

"Then, according to these articles, the Energy Department archives should have the independent environmental study of strontium in the soil at Rocky Flats," he stated.

I nodded. "I know. I filed a Freedom of Information Act request to get it and they told me there wasn't one. I finally managed to find a real human I could talk to, and asked him to help me. Eventually, I was able to speak with one of the researchers who'd actually worked on the environmental surveillance studies around the time of the raid. He still works there. He still has the soil samples that were collected."

Lipsky looked at me eagerly.

"He says there was never any study done on strontium," I told Lipsky. "He was part of the team and they never studied it."

Lipsky looked puzzled. Then he started to get angry. "I saw the data," he insisted. "I read it and the analyst who showed it to me also remarked to me about the high strontium levels."

I nodded again.

Then Lipsky's jaw set and he started thinking along a different track.

"So what does all this mean?" His question hung in the air for a moment while we both tried to figure out why the Energy Department had given congressional testimony about a study that a researcher involved in the project says never took place, but that Jon Lipsky had seen.

"We'll never be able to prove what's really true. Maybe the studies got stuffed somewhere, after you saw them," I said finally. "That way, the Energy Department can tell the public and Congress pretty much whatever it wants and there's nothing to contradict it."

"Could they really do that? Stuff data just because they didn't like it?" Lipsky looked incredulous. I said nothing. Then he got a kind of sheepish look on his face.

"Doesn't the Bureau ever do things like that?" I asked him quietly.

Lipsky just looked at me. It was a who-are-you-kidding kind of look.

"Who's going to stop them?" he asked quietly.

"Exactly," I said. "Who's going to stop them."

Lipsky had to leave for work. He took the environmental surveillance reports with him.

When we met the next afternoon, his wife, Patti, was with him. It was Saturday and they both had a few hours for me before they were to leave for their youngest daughter's softball game.

We sat looking over at each other across the restaurant table while families around us ordered barbecue. Patti was attractive, bright, and worried. Jon was risking his pension and their future talking with me. I didn't blame her at all for being nervous.

Patti nicely told us to just pick up where we'd dropped off the day before. "Jon filled me in on the way here," she explained. Jon handed me back the surveillance reports with a shrug.

"Like you said, there's nothing in there about strontium," he said. "And these definitely aren't the studies I saw. They don't look anything like them."

I nodded, knowing I'd never be able to force the Energy Department to cough up the reports Lipsky had seen so long ago during the FBI investigation. If they hadn't been shredded by now. But the important issue was, how did elevated strontium readings affect the clean-up plans? If the people in charge of cleaning up Rocky Flats don't know about the strontium, how can they make sure it's cleaned up?

"You were the lead agent on the case, but now I understand you were kept in the dark about a lot of things," I began after he'd been quiet for a while, remembering. Lipsky nodded, slowly, wondering what was coming next.

"Did you know about the EPA and FBI interviews with Rockwell employees who talked about some of the data falsification that went on there?"

I showed him copies of the interviews I'd sent John Till, where former Rockwell employees talked about finding out that some of the workers had been cheating on the water testing that determined the amount of radioactivity that was in the Rocky Flats discharge to the community drinking water reservoirs. Falsifying the test results that determined whether the workers were being over-exposed to dangerous radiation. Faking the filter testing which determined whether the public was being exposed to dangerous levels of plutonium from the Building 771 incinerator.

Lipsky nodded without reaching for the interviews, looking frustrated. I handed Patti the file.

"I knew about them. Some of those interviews I took myself," he told me. "And I know your next question. No, the prosecutors weren't really interested in what these guys said because the Justice Department had already decided to settle the case. And evidence of cheating would've brought the settlement to a screeching halt. Rockwell had already told us it would not plead guilty to any fraud or deceit charges."

I'd checked the Justice Department's status reports that had been filed as the investigation had progressed.[132] The evidence of Rockwell's cheating on environmental reports and falsifying test results had made it to an early list of allegations to be investigated. But less than a year into the investigation, this serious issue, as well as allegations of false statements and fraud, had been abandoned.

Yet, that didn't stop Justice Department headquarters and the prosecutors from telling the court and swearing to Congress that there'd been no off-site public health or environmental damage from Rocky Flats. They said it even though they knew they'd never fully investigated the issues raised in these interviews and even though they had first hand evidence that Rockwell had been cheating on the very tests which measured off-site contamination. They said it to get the case settled. They said it because Rockwell required them to say it before the company would agree to settle the case.[133]

I'd never even have found out about this laundry list of fraud and public endangerment if Edith Holleman hadn't let me review and copy the thousands of pages of documents that had been delivered under subpoena during the 1992 congressional hearings about the Rocky Flats Grand Jury investigation.

Patti glanced up from the interviews she'd been reading, looking angrier by the minute. She waited until the waitress had refilled our drinks before continuing. Then she leaned forward over the polished wood table. She was agitated, twirling the straw in her Coke.

"Those statements Rockwell made the Justice Department agree to about no off-site harm from the Plant really made us mad. Why does a defense contractor have enough clout to convince the US government to lie to the American people? And to Congress? What about the Blue Baby syndrome the City of Broomfield was so worried about?[134] The Broomfield health officials were complaining about high nitrate levels in the streams from Rocky Flats that fed their drinking water supplies. Nitrates keep the fetus from getting enough oxygen, and the City already knew that several infants had been born with birth defects.

"If there really wasn't any problem, why'd Broomfield stop taking their drinking water from the streams that ran from Rocky Flats? Do you think Broomfield city officials just woke up one morning and said, 'Hey, let's spend millions of dollars changing our water supplies just for the heck of it?'"

I nodded but didn't interrupt her.

"It's a betrayal of everything Jon risks his life for as an FBI agent for Justice to lie to the public and Congress, just because some defense contractor insisted on it. It's like Rockwell was pulling the strings on a puppet."

Patti was quiet for a while. She stared out the big glass window to the parking lot, the stream of cars going by on the freeway. She took a deep breath and looked directly at me.

"How can the Energy Department possibly be so sure they can clean that place up enough to let kids play there when this kind of cheating and lying went on for so many years? They haven't got the slightest idea how much dangerous stuff is spread all over the place out there.[135] Or what else people might have been lying about.

"And now the Bureau is telling *Jon* to lie. Where will it all end?" she said sadly. We were quiet, not knowing the answer to that very important question. I asked Jon if he'd known there'd been a lawsuit by surrounding landowners claiming that Rocky Flats had contaminated their property.

"We knew about it," Jon acknowledged. "Ken Fimberg initially told me to go get the court file because there should have been some great evidence about off-site contamination in there. Then, for some reason, he called me off and said he'd do it himself. Later, Ken told me the file was sealed and we couldn't get anything out of it.

"He never told me the US Attorney's Office was the ones who'd asked to have it sealed. And *you* got some information even though the file was sealed. So Ken should have, too"

I didn't know what to do except plunge ahead.

"Actually, there was an even larger property owners' lawsuit filed against Dow Chemical and Rockwell after the raid.[136] Did you know about it?"

He shook his head.

"About 11,000 property owners who lived within a five mile radius of the Plant sued the defense contractors who'd been operating Rocky Flats up to the time of the raid. They claimed their property had been contaminated by Rocky Flats. And they have expert witnesses who say they're right."

Both Lipskys were looking at me expectantly, so I continued.

"That case was filed in 1990. And the landowners have been trying to get a trial date since then. But, again, no ruling from the judge. In fact, it's now more than a decade since the case was filed, and *still* no trial date.[137]

"The landowners also conducted their own tests.[138] They have a lot of proof of what went on at Rocky Flats, and how it contaminated the surrounding neighborhoods. But they can't get to trial, and the evidence they have just sits in their lawyer's files gathering dust."

"And the public remains in the dark," Patti Lipsky finished for me. "And the wildlife refuge opens and the public is invited in."

We were all a little agitated, twiddling straws, tapping pencils, looking around. I wasn't sure what Jon and Patti were thinking.

"There are some other strange legal cases dealing with Rocky Flats," I continued. We were all overwhelmed by now, but I felt I had to continue the information download. Jon knew about the Grand Jurors' lawsuit[139] but Patti didn't.

"After the Grand Jury Report was leaked to the press, the Grand Jurors started talking in public a little about how unhappy they were with the Justice Department's plea bargain. The Grand Jurors weren't violating their oaths of secrecy, but just by appearing publicly and stating their dissatisfaction with what the Justice Department had done during the Grand Jury investigation, the whole issue was getting a lot of publicity, and some attention from Congress as well.

"Then the FBI started investigating the Grand Jurors. There were rumors they might be prosecuted for leaking the Grand Jury Report, even though there was no real evidence that it was one of them that had done it. Well, all of the Grand Jurors except the foreman hired a lawyer, Jonathon Turley. He's a law professor from Washington, DC. Turley decided the best route was to ask Congress to grant the Grand Jurors immunity from criminal charges so they could testify before Congress about what the Justice Department had done to the Grand Jury investigation. When that didn't work, Turley filed a petition in federal court in Denver asking the court to allow the Grand Jurors to speak.

"Turley got the Grand Jurors all to agree not to make any more public appearances about Rocky Flats, even if they didn't violate their oath of secrecy, until after the court ruled. So that's why there hasn't been anything further from the other Grand Jurors in the press."

"Why didn't the Grand Jury foreman join the lawsuit?" Patti asked.

I had to be a little careful here, but I wanted to answer them.

"Well, he *was* part of the lawsuit in the beginning, along with the other Grand Jurors. But then Turley and some anti-nuke activists, independently of each other, came up with the idea that Wes should run for Congress. Members of Congress have complete immunity for what they say in Congress. Turley thought it'd be a good idea to have a two-pronged attack: Wes trying to get elected so he could talk about Rocky Flats in Congress, and Turley running a lawsuit trying to get a judge to let the Grand Jurors speak."

Patti and Jon nodded. They'd known about Wes' unsuccessful run for Congress. What they didn't know, though, was that Wes had also been very skeptical about the possibilities of a federal judge allowing the Grand Jury to speak the truth about Justice Department manipulation and deceit behind the closed doors of the Grand Jury chambers.

I was a little uncomfortable talking with them about Wes; they still didn't know he was part of the Citizens' Investigation. I changed the subject.

"The Grand Jurors' petition to the court was filed in 1996," I finished, looking at them.

"And?" they both asked, almost simultaneously.

"And all these years later, there's still no ruling from the judge."

We sat there, uncomfortable, angry, and not knowing each other well enough to talk about it. I figured I might as well tell them the rest of what I'd found.

"In 1998, the Colorado Health Department released a study they'd done of the incidence of cancer in the areas around Rocky Flats," I said quietly.[140]

Jon looked over at Patti. "The State Health Department is very political, Patti, and never was on top of what was going on at Rocky Flats."

"The cancer study was designed to determine whether the areas surrounding Rocky Flats had a higher incidence of cancers than the rest of metropolitan Denver," I continued.

They were both nodding that they understood.

"The study compared the areas around Rocky Flats with the rest of metropolitan Denver and . . ."

Jon interrupted me, leaning forward across the table. "But that's no kind of comparison." He was talking loudly, and some people near the cash register looked over curiously. Jon leaned back and lowered his voice.

"Metropolitan Denver was dosed by Rocky Flats, too. It's only 16 miles away, directly downwind. If you compare metropolitan Denver to the areas around Rocky Flats, they're just not going to be much different. They need to compare the areas around Rocky Flats to an area *away* from Rocky Flats. That study's worthless."

"Well they also included Boulder in the areas considered as potentially dosed."

"But Boulder's a college town. Denver's an urban center. There's plenty of studies showing that urban areas usually have higher cancer rates than non-urban areas, even without nuclear weapons plants nearby. So, on that basis alone, you can't compare Boulder to Denver."

Patti nodded that she understood, so I took out a folder and showed them the study's conclusion: "...the incidences of cancer combined for persons of all ages and for children during 1980-1989 was not higher than expected compared to the remainder of the Denver metropolitan area."

Then I gave them the interviews I'd obtained from an independent radioecologist. "It appears that the study design was chosen for public relations purposes, to calm people down, rather than for any real scientific reason," stated Bernd Franke, after reviewing the Colorado Health Department's study.[141]

I also gave them some reports from the former Jefferson County Health Director, Dr. Carl Johnson—reports the Justice Department had not managed to get sealed in the court file—showing his findings of excess cancers and increased infant death rates around Rocky Flats compared to the rest of the country.[142] More recent epidemiological evidence supported some of these findings and I showed them that, too.

> *"The manner in which these operations were conducted exposed people living in the vicinity of the plant to a variety of radioactive and non-radioactive toxic material. In my judgment these exposures were significant and were sufficient to cause latent diseases among members of the exposed group."*[143]

> *"There is a continuing excess of lung cancer in the area closest to the Rocky Flats plant which supports previous findings and analyses. Further, there are several other types of cancer which are increased in populations which may be exposed to plutonium and other emissions from the Rocky Flats plant."*[144]

The State of Colorado and the Energy Department had established a Rocky Flats Future Site Use Working Group. After studying the issue, the working group decided that the former nuclear weapons plant should be turned into open space, and closed off to human access until the radiation levels on the site were cleaned up to average background levels.

But the Energy Department didn't like that conclusion. It's applying less protective clean-up levels, less than what would be required for an industrial site, in spite of the plans to open Rocky Flats for recreation. A plan is being implemented throughout the country turning contaminated sites into wildlife refuges or other areas open for public recreation, using these less protective clean-up standards.

Since 1993, former Superfund sites have been returned to communities as soccer fields, golf courses, and wildlife refuges, thereby promoting human access to the sites. In fact, the EPA is working closely with private organizations like the US Soccer Foundation, the National Football League, and major league baseball to obtain their support for turning Superfund sites into recreational areas.[145]

Jon Lipsky hadn't known any of this when he'd d started the investigation of Rocky Flats back in 1987. He was just trying to enforce the nation's environmental laws against the government and its defense contractor the same as he would against any private citizen.

The Bureau had already retaliated against him just for testifying truthfully to Congress back in 1992. And now here I was asking him to take still more risks by joining our Citizens' Investigation.

Within three days of publication of the Wolpe Report to Congress, which heavily relied on his testimony, Lipsky had received orders that he was being transferred out of Denver. He protested, but it was useless.

Lipsky was never again to work environmental crimes. The FBI's star environmental crimes investigator, the agent with nine years of specialized training, the man who gave lectures to other agents and Justice Department employees on the intricacies of investigating these technical crimes, was assigned to work gangs in the streets of South Central Los Angeles.

"Our life has been ruined because of that Rocky Flats investigation," stated Patti Lipsky. "We didn't want to transfer to LA; we'd just bought a house in Denver. It's actually against FBI policy to transfer us to LA, because that's where we'd started. And it's so expensive. We have three daughters. We were told it was Mike Norton's direct request to the FBI.

"Before we got here," Patti continued, "someone from the Justice Department had already talked with a few of the men Jon was going to be working with. Told them the Department's version of what happened during the investigation and the congressional hearing. After that, no one wanted to work with Jon. They wouldn't have anything to do with him. I don't know what the Department said, but it sure wasn't good."

Patti Lipsky was understandably bitter, despite the brave bright smile.

"The Bureau is Jon's life. He worked the Rocky Flats case for years before the raid and for years afterwards. They wouldn't even let him take a promotion to go work in DC; said he was too important to the case. And then they transferred him to LA, bad mouthed him, and every time he tries for a promotion out, he gets stopped.

"And now, to find out the cover-up had started almost from the beginning . . . that he was used. All that time, he was being used. . . ."

I wondered what it had been like for her, all these years, knowing how badly the Bureau had hurt Jon, and disappointed him, and betrayed him. And then she watched him go to work and risk his life again with them anyway. I knew she wanted to help the Citizens' Investigation—she already had—but I understood her worries.

Then her chin tilted up again, and the big smile started to come back.

Jon sat with his arm across the back of the booth behind her. He watched her with a worried look. He'd told me yesterday how hard Patti had taken the Bureau's retaliation against him.

"She actually feels it worse than I do," he'd told me yesterday as he was offering to bring her along to our last meeting. "And that's saying a lot. We've both felt angry, and hurt and used. And worried about the people living around Rocky Flats. We've wanted to do something and not known how. So we've both been really frustrated about it all these years."

His already troubled face became even sadder.

"And Jacque Brever. I've felt so bad about what happened to her. The Bureau just used her up, spit her out, never even tried to protect her. I've never had that happen to any witness in any of my investigations. It feels terrible. I still worry about her, after all these years."

Patti took his hand and squeezed it. I could only imagine what it must have been like for them for the past ten years. Shunned by their former friends, retaliated against by the agency Jon had devoted his life to. Worrying about a brave witness who might be dead by now because of his investigation. Jon working street gangs in South Central Los Angeles instead of environmental crimes. Knowing a huge injustice had been done, knowing the people living around Rocky Flats might still be in danger, even though the Plant had been closed. Knowing some terrible things about the Justice Department and Rocky Flats, but not knowing what to do about it.

And now, the plans to open Rocky Flats to recreation. . . .

"There's something I want to tell you about that I didn't tell Congress," Lipsky said quietly. He looked a little subdued.

"They never directly asked me anything which would have made me answer it. And I'd been ordered not to volunteer it. But I also think I was still just so shocked it had happened that I didn't know whether to say anything or not."

I nodded and looked at him, pen ready.

"One day right before I was supposed to appear for my second round of testimony to the Wolpe subcommittee, Ken Fimberg called and asked me to come down to his office. Things were already pretty strained by then, because Ken knew I disagreed with a lot of what had happened with the Grand Jury investigation, and I'd already testified to some of it.

"When I got to his office, Fimberg handed me an affidavit and asked me to sign it."[146]

"Jon was already worried about what Ken might be up to," Patti joined in, remembering back. "And there was another strange thing."

She looked around to make sure no one was listening. I'd noticed her doing it before. She laughed with a little embarrassment, and continued.

"Anyway, Jon told me that Ken had been sued for threatening one of the witnesses in the case.[147] And Jon was worried that Ken was about to threaten him, too."

Lipsky nodded as he finished the story.

"I didn't read the affidavit right there, just told Ken I'd read it later and think about it. I got out of that office as fast as I could. There was no reason for Fimberg to be giving me an affidavit. I wasn't a witness in some case Ken was handling. We were *both* witnesses before Congress. Why was Fimberg trying to get me to sign an affidavit?

"I read the affidavit in the elevator. Fimberg wanted me to swear I agreed that there'd never been enough evidence to indict Energy Department individuals. Norton had testified to that. Fimberg, too. If they could just get me in line. . . .

"But I didn't agree. Not the way Fimberg and Norton had said it, like we'd done a complete investigation and there just wasn't enough evidence of Energy Department criminal acts. That wasn't true. We never really investigated the Energy Department officials, never got that far before they shut the investigation down."

"But why did he ask you to sign an affidavit? Why not just talk to you?"

Lipsky just looked at me quietly and shook his head with a look of sadness in his eyes. Ken Fimberg had been one of his best friends.

"The whole Rocky Flats investigation team was under orders not to talk to each other about our testimony," was all he'd say about it.

Jon slipped the affidavit across the table and they both went quiet as I reached for it. Then I heard Patti start chuckling as I finished reading the affidavit Jon Lipsky had never signed.

She smiled as she told me, "Jon's reaction is on the back."

I turned the affidavit over. FBI Special Agent Jon Lipsky had scrawled "Bullshit" in large angry letters, and had never talked to his former friend again.

"Ken and I were very close friends. I lost my career and a friendship that really mattered to me over Rocky Flats."

He darted a quick look at me, and then stared off again into the distance. A man who had done the right thing. And paid for it. It's tough being a whistleblower. Hard to do the right thing when your friends and colleagues aren't.

I looked over at the two of them, across the table in our quiet corner booth. Patti and Jon Lipsky laughed alike and they sounded alike on the phone. They went to their daughters' sports events and acting events together. They'd lived this nightmare together.

It was time to tell them that Wes and Jacque were involved in this Citizens' Investigation, I realized. Jon and Patti had trusted me, and it was time to trust them, too.

"That's great!" Lipsky said after my short explanation. "If they're willing to take the risk, so am I."

Patti still looked worried, but she smiled and started slowly to nod.

"How is Jacque's health?" Jon asked carefully, as though not sure he had the right to know.

"She's sick," I answered honestly. "She's got health problems. But she's part of this Citizens' Investigation no matter what it takes."

Jon sat quietly for a while, remembering, looking troubled. Then slowly he started to smile.

"What?" I asked, perplexed.

He laughed out loud. "I'm remembering a sign that popped up on the wall in the Bureau's investigation office during the congressional inquiry.

"It said 'Free the Rocky Flats Grand Jury.'"

CHAPTER THIRTEEN

We Prove the Justice Department Cover-Up.
Now What?

A short while later, we really got lucky. Everything the Justice Department had said about the Rocky Flats case was now thrown into question.

I found copies of the infrared reports.[148] After the Justice Department had refused to provide copies under the Freedom of Information Act, I'd called the regional EPA offices in Las Vegas, Nevada, where the work had originally been done. Much to my surprise, they promptly and politely sent me the two reports.

More than one way to get around the government's usual FOIA blockade, I thought with satisfaction, as I pored over the graphs and annotations.

And the reports led me straight to the infrared expert.[149] There was his name, right on the front page of the reports. Al Divers was listed in the phone book; he still lived in Las Vegas. And he remembered this Rocky Flats project quite well.

He listened to me politely as I explained why I was calling. His first words stunned me.

"I don't know why anyone would say my testimony was different than my reports. I certainly did not change my position," he told me.

At first I thought I'd misunderstood him. His change of position was the main reason the Justice Department had dropped the midnight plutonium burning charge, according to all the Justice Department public and congressional statements.

But he repeated himself. "I did not change my position. I said the same thing in the Grand Jury room as I said to those men who interviewed me before my testimony, same as I said in the reports."

Fimberg and Lipsky had both interviewed Mr. Divers, I remembered. I was very quiet on the other end of the line as he explained how the infrared photography worked.

With the infrared equipment the FBI had used, you can't tell how hot something is, absolutely, you can only tell the heat relatively, compared to other things, he explained. It reads in colors from white to black. He had determined from the infrared photography that the incinerator had been operating, and that's what he'd told the Grand Jury in response to their questioning. He couldn't tell them how hot it was, but by comparison to other parts of the building, to the steam lines, and to a nearby electric plant, he could tell that the 771 incinerator was thermally active.

Most important was the comparison between the first infrared overflights in December, 1988—when Rockwell and the Energy Department denied the incinerator was operating—and the overflight in February, 1989, after they admitted that the incinerator had been re-started.

The heat signatures are the same. According to Divers' second report for the February, 1989 overflight: "This stack, located on the east side of building #771 is hot. The temperature of the stack appears equal to that of previous taping."

How could the heat signatures possibly look the same if the incinerator was operating during one photo and supposedly shut down during the other?

I told him about Rockwell's position that the 771 incinerator exhaust was just 1.5 degrees centigrade hotter than room temperature. This supposedly explained why the infrared photos looked the same when the incinerator was shut down as when it was operating.

Mr. Divers actually laughed.

"That's ridiculous," he told me.

Divers firmly rejected that explanation, stating that he'd seen videotaped infrared images of people moving around outside the buildings. He used the shade of gray registered from their bodies as a baseline for human body temperature. His report had also compared the white of the 771 incinerator stack with the other parts of the 771 building, which were only light gray, and with the room exhaust from HVAC systems on other buildings.

"If it's white on the photo, I'll guarantee the stacks were hot," he said. "That incinerator was running and the exhaust was much hotter than room temperature."

I sent Mr. Divers copies of the reports he had written for the FBI. When I called to make sure he'd received them, he had, and had reviewed them, and his opinion was unchanged. The 771 incinerator had been operating during the December, 1988 FBI overflights.

He still seemed perplexed about why the Justice Department was claiming he'd changed his story. And had no idea of the bombshell he'd dropped on our little Citizens' Investigation.

What Divers had told me sounded like pretty good proof that the Justice Department had lied about the real reason they'd dropped the secret midnight plutonium burning charges. And it sounded like pretty good proof that the secret midnight plutonium burning had really happened.

Wes had been sitting in my office while I was taking with Divers. He looked at me quizzically after I slowly hung up the phone. We both got excited as I explained what Divers had said.

"So Rockwell's position about room temperature incinerator exhaust is just a bunch of bull," he said. "And the Justice Department's position about the infrared analyst changing his position is even more bull. They *knew* there was plenty of evidence that the incinerator had run during the shutdown, but they insisted it had never happened. And labeled Jacque and Karen not reliable sources to boot."

Wes was agitated.

"The prosecutors didn't just drop it; they insisted it never happened. Not, oh, there's conflicting evidence, oh, Rockwell says they never did it. Nope, the Justice Department just insisted it never happened. And told the court that, too. Seems like an awful lot of what the Justice Department said was just a bunch of bull."

But then we started getting excited again. I couldn't wait to tell Jon and Jacque.

Their responses were quite different. Lipsky was quiet for a long time on the other end of the phone. And his voice was sad when he finally spoke.

"Ken told me personally that Divers had changed his position. We'd both interviewed him before the raid. His findings were used as the basis of my affidavit, and he corroborated it later, right before he testified, when we interviewed him in person. But Ken told me Divers had changed his position when he testified to the Grand Jury, and that's why they dropped the secret midnight plutonium burning charges. And of course I didn't hear him testify myself."

I said nothing, knowing he was really talking to himself, trying to find a way to make sense of the terrible waste of it all.

I heard him sigh. And then his voice became analytical and he told me how Mr. Divers' statement that he'd never changed his testimony proved that the Justice Department had covered up the secret midnight plutonium burning charges.

"And since the Citizens' Investigation has proved one cover-up, Congress ought to be willing to look at what else got covered up."

His voice was firm, and he thanked me for telling him, but I knew he was a sad and angry man.

Jacque Brever was ecstatic. She immediately understood the importance of Divers' statement. "So that means there *was* corroborating evidence for what Karen and I were saying," she said emphatically "They just hid it."

———————————

I was flipping through Wes' steno pads again when I found still more evidence of the Justice Department cover-up. I hadn't been able to read too much of the steno pads at once. His handwriting was *so* bad.

Getting the steno pads out of the Grand Jury room was a story in itself.

Wes' journal Mar. 1992: My thoughts had been anything but pure when I walked by the security guards, guys I had become friendly with, my back stiff due to the steno pads I had wedged between my back and my belt, covered by the faded sports coat I wore just for this occasion. I was afraid the guards would notice my coat and comment on me wearing it. The weather was certainly cool enough for a jacket but then, I never wore a sports coat.

The guards were their usual friendly selves but never mentioned my coat. I exchanged farewells with them and walked out of the courthouse. All the way till out of sight of the courthouse, I was afraid the bounty from the Grand Jury room would suddenly become visible through the back of my jeans and through my coat and announce its presence. The homeless man I had seen on every trip to Denver I now suspected was a government agent, and I now expected him to lash out a hand, feel my butt, and discover the steno pads slipping lower.

The safety of my room gained, I hid the steno pads in my dirty clothes, stuffed in the tied off leg of my soiled jeans.

They were my journals, after all. I wasn't stealing anything. But I knew if I'd asked the prosecutors could I take them home, they'd have refused.

And somehow, I'd thought, as I gave an extra yank to the leg of my jeans, someday, I'm going to need these.

I remembered back to that grin I'd caught on Wes' face, way back in the beginning, when I'd asked him if he had anything to prove the cover-up. He couldn't have known that a date on one of his journal entries would be so important. But he must have felt certain those journals would come in handy somehow.

And there it was, in the pages of nearly illegible scrawl and cowboy slang, rough grammar and skewed syntax in his notebooks. It was only a date. Something I hadn't noticed before. But it made everything fall into place.

Two weeks after the October 1989 Grand Jury session where Jacque Brever and Karen Pitts—the supposed star witnesses for the Grand Jury investigation—had testified, the Justice Department started sabotaging their testimony. Sabotaging the testimony of their own star witnesses.[150]

The prosecutors called an Energy Department employee to the stand. He testified that the midnight burning had never happened.

Wes' journal Nov. 16, 1989: What's this? Last session we heard from two honest sincere ladies who took to heart the oath to tell the truth. Today, this Energy Department guy said exactly the opposite of what Pitts and Brever said in the last session. He swore the incinerator hadn't been operating during the shutdown, and that when it did it was only 1.5 degrees centigrade hotter than ordinary room temperature.

"I'd forgotten all about that witness," Wes told me. "But what are you staring at? We already know that bull that the incinerator exhaust supposedly wasn't hot. It was in the newspapers. That's nothing new."

But I couldn't take my eyes off the steno pad in my hand. Wes looked at me strangely.

"It's the evidence of criminal intent we've been looking for," I explained, still staring at his steno pads. "This proves they we're lying about why they dropped the midnight burning charges."

I held the steno pad out to him. "The Justice Department swore to Congress that they'd dropped the secret plutonium burning charges because the infrared analyst had changed his position. We've proved that he didn't change his position. But what if the Justice Department was just wrong? What if they'd misunderstood what Mr. Divers was saying? A cover-up requires proof that they were actually lying or intending to deceive Congress. And here it is," I said as calmly as I could.

Wes took the steno pad, and then looked up at me curiously.

"It's the date, Wes, the date the guy testified about how the midnight burning hadn't happened. He testified *before* the infrared analyst took the witness stand.

"The prosecutors were sabotaging Karen and Jacque's testimony *before* the infrared expert had even testified."

We looked at each other.

"And two weeks later, the story gets leaked to the press, so Rockwell knows the prosecutors are going to drop the midnight burning charge. Paved the way for Rockwell to argue there was no criminal intent, no cheating, no sneaking, no bad faith, and then wangle its way into a plea bargain under the Justice Department's policy of only prosecuting intentional environmental crimes."

Jacque Brever had thought her Grand Jury testimony mattered, that it was worth risking her life to have the truth come out about Rocky Flats. It was hard to think about her, knowing someone had tried to kill her to shut her up, knowing how she'd braved it out and testified to the Grand Jury anyway. It was hard to believe she was still so willing to help.

———

Out of the blue, Jacque sent me a teasing e-mail. "Found Ron Avery. Want to talk with him?"

I called her immediately. Would the Rockwell foreman corroborate her testimony? Or call her a liar? Or just not remember?

"Thought that might get your attention," she laughed. "Ron was the guy they always called when they had something dirty they wanted done," Jacque explained by way of prelude. "He was the guy they could rely on."

I said nothing, anxious for her to get to the point. But she was enjoying keeping me in suspense.

"It didn't take long to find him. He's in the phone book." Jacque started telling me the details of how they'd gotten reacquainted and then laughed as I interrupted her.

"Will he talk to me, Jacque? I need to talk with him," I said urgently.

She kept talking as though she hadn't heard me.

"I'm in Colorado," she said rather casually.

I was surprised. Last place I thought she'd be after all the effort she'd made to disappear from there. "Okay," I said, waiting for more.

"With Ron."

I was even more surprised. Apparently, when she'd contacted him, they'd started talking about more than just their years together at Rocky Flats. Back in the old days, they'd lived together for almost four years before Jacque had left because she couldn't take his drinking and partying. She hadn't seen him in thirteen years when she'd tracked him down for the Citizens' Investigation.

Jacque laughed into the silence from my end of the phone.

"I can tell you're surprised. And so am I. But he's been calling me every day since I found him. Last week, he flew out and helped Jessica and me pack up the car and then drove us back to Colorado.

"We're getting married."

My immediate reaction was to be happy for her. She'd been terribly alone since the attacks by her former co-workers and friends at Rocky Flats. She was afraid to trust anyone, didn't date. And although she'd conquered her fears of going out of the house and had successfully completed her advanced education degrees, her personal life was still in shambles.

Her daughter—now 19—was always urging her to date, and Jacque's reply was always that she'd rather stay in her room and paint.

Until now.

What a sudden shift. Then I started worrying. Why back with Ron? There were lots of men in the world.

She must have sensed my hesitation.

"He stopped drinking and partying the day he left Rocky Flats," she told me quietly. "He knew that's why I'd left him, and he couldn't stand being like that any more, either. We never stopped loving each other, Caron," she said quietly. "But that place was killing us.

"Lots of workers at Rocky Flats were into drinking and cocaine.[151] On and off the job. People would come in drunk and go to their stations and just pass out on the floor. One time the nitric acid tank overflowed and contaminated the place because the chem operator was drunk and passed out and didn't hear the alarm. He was a known drunk who often slept on the job. But no one ever did anything about it.

"Even when people weren't drunk, there was a lot of sleeping on the job. People were working too much overtime because Rockwell was pushing production so hard. . . ."

I heard her catch herself from going back too far into those memories.

"Anyway, Ron's stopped partying and we still love each other and we're getting married. I'm sorry I didn't call you right away so you could talk with him. But Ron and I have thirteen years to make up for.

"Wanna meet him?" she asked playfully. And of course I did.

Ron and Jacque held hands the entire time they were down in Santa Fe for the interview. Every time I saw them together, when I passed them sitting on the portal after dinner, or when they were off taking a walk, they were talking and holding hands. Thirteen years to make up for.

Ron was a large man with a lot of thick hair curling around a face that seemed to be smiling all the time. He was attentive and courteous to Jacque and didn't mind talking about how he'd blown it thirteen years ago and wasn't going to do it again. "She's the only one I've ever loved," he told me one night over dinner.

Since getting back together, Ron and Jacque hadn't talked very much about Rocky Flats and it was interesting to see their different perspectives on the place. Jacque had started reporting safety problems at the Plant long before she'd become a whistleblower for the FBI. She'd been wary of the safety conditions and knowledgeable about many of the regulatory violations.

Ron had always thought the place was fairly safe. He was angry about what his co-workers—some of them probably friends—had done to Jacque after he'd retired from the Plant. But he didn't think that meant the Plant itself was unsafe. He knew you had to be careful, but, basically, he believed the government's statements that if you followed the safety rules, you weren't going to get hurt.

He shrugged when I asked him why he thought it was safe.

"The government said it was," he answered.

I just looked at him. Obviously he and Jacque hadn't been talking all that much about the Citizens' Investigation and what we'd already uncovered.

I confirmed that with Jacque later.

"I didn't want to prejudice him one way or the other," she explained and I nodded gratefully. I wanted his independent recollection before he learned everything we'd found out.

"I told him you were interested in Rocky Flats, and wanted to know what he remembered. I didn't tell him about the Citizens' Investigation. Otherwise, we've been catching up on our lives."

Jacque and I decided that I'd interview Ron alone. Ron was agreeable. It was the first time I'd seen them apart since they'd driven down two days before.

Ron Avery had started working at Rocky Flats in 1970. He became a crew leader within a year, and a foreman in 1984. Almost all that time, he'd been a chem operator in Building 771.

"I know all the processes, and I know the entire building," he told me. "I can see it now, even so many years later."

We talked about other things at first, not the secret midnight pluto-nium burn. I didn't want to scare him off, but the main thing I wanted to know was whether he'd violated the shutdown order. How do you ask somebody that without scaring them off?

I muddled about for a while, telling him I was learning what I could about Rocky Flats, that I'd already interviewed Jacque and some other people. He told me he'd left Rocky Flats in 1989, shortly before the FBI raid.

"Why'd you leave?" I asked. "Did you know the raid was happening in advance?"

He laughed at that. "No, I found out about it on the tube, like most other folks. Only I was in Florida. I'd just had enough of the whole busi-ness by then. I said to myself, 'Boy am I glad I ain't there.'"

"But you were just a few months short of your pension," I protested. "Why were you willing to give that up?"

"I was vested by then," he answered. "I didn't give it up. But I had to get out of there. I had turned 40 years old and it felt like my life just wasn't going anywhere."

"Do you know how the incinerator filter system worked?" I asked him. I assumed that as a foreman, he'd known a lot about how everything worked.

He confirmed this assumption. "Yeah, we changed the filters our-selves a lot of times." I could see him brace for more questions. This guy was really uncomfortable talking about Rocky Flats.

"Did you ever notice any problems with the filters when you changed them?" I asked.

"Well, they were always black with soot, and sometimes wet."

That one stopped me.

"What does that mean?" I asked.

"It means the scrubber system wasn't set right for the blowers and too much caustic was going up towards the filters. The soot is from the incinerator exhaust. It interrupted the vacuum and means the filters weren't working as effectively as they were supposed to. Also, wet filters can sag and let more contamination through or around the edges.[152] It was not a good thing."

"Did you see wet filters frequently?" I asked.

His voice sounded sad as he told me he'd seen it a lot.

Later that night, after dinner, I listened while Ron explained what had to be the standard line for workers at US weapons plants.

"I had no reason to believe I was getting an unsafe radiation dose," he told me. "I always wore my dosimetry badge.* Rockwell had them read regularly," he started out.

"Do you know what the legal dose limit was for plutonium workers back when you were at Rocky Flats?" I asked, my voice neutral. I refused to use his terminology of "unsafe dose," as though there were proof that any dose could be safe.[153]

He hesitated, thinking back. After a while he looked sheepish.

"No, I guess I don't. But I was working for the US government, even though Rockwell paid me. I don't have any reason to believe they would expose me to a radiation dose that was unsafe. Or lie about what was safe and what wasn't."

I pulled out *Dead Reckoning*,[154] a booklet put together in 1992 by Physicians for Social Responsibility. They'd shared the 1985 Nobel Peace Prize for their work on nuclear disarmament.

"Let's see what the legal dose limit was," I said to Ron, although I was sure I already knew.

"It was 5 rem per year for workers in 1987," I read, pointing and showing him the page. I watched as he read that line, and then kept reading the next line of the little chart. When he sat back his face was red.

"But in 1990, the International Commission on Radiological Protection recommended lowering the legal dose limit to 2 rem per year," Ron read from the chart. "Why such a big change?" he muttered out loud.

Ron's face was getting redder. I showed him the article where the National Academy of Sciences admitted that the danger at low levels of radiation exposure was three to four times greater than previously thought.[155]

Ron Avery was now one angry man. But he asked the right question.

"So did the Energy Department follow the recommendation and lower the limit?"

He must have seen it in my eyes. Before I'd started to answer, he was already shaking his head in disbelief and anger.

"The government never adopted the recommendation," I said qui-

---

* A personal radiation badge that measured each worker's exposure to some types of radiation from the materials they were surrounded by. A cumulative dose over time could be arrived at, so that a worker could be removed from high exposure work areas once the readings got too high.

etly. "The legal limit is still 5 rem. But the Energy Department's contractors have voluntarily agreed to use the 2 rem limit at Rocky Flats. At least for now," I told him.

"Why don't you take a walk with Jacque? Ask her about Karen Pitts' dosimetry badge," I said, hoping to lower his blood pressure but not lose his attention. I knew how quickly denial could set in again. Denial is what kept people working at those dangerous jobs. That wonderful cocoon of self-imposed ignorance, where you don't let in any information that might conflict with what you've already decided you want or need to do.

As Jacque Brever had ruefully told me, admitting to her own years of denial when she'd worked the plutonium gloveboxes, if you want the highly paid jobs, you had to forget about the danger.

"And you had to keep going even when you knew they were lying to you about safety issues," she'd added. "If you paid too much attention to safety, you'd never work there. And we all had mortgages and other bills."

Jacque had told me some of the risks she and the other workers had taken at Rocky Flats.

"Needless risks," she said. "It was bad enough we were taking risks every day we worked there. We got dosed all the time. But instead of quitting, or pushing really hard to get Rockwell to fix the problems, we laughed about them.

"Midnight mouth, for instance. We had this funny metallic taste in our mouths, almost all the time. We called it 'midnight mouth.' Turns out it was the same thing the people around Three Mile Island had after that nuclear accident" She looked sad, but continued.

"Workers slept on the job a lot. We were always so tired, probably because we worked so much overtime. We all wanted the big bucks. So people would fall asleep leaning on the fluorinator heater. It's really contaminated with gamma and neutrons that dose you just by being near it. But it didn't stop anyone. It was cold in the building, and if we were cold and tired, we'd go warm up on the fluorinator heater."

I was shaking my head, and so was she.

"It's not that we didn't know gamma and neutrons were bad for us. It's not that we didn't know the fluorinator was radioactive and dangerous to be near. We knew. But somehow, we put it out of our minds. With Rockwell's help, we'd taught ourselves to deny there was any danger, just so we could keep working there. And this was just part of the same denial."

Jacque and Ron came back from their walk a short while later, hold-ing hands again. Ron's face wasn't red anymore, but he was still angry.

"Karen never turned in her dosimetry badge when she quit Rockwell." He repeated the conversation he'd just had with Jacque. I nodded. I already knew the story. "But Rockwell sent her some readings from the badge anyway. They had to have been fake, because she still had her badge."[156]

Ron started shaking his head and muttering. Jacque looked sad.

"Karen told an official government committee about the falsified records—it's a crime—but no one ever did anything as far as we know."

I nodded again. I'd read Karen Pitts' testimony in the public record. And I'd heard about the same thing going on at Los Alamos National Lab, too. In 1997, the US government finally admitted that the radiation expo-sure of workers at its nuclear weapons plants had not been properly mon-itored and that its own data was suspect.[157]

Ron's face was getting red again. Jacque pulled him outside for another walk.

It was time to ask him about the secret midnight plutonium burning. He needed to leave soon to get back to work. So, when he came back inside, I told him I was trying to find out more about an overtime Sunday he'd given Jacque and Karen Pitts, assigning them to clean up after an incinerator run. There, that didn't seem too threatening.

Avery was very forthcoming. The simple truth stunned me. After so many years of piecing together circumstantial evidence, here was the man who'd actually done the secret midnight plutonium burn.

And he was admitting it.

"I ran the incinerator on Saturday night, and Jacque and Karen Pitts worked that Sunday morning cleaning it up," he told me. "I remember it because it was right before my birthday. Last birthday at Rocky Flats before I quit."

I was scribbling fast.

"In fact, we ran the incinerator the entire weekend, starting the Friday night before. It was a special run; they wanted me to get rid of a lot of high gram count barrels of waste. We can only do about 10-15 bar-rels of that stuff a shift. It took us through Saturday night to do what they wanted."

"Was this during the Energy Department-ordered shutdown?" I asked him, holding my voice neutral. I couldn't believe we'd finally found someone who would admit to running that incinerator.

"Well, *now* I know it was during the shutdown, but I didn't know the government had shut us down until I heard it on the tube after the FBI raid," he explained. "And by then I was gone."

There it was. Conclusive proof of the secret midnight plutonium burning. We finally had direct evidence to add to the growing pile of circumstantial evidence we'd been collecting for the past four years. And we'd already proved that the Justice Department lied about why they'd dropped the charges. Surely this was enough to get Congress to do something about Rocky Flats.

"The Energy Department nuclear inventory was starting the following Monday," I said. "Did that have anything to do with the secret burn?"

"Could have," he agreed. "They could have gotten in trouble for all the excess barrels of waste they had and for those barrels of really high-level waste."

"Do you have any idea what was in the barrels you burned that weekend?" I asked, thinking about the "black projects" and the secret experiments we'd heard so much about.

"Nope," Ron Avery answered. "And I don't want to know."

And then I had one more question.

"Did the FBI ever try to reach you?"

"No, no one asked me anything at all," he answered. "I wasn't trying to hide; all my friends at 771 knew where I was."

"I guess the good part is that we've finished the investigation, Wes. We can stop now. Even though we have lots of lines in the water, lots of angles still to pursue. If we keep looking, we'll always find something else. I think we've found enough evidence to show the Justice Department covered up the secret midnight plutonium burning."

"And we've found enough to prove that place isn't fit for recreation, no matter how much they say they're going to clean it up," Wes added. "And why should we believe anything they say about it anyway, now that we've seen what kind of cheating goes on?

"But you're right, Caron. Looks like our part of the investigation is over. Finally."

Then we enjoyed a moment or two of silent satisfaction.

"Wes, Jan okayed us sending this information to Congress, right? Remember, we agreed she'd have the last say?"

"Yep. She said for you to tell the Lipsky family that if Jon loses his job, they should to come on down to the ranch. They can eat organic beef and haul hay with the rest of us."

"Does that mean yes, Wes?" I was sort of insistent on this. A promise was a promise.

He gave me one of those funny looks. Then he smiled.

"She didn't say yes, Caron. She said, 'Absolutely yes. For sure. Do it. Hurry up about it. What are you all waiting for?' That's what she said."

We started grinning. I tossed file folders into boxes for storage somewhere far, far out of sight. One of my favorite rituals when a case is over.

I looked over at Wes. He had leaned back against the banco, staring out at Los Alamos, picking out his cowboy song, enjoying the feeling of freedom that had just washed over him after more than ten years.

———————

Hopefully, we had enough evidence to convince Congress to hold hearings about Rocky Flats and the plans to open it for recreation. I called Edith Holleman the next morning. Edith had been in touch periodically throughout the Citizens' Investigation, encouraging us, helping when she could. And she was still an attorney for the Democratic staff of the House Energy and Commerce Committee.

"Of course I'll help," she agreed immediately. "I'll call around and see which Member might be likely to hold hearings. But how am I going to present it to them? Have you written a summary of what you've found?"

The question I'd been dreading. We had our file notes, our original research, our interviews and investigation summaries. We had copies of the few documents we'd been able to obtain from the government. But to get Congress interested, we were going to have to write it up. And none of us wanted to do that. We were just a bunch of concerned citizens, not professional writers.

I sighed. It must have been a loud one, because Edith said kindly at the other end of the line. "I know how you feel. Bet you thought you were finished."

Indeed I had, but I knew we had to write this up for Congress. Wes and I started working on it that afternoon.

It took months. There were over twenty boxes of documents. Luckily, we'd kept logs and summaries as we went along, knowing we'd have to summarize the findings someday. But it was difficult deciding what to leave out. We couldn't send Congress everything.

What finally emerged was a Citizens' Investigation prosecution memo.[*] The government uses prosecution memos as it decides whether and when and who to prosecute. Our prosecution memo detailed the evidence of crimes by Rockwell and Energy Department officials who hadn't been charged as part of the plea bargain. Serious crimes, crimes that could have resulted in debarment of Rockwell from future government contracts, if the Justice Department hadn't dropped them. Crimes that could have sent high-level Rockwell and Energy Department officials to prison. And sent a message to the rest of the government and defense contractor community that environmental laws were going to be enforced against them just as they were against ordinary citizens.

Our prosecution memo also detailed the evidence of criminal conduct by the Justice Department in obstructing the Rocky Flats Grand Jury.

Congress would be able to see how the secret midnight plutonium burning charges had been obstructed by the Justice Department, how the cover-up had toppled the Grand Jury investigation and hidden the truth about the dangers of Rocky Flats.

And Congress would be able to see why recreation at Rocky Flats is such a dangerous plan.

———————————

But Congress didn't see. Or, more accurately, no one looked.

I could hear Edith's disappointment on the phone.

"I've talked to everyone I can think of, Caron. They all say they'd never be able to convince their committees to hold hearings. Democrats have no power now, and the few Republicans who might be interested are swamped with other issues.

"You'd better think of some other way to stop the recreation plans."

I tried to call Wes to tell him the bad news, thinking as I waited for him to answer how sad it would be to close my files and end the Citizens' Investigation. I'd come to like and admire Wes tremendously, Jon and Jacque, too. And I was as worried as they were about the plans for Rocky Flats. I was worried about all the other contaminated sites that were being turned into recreational areas, too. I'd thought if we could prove this cover-up at Rocky Flats, Congress would take a look at this dangerous policy of allowing lowered clean-up standards at these contaminated

———————————

[*]   See, www.Ambushedgrandjury.com

sites, and then turning them into recreation areas.

But there was nothing more for me, as a volunteer lawyer, to do.

When Wes didn't answer, I left a neutral message asking him to call, and sat there staring at the piles of boxes in my office. Wes and I been at this Citizens' Investigation together for over four years; Wes been at it alone for more than five years before that. But with this final door being slammed in our faces, there was nothing more to do. It was time for me to say good-bye.

I got a call from Jacque. Before I could tell her my bad news, she told me hers. She and Ron had both undergone medical tests offered by the Energy Department to former radiation workers. Thanks in large part to the efforts of activist groups and scientists, the Energy Department finally agreed to offer limited medical screening to the former radiation workers who had helped build the nation's nuclear arsenal. New legislation—the Department of Energy Employees' Occupational Exposure Compensation Act—also offers limited compensation to former workers for a limited number of ailments.

Ron and Jacque were both worried. In typical Energy Department hedging, one of the letters Ron had received from the health studies physicians said, "There may have been some abnormalities that are very significant for you so we provide this information so that you may share it with your physician." Months later, on his own, Ron saw another doctor. He was diagnosed with a rare form of cancer on his right eye. Surgery and radiation have left Ron with partially limited vision and new concerns about his exposures at Rocky Flats.

Jacque was steadily getting worse. Her doctor had told her that her spine was deteriorating rapidly, her breathing was worse, she had a growth in her left lung and on her thyroid, and she could no longer work. The woman who had refused to be turned into a victim, who had fought death threats, harassment and abuse, her own fear and post-traumatic stress disorder, the woman who raised her daughter by herself and worked for every penny she'd ever had, despite persistent pain, was now unable to support herself.

And none of the medical problems plaguing Jacque Brever was on the short list of diseases the government had reluctantly agreed to compensate.

We talked a bit about her plans for trying to improve her health. After hearing Jacque's sad news, I hadn't even wanted to tell her what Edith had said. But Jacque wanted to talk about the Citizens' Investigation. Strangely, she wasn't as upset as I was about Edith's news.

"We'll just have to think of something else," she said firmly.

I said nothing, wondering how she could even think about the Citizens' Investigation with such overwhelming problems of her own.

She must have heard my hesitation on the phone. "I may not be able to stand or walk very well, but I can lie down and I can still think," she said firmly. "We each have to do what we can. We should meet and come up with a solution."

Of course we needed to meet for other reasons, too. Wes, Jon and Jacque hadn't seen each other since the Grand Jury investigation had ended almost a decade ago. And they'd each learned of the other's participation in this Citizens' Investigation only through me. It was *their* lives and careers at risk here; their pasts. They should discuss it face to face, I thought, not through me.

Wes drove down bringing some more beef for a re-union dinner, and together we went to meet Jon at the Albuquerque airport. It had stopped snowing, a beautiful cold day and clear roads in front of us. Normally, I enjoyed any time I spent with Wes. But I was not looking forward to seeing the disappointment on his face.

They'd all been upbeat on the phone, saying that we'd get together and think of something else, but I was discouraged. I thought their continued confidence was naïve.

I tried to make conversation with Wes, but I wasn't in a mood for any more Citizens' Investigation. Almost out of habit, I asked Wes how he felt about meeting Jon and Jacque after all this time. He just cocked his hat back, moved his toothpick to the other side of his mouth, and grinned at me. It had become almost a game, me trying to find out how he felt and him denying he had any such thing as emotions.

Wes and I stood together in the waiting area at the airport for awhile. Then I moved off to the side, behind a column, out of the line of sight from incoming passengers. I wanted to see if Jon and Wes would recognize each other and what would happen when they met.

Jon spotted Wes from a long way off. I saw his head swivel and a smile of recognition start. Wes was pretty easy to spot, standing there in his fringed leather jacket and cowboy hat. But Wes had seen Jon, too. They both started grinning and I was treated to the sight of the big FBI agent and my cowboy friend wrapped in a bear hug in the middle of Albuquerque airport.

Then I got a bear hug from Jon Lipsky, too.

We talked all the way back to the house, where Jacque was due to meet us later that afternoon.

Jacque looked ill, sicker than the last time I'd seen her. Her breathing was audible, and fast, and I saw it was hard for her to walk without pain. She couldn't stand up straight.

But she looked excited. Wes and I got hugs from Jacque, but she pretty much ignored Jon Lipsky. Just gave him a cool nod and went to pet my dog.

Uh, oh, I thought, remembering how angry Jacque had been at the FBI. I guess I'd assumed she'd be over that by now. I'd assumed wrong.

We sat inside, watching the sunset on the snowy mountains, casual catch up conversation. Some of the other Citizens' Investigation volunteers who'd joined up along the way had arrived for the supper. I was trying to ignore the uneasy feeling I was starting to get about how Jacque was treating Jon.

It was Wes who brought up the question on everyone's mind.

"Okay, we have to decide what to do next. We've proved the Justice Department cover-up. And we've proved the secret midnight plutonium burn. But, unless we get Congress to do something, and soon, Rocky Flats is going to have horseback riding and nature trails."

"But Congress isn't interested," I started.

"Then we have to *make* Congress be interested," Wes continued. "Congress needs to hold hearings where the Justice Department doesn't just stonewall things. And where they listen to what the Rocky Flats Grand Jury has to say.

"We also need to get some cover for Jon. As soon as his bosses hear about his participation in this Citizens' Investigation, he's gonna lose his job quick unless he's got some strong allies in Congress."

Everyone nodded at that one, too. "Jon's got three young daughters," I said to Wes. "You know how it feels to take risks when you've got that kind of responsibility."

Wes nodded, a remembering kind of look in his eyes.

"He just feels he has to do what he can."

Now I had the remembering look in my eyes. It was that sentiment from Wes that had gotten me into this thing to begin with, so many years ago.

That memory at least felt better than the disappointment I'd been swamped with since Edith's phone call.

Wes was still reviewing our options.

"We'll turn this into a book, so the readers themselves can be Citizen Grand Jurors. They can review our evidence, and then they can tell Congress *themselves* that former nuclear weapons plants and other hazardous sites shouldn't be opened up to recreation."

"What about drafting up a Citizens' Indictment that lets the readers, as Citizen Grand Jurors, decide whether the crimes were committed? We could put it in the back of the book," Jon suggested.

Everyone got excited about that idea. An easy way for citizen readers to make themselves heard to their elected representatives.

Wes nodded. "Hand up an indictment against the Justice Department and Rockwell and the Energy Department, and recommend 'No recreation at Rocky Flats Nuclear Weapons Plant.' Or any of the other contaminated sites around the country scheduled to be opened to recreation.

"And then we'll send them all to Congress."

The enthusiasm was catching. They all started talking at once, figuring out how to get the book written as fast as possible, how we could work together when we lived in three different states.

But I was starting to get worried. I didn't know if anyone else had caught the look Jacque had given Jon, but he certainly had and was looking more uncomfortable by the minute. He was standing by the fireplace, as far across the room from Jacque as he could get.

Jacque had been quiet for a while. Suddenly, her voice sounding strange, she chimed in. "Yeah, the Citizens' Investigation did the job the FBI should have done." She shot Jon a hard look. "So the readers can be like a Citizens' Grand Jury and finally do what the Justice Department stopped the Rocky Flats Grand Jury from doing back in 1992."

The rest of the group suddenly grew quiet. Jacque got slowly to her feet. She walked with obvious pain, stooped over to the side. She stopped in front of Lipsky, moving right in front of him, and I saw Jon tense. Too close for an FBI agent, especially because Jacque was acting sort of weird.

Jacque kept staring in Jon's face, but raised her voice to talk to the entire room. "Last time I talked to Jon I called him a dumb fuck and to never call me again," she announced to the room at large, her eyes never leaving his face.

Lipsky stood there. He met her eyes. But he didn't move away, and he didn't protest what she'd said.

I didn't know what to say or do as Jacque continued to stare at Jon. Her voice was a flat monotone, as though she were speaking in a trance.

"Right before the plea bargain, Lipsky here called me. Actually, he called Karen Pitts first, and she hung up on him. She called me to warn me, so when he called a few minutes later, I was ready. We were so sick of the FBI by then. We'd been used and abandoned by them, and they should have protected us.

"The harassment had gotten so bad, I had to hire a private investigator. Almost the day after I hired him, he found one of the people who'd been breaking glass in our driveway. He followed the guy and went and talked to him. Never had that problem again.

"But the FBI never caught anyone. Never stopped anything. They wouldn't even go on Plant site with us to show that we were still part of the FBI investigation, give us a little protection."

She hadn't moved away from Lipsky. She was really in his face.

"So when Lipsky called, I just let him have it. I told him he was an asshole and a dumb fuck and to never call me again in his entire life. And I hung up on him."

It was an incredibly sad image. And now I was wondering how I'd managed to make things worse for everyone by bringing them together.

Jacque's voice got firmer.

"So now I have to apologize, Jon, because now I know it wasn't your fault after all."

This time I did see a reaction from Lipsky. He blinked, and looked confused.

"Now I know you were trying to help. I've had you wrong all these years," she said. "And now I know they were using you, too. So, I'm sorry I called you a dumb fuck."

She started to laugh, clearly enjoying herself.

The relief on Jon Lipsky's face was clear. The rest of the room relaxed, too, and conversation started up again.

I was also relieved. Jon Lipsky had felt bad about Rocky Flats for over a decade. Thinking that he should have tried harder, that there was something else he could have done. And he'd felt terrible about what had happened to Jacque Brever, too. Her own co-workers had tried to kill her just for telling the truth. And then it turned out she'd taken that risk for nothing, because the Justice Department Jon had dedicated his life to had twisted his investigation to cover up the truth.

Learning that Jacque Brever had forgiven him was probably the most important outcome for Jon Lipsky of anything that happened in our odd little re-union.

I had something for Jacque, and now seemed the right time to bring it out. She'd gone to a large leather chair by the fire, talking avidly with Jon now that she'd had her fun. I walked over and casually dropped a large manila envelope in her lap. I waited next to her while she opened it and read the typewritten pages.

"This is a complete set of Jacque's FBI interviews," I explained to the rest of the group. They were watching Jacque, who'd gasped loudly and was staring at the pages in her hand, reading them intently.

"I've been trying to get these for a long time.[158] All we've ever had are the copies with six blacked out pages that the Justice Department sent to Congress. The ones I got from Edith Holleman.

"I was so curious about what they'd blacked out. Jacque'd never seen the original interview reports, so she didn't know what was blacked out on those six pages, either. But remember how the Justice Department kept saying Jacque wasn't reliable? Mike Norton said she couldn't even place the date of the midnight burn within a six month time period, so how could she know if the incinerator burn she was talking about was during the shutdown or not?"

Jacque cut in here, her voice strangely hesitant. "But I *did* know, and I told the Grand Jury all about it. I told the FBI and the prosecutors, too. And I gave them a bunch of ways they could prove I knew it was during the shutdown. Instead, the Justice Department started saying I wasn't reliable. But there was nothing I could do. I didn't have any proof of what I'd told the Grand Jury or the FBI."

She gulped and looked down at her hands, clenching and unclenching in her lap.

"Jacque's been suffering over this for ten years," I said. "Thinking the Grand Jury didn't believe her, that everyone thought she was lying, stupid, that she wasn't reliable."

Jacque nodded, tears flowing freely now.

"And yet right here in the copy of her FBI interviews I just received, she tells the agents exactly how she knew the secret midnight burn was during the shutdown. She gives them all sorts of corroborating information to prove when it was and to support what she was saying.

"But in the copy the Justice Department sent to Congress, almost all the details of Jacque's story about the secret midnight plutonium burning, and when it occurred, as well as other crimes she knew about, are blacked out."

"I guess so they could call her an unreliable source and get away with it," Jon said angrily.

"Until now," Jacque added. She was crying quietly, her hand shaking as she clutched the pages.

Jon Lipsky was the one who comforted Jacque first, a big hand on her shaking shoulder. Soon we were all clustered around, patting her back and trying to comfort her as she cried out ten years of painful humiliation.

Then we all sat down to start planning the book.

Wes put his cowboy boots up on the office table and grabbed a steno pad and pen. "Democracy is *not* a spectator form of government."

The Citizens' Grand Jury Indictment

is on page 281.

Or, go on line at

www.Ambushedgrandjury.com

Updating Our Story

- In 2003, at Los Alamos National Laboratory, the Energy Department, on a limited basis, resumed the Rocky Flats' mission of plutonium pit production which had been closed down since the FBI raid in 1989. A new bomb production plant called the "Modern Pit Facility" is planned for increased weapons production. Five Energy Department sites—Los Alamos National Laboratory and the Waste Isolation Pilot Plant (WIPP) in New Mexico; the Nevada Test Site; the Pantex Plant in Texas; and the Savannah River site in South Carolina—have been targeted by the Bush II Administration as the potential location for "Rocky Flats II." Environmental and nuclear activist groups are fighting the plans.
- The 1989 FBI raid of Rocky Flats was the first and last FBI raid on a nuclear weapons facility. Arjun Makhijani advises that a high-level Energy Department official, who insisted on anonymity, told him that shortly after the raid on Rocky Flats, Energy Secretary Watkins and the Justice Department had made a deal: if the Energy Department would do Tiger Team reports (basically, quasi- independent self-reviews with no enforcement or penalty power) at the weapons facilities, the Justice Department would agree not to raid any other weapons sites. In effect, the Justice Department abandoned its responsibility to enforce environmental laws at nuclear weapons plants and again left it up to the weapons builders whether and to what extent they would comply with public health and environmental laws.
- In 2002, Wes McKinley ran for office again, this time for the Colorado State Representative seat in District 64 in southeastern Colorado. He came within 489 votes of unseating the incumbent, although he had no professional organization and had raised only $13,000. He ran so he could talk about Rocky Flats, claiming legislative immunity. Again, he rode Marvin the Mule (who is always referred to by his full name) around

229

the district.   Wes will run again in 2004 and again for succeeding years until the plans to open Rocky Flats to recreation are stopped.
• Jon Lipsky still has his job with the FBI.
• Jacque Brever has now been diagnosed with thyroid cancer, and is undergoing treatment. In the meantime, she started **United to Keep Rocky Flats Closed**, a Colorado-based informational program dedicated to stopping recreation at Rocky Flats.
• Edith Holleman is still looking for ways to help us convince Congress to investigate what happened at Rocky Flats.
• Former US Attorney Mike Norton has never again run for public office. However, his wife, Jane Norton, was elected Lt. Governor of Colorado in 2002.
• Judge Sherman Finesilver retired unexpectedly from his life time appointment as a federal judge. He went to work as a mediator. [159]
• Ken Fimberg/Scott is still prosecuting war criminals at The Hague. [160]
• Mark Pitts, husband of whistleblower Karen Pitts, committed suicide in October 2001. He had continued to work at Rocky Flats until his death. Mark Pitts had attempted suicide once before, back when the FBI investigation was underway and the Pitts and Brever families were being harassed and threatened by their co-workers. "He was a sensitive man, and the pressure was very hard on him," according to Jacque Brever.
• After Rockwell had signed the plea agreement, paid the fines, and stopped doing work for the Energy Department, then-Colorado Governor Roy Romer gave Rockwell $26.2 million in tax breaks and a fast-track pollution permit to lure Rockwell back into business in Colorado. This time, Rockwell wanted to build its new semiconductor plant in Colorado Springs.
• In 1992, Rocky Flats stopped producing nuclear bomb cores. In 1995, Kaiser-Hill took over operation of Rocky Flats Nuclear Weapons Plant— now renamed the Rocky Flats Environmental Technology Site. Its mission: clean-up. The Rocky Flats clean-up is not yet complete, and, at this time, Rocky Flats has not been opened up for recreation.

Afterword by Arjun Makhijani[1]
Back to the Bad Old Days[2]

During the long Cold War, the government of the United States, like that of the Soviet Union, deliberately sacrificed the health of its own people without informed consent in the name of national security. The production and testing of vast numbers of nuclear weapons contaminated neighborhoods and the environment surrounding the nuclear weapons plants with radioactive and hazardous elements that will remain dangerous for thousands of years.

As the Cold War came to an end, and people began to wake up to the radioactive contamination of their neighborhoods, there were official expressions of contrition. The United States government seemed willing to cease or cut back its nuclear weapons production. It appeared ready to address and remedy the legacy of cancers and contamination it had created among workers, armed forces personnel, and people downwind from nuclear weapons plants by its rush to produce nuclear weapons.

As people around the country organized against the contamination and damage, many nuclear weapons plants were shut, especially during the administration of Bush I, who also initiated a nuclear test moratorium in 1992, which Congress enacted in 1993. An historic step was taken in 1993 by then-Secretary of Energy Hazel O'Leary when she announced an unprecedented openness initiative. From the late 1980s to late 2000,

---

[1] Arjun Makhijani is president of the Institute for Energy and Environmental Research in Takoma Park, Maryland. He received his Ph.D. in nuclear fusion from the Department of Electrical Engineering, UC Berkeley.

[2] This Afterword is mainly drawn from Arjun Makhijani and Lisa Ledwidge, "Back to the Bad Old Days," *Science for Democratic Action*, September 2003, at www.ieer.org, the web site of the Institute for Energy and Environmental Research. References are to be found in that article or in other material posted on the IEER website.

laws compensating various categories of affected workers, atomic veterans, and downwinders were passed.

In 1989, as part of its effort to demonstrate a new face to the public, the FBI raided Rocky Flats, where most of the US plutonium bomb cores were made during the Cold War. Rocky Flats was part of the nuclear horror show. There was massive contamination of the site, even though most of the waste had been shipped to Idaho. There was evidence that laws had been broken.

Then-Deputy Secretary of Energy W. Henson Moore, on his visit to Rocky Flats in the aftermath of the FBI raid, explained the Cold War attitude of the government thus: Nuclear weapons production, he told the press, had been "a secret operation not subject to laws . . . no one was to know what was going on." He added that "the way the government and its contractors operated these plants was: This is our business, it's national security, everybody else butt out."

The "everybody else" he was referring to was not a foreign power, but the people of the United States.

A three-year Grand Jury investigation of alleged government and contractor crimes at Rocky Flats ensued. It seemed that the US government might be serious about nuclear weapons reform. But the Justice Department's later ambush of the Rocky Flats Grand Jury in 1992, and its cover-up of the Grand Jury proceedings, of which this book is a gripping account, was possibly the very first solid piece of evidence that the nuclear weapons establishment was not really serious in its contrition.

A decade later, in the new century, an "axis of evil" was proclaimed by the President of the United States. New nuclear weapons are being designed. The Nevada Test Site is being kept in readiness for resuming nuclear weapons testing. The nuclear boys seek to again ride the high horse they call national security. The bad old days are back.

Evidence is increasing that the nuclear establishment is now back to sacrificing people and the environment in favor of nuclear weapons production. Plans for building a "Modern Pit Facility," the replacement for Rocky Flats that would put the United States back in the business of building hundreds of new nuclear weapons every year, are marching ahead. Nuclear weapons designers are eager to resume design of new nuclear weapons. There is more and more serious talk of abrogating the Comprehensive Test Ban Treaty, whose ratification the US Senate rejected in 1999. Environmental and health considerations are once more being shoved into second place, if that. Secrecy is back, too.

There are also signs that the government is now more brazen than before in imposing health risks on workers and the public. According to the radiation dose estimates published by the Department of Energy itself, the Modern Pit Facility would violate its own guidelines regarding worker doses. More than one in four of the potential accidents analyzed for the proposed facility would violate the Department's guideline for radiation exposure to the public, some by as much as 400%. In addition, the potential accidents analyzed by the government represent only a fraction of possible scenarios, masking the full truth about the overall risk posed to the public.

The Department of Energy argues that making new plutonium pits is necessary because the pits might get old and not explode destructively enough. However, according to data from the Department's own plutonium geriatrics program, there is no scientific basis for a decision to build a new pit facility for the purpose of replacing aging plutonium pits in the current arsenal.

So if plutonium pit aging is not the main reason for building a new bomb plant, what is? The principal motivation appears to be to replace Rocky Flats, to re-create a capability to mass manufacture entirely new nuclear weapons that require pits of new designs.

New nuclear weapons plants and plans will carry a very high price in terms of reduced security, increased proliferation risks, and greater health and environmental damage. Could it be that these programs mainly benefit a nuclear weapons technocracy trying to perpetuate itself despite the great cost to the public and to future generations, as it did back in the bad old days?

Take a look at some of the features of those bad old days as a reminder of the kind of world that we may re-visit:

- During the 1950s and early 1960s, the era of atmospheric nuclear testing, the US government was secretly informing photographic film producers of expected fallout patterns so they could protect their film supply. This practice started after Kodak threatened to sue for damages caused by exposure of their film products to radioactive fallout (via contaminated packaging material). The US government provided advance data on anticipated fallout patterns to Kodak and its fellow film manufacturers, but did nothing to inform downwinders so they could take precautions. Nor did the government inform milk producers so they could protect that vital component of the food supply. The government's estimates now indicate that about 80,000 people in the United States have gotten or will get cancer due to exposure to

testing fallout. Of these, 15,000 to 20,000 are estimated to be fatal cancers.
- From the 1940s into the 1970s, the United States government sub-
jected more than 23,000 people to radiation experiments, many without their informed consent. One experiment involved feeding oatmeal
with radioactive trace elements to more than 100 boys at a
Massachusetts school. There were also testicular irradiation experiments on prisoners. There were experiments on pregnant women. In
1993, upon learning of a particularly troubling experiment involving
the injection of plutonium without informed consent into subjects,
then-Secretary of the Department of Energy Hazel O'Leary remarked,
"The only thing I could think of was Nazi Germany."
- In the 1950s and early 1960s, most workers at the Fernald nuclear
weapons plant near Cincinnati were overexposed to uranium without
their knowledge or consent. Because of the toxicity of uranium as a
heavy metal, many workers probably also suffered kidney damage.
Here, and at other nuclear weapons plants, workers were falsely reassured that they were not being harmed.

In one of the more alarming and telling signs of regression to the bad
old days, in 2003 the Department of Energy asked Congress to allow it
to reclassify wastes designated under current law as "high-level," and
hence requiring deep geologic disposal, as "incidental waste" that could
be disposed of in shallow burial sites. As of this writing, it has not succeeded. But if it is actually permitted to leave vast amounts of radioactivity, including high-level waste and waste highly contaminated with
plutonium, in place in shallow dumps, capped or grouted, the
Department of Energy would be putting some of the most precious water
resources of the United States at risk, including:

- The Columbia River in Washington and Oregon, the largest river in
the West.
- The Snake River Plain Aquifer in Idaho, a sole source aquifer for
much of southern Idaho, where 75 percent of the country's commer-
cial rainbow trout are grown.
- The Savannah River in South Carolina and Georgia.
- The Rio Grande.

As *The Ambushed Grand Jury* goes to press, the United States is
leading the world headlong in the retrograde direction of greater reliance
on nuclear weapons and force, against its own best traditions of the
rule of law. "Do-as-I-say-not-as-I-do" is the nuclear tipped norm

for the US government.

This book, with its real cowboy protagonist—a cowboy who knows mathematics—and its courageous FBI agent and Rocky Flats whistle-blower, is far more than a cautionary tale. It is a true story of public empowerment, based on solid research and told with style and vigor. If we pay no heed to its message, we risk sliding down a steep slope into the nuclear abyss. But should we be awake enough to attend to it, we will surely be moved to put people back in the saddle and nuclear weapons where they belong in the dust bin of history.

Appendix

Who's Who and Timeline

Who's Who
(in order of appearance)

The Citizen Investigators

Jon Lipsky – FBI Special Agent who headed the 1989 FBI raid of Rocky Flats. Later became a Citizen Investigator. Still works for the FBI.

Jacque Brever – former Rockwell International plutonium worker at Rocky Flats. Became a whistleblower during the FBI investigation, and later a Citizen Investigator.

Wes McKinley – cowboy and physics teacher. Foreman of the Rocky Flats Grand Jury. Later became a Citizen Investigator and co-author of *The Ambushed Grand Jury*.

Caron Balkany – volunteer lawyer for the Citizens' Investigation. Long-time attorney for citizen and nuclear safety groups. Co-author of *The Ambushed Grand Jury*.

The US Justice Department

Ken Fimberg – Assistant US Attorney for Colorado. Lead prosecutor during the 1989-1992 Rocky Flats Grand Jury investigation.

The Hon. Michael Norton – US Attorney for Colorado during the Rocky Flats Grand Jury investigation.

The Hon. Sherman Finesilver – federal judge assigned to the Grand Jury and the Rocky Flats criminal case.

Peter Murtha – Prosecutor with the US Justice Department in Washington, DC. Assigned to Colorado to assist with the Grand Jury investigation.

The Congress of the United States

The Hon. Howard Wolpe – Congressman from Michigan. Headed the 1992 hearings by the House of Representatives, Subcommittee on Investigations and Oversight, Committee on Science, Space, and Technology on the Justice Department's handling of the Grand Jury investigation.

Edith Holleman – staff attorney for the "Wolpe hearings."

Defense Contractors Operating Rocky Flats

1952-1975 – Dow Chemical Corporation

1975- 1989 – Rockwell International Corporation

1989-1995 – EG&G, Inc.

1995-present – Kaiser-Hill, Inc.

Other Important Characters

Jim Stone – engineer working with Rockwell International, later became a whistleblower.

Dominick Sanchini – Rockwell International's Manager of Rocky Flats.

Karen Pitts – Rockwell plutonium worker who became a whistleblower.

Ron Avery – Foreman for Rockwell International at Rocky Flats.

The Government Agencies

US Justice Department – The Attorney General of the United States is head of the Justice Department and is a Presidential appointee. The Attorney General holds a Cabinet level position. The US Attorneys for each of the States and US territories report directly to the Attorney General. So does the Director of the FBI, also part of the Justice Department. Among other things, the Justice Department is responsible for enforcing federal law. At the time of the raid, the Attorney General was The Hon. Richard Thornburgh, who served under Presidents Reagan and George HW Bush.

US Energy Department – Headed by the Secretary of the Department, a Presidential appointee. The Secretary holds a Cabinet level position. The Energy Department owns the nuclear weapons plants on behalf of US citizens. It arranges for defense contractors—usually large, private for-profit corporations—to operate the weapons labs under contract. It is supposed to oversee the work done by the defense contractors. At the time of the raid, the Secretary was The Hon. James Watkins, Admiral, US Navy (ret.), appointed by President George HW Bush.

The US Environmental Protection Agency – The Administrator is the head of the EPA, and is appointed by the President. The Administrator holds a Cabinet level position. Among other things, at the time of the raid, the EPA was charged with limited regulation of environmental impacts from nuclear weapons production. At that time, upon determining that a violation had occurred, the EPA usually referred the matter to the Justice Department for prosecution. Historically, the US Energy Department has disputed the EPA's authority to regulate most things involving Rocky Flats. At the time of the raid, the EPA was headed by The Hon. William K. Reilly, appointed by President George HW Bush.

The Colorado Department of Health – had limited regulatory authority over Rocky Flats. At the time of the raid, the Executive Director was Dr. Thomas Vernon. Historically, the US government has disputed the State's authority to regulate most things involving Rocky Flats. The dispute over state jurisdiction to enforce environmental laws involving nuclear weapons production continues to this day.

Timeline

1950-1980s – persistent accidents and safety problems at Rocky Flats.

October 14th, 1988 – The Building 771 plutonium incinerator at Rocky Flats is shut down because of repeated, unremedied safety problems.

December 9th, 10th, 15th, 1988 – The FBI, under cover of darkness, flies over Rocky Flats in a Night Stalker and takes infrared videos of the 771 plutonium incinerator during the time the incinerator was ordered shut down.

June 6th, 1989 – The FBI raids Rocky Flats Nuclear Weapons Plant based in part on evidence of secret midnight plutonium burning.

June 13th, 1989 – Rockwell International, the defense contractor operating Rocky Flats for the Energy Department, warns workers that whistleblowers will be dealt with severely.

June 16th, 1989 – Plutonium workers Jacque Brever and Karen Pitts go to the FBI to blow the whistle on secret midnight plutonium burning.

August 1st, 1989 – Colorado's first Special Grand Jury is impaneled. Later known as the Rocky Flats Grand Jury. Wes McKinley is later named Foreman.

September 14th, 1989 – Jacque Brever is intentionally contaminated with plutonium while on the job; the suspects tell her "that's what you get for making waves."

October 24th-25th, 1989 – Jacque Brever testifies to the Rocky Flats Grand Jury about secret midnight plutonium burning and other safety problems.

November 9th, 1989 – Berlin Wall falls; the beginning of the end of the Cold War.

November 22nd, 1989 – Infrared analyst testifies to the Rocky Flats Grand Jury about secret midnight plutonium burning.

November 30th, 1989 – Governor Roy Romer and Congressman David Skaggs, after discussions with Justice Department officials, announce to the press that they believe that the secret midnight plutonium burning never happened.

January, 1991 – Rocky Flats is officially closed and weapons production at the Plant ceases.

March 24th, 1992 – The Rocky Flats Grand Jury is formally discharged.

March 26th, 1992 – The Justice Department announces a plea bargain with Rockwell International.

September 11th, 1992 – Special Agent Lipsky, lead agent for the FBI raid of Rocky Flats, becomes the first witness before Congress in hearings directed at the Justice Department's actions during the Rocky Flats Grand Jury investigation.

September 25th, 1992 – Judge Finesilver seals the Rocky Flats Grand Jury Report.

September 30th, 1992 – *Westword* breaks a story of Justice Department obstruction based on a leaked copy of the sealed Grand Jury Report.

October 16th, 1992 – Judge Finesilver requests the Justice Department to investigate the Grand Jurors for breaking their secrecy oaths.

October 17th, 1992 – US Attorney Michael Norton requests the FBI to investigate the Grand Jurors for breaking their secrecy oaths.

November 19th, 1992 – the Grand Jurors hold a press conference and ask President-elect Clinton to investigate the US Justice Department.

January 4th, 1993 – The Wolpe congressional subcommittee publishes a report on its hearings into the Justice Department's handing of the Rocky Flats Grand Jury investigation.

April 8th, 1994 – The Justice Department publishes its self-review of the Justice Department's handling of the Rocky Flats Grand Jury investigation.

1995 – Kaiser-Hill takes over operation of Rocky Flats from EG & G with the mission of clean-up.

1995-1996 – Wes McKinley continues his speaking engagements, trying to talk about Rocky Flats without breaking the Grand Jury secrecy oath.

1996 – Wes McKinley runs for Congress so he can talk about the Justice Department's actions at Rocky Flats.

Fall, 1997 – Wes McKinley gets a volunteer lawyer and starts the Citizens' Investigation.

Acknowledgements

Dedicated to Special Grand Jury 89-2, courageous men and women all, who stood up to the government's abuse of power.

We couldn't have done the Citizens' Investigation without Jacque Brever and Jon Lipsky.

Lee Lysne, Judy Goldberg, Lisa Law, and Candida Jones gave us invaluable help.

Also, we are indebted to Patti Lipsky, Jan McKinley, Paul Trachtman, Edith Holleman, Arjun Makhijani, Ron Avery, Marilyn Balkany, Bruce MacIntosh, Forouz Jowkar, Lee Katherine Goldstein, Michael Lessac, Larry Mitchell, John Till, LeRoy Moore, Bart Main, Grahm Balkany, Jerry and Mike Tinnell, Pame Jean Kingfisher, Beth Harris, Doug Hartnett of The Government Accountability Project, Marcy Rosenbaum, Rick Brull, Barry Nierenberg, Georges Hemund, and Dean Ormistead.

With many, many thanks to CT Rich, who stepped in and saved the day with eagle eye, red pen and computer.

Any mistakes are ours.

BIBLIOGRAPHY AND ENDNOTES

General Sources

In re Rocky Flats Grand Jury Investigation, Case # 89-2, United States District
    Court, Denver, Colorado:
        Application and Affidavit for Search Warrant
        Oath and Instructions to the Grand Jury
USA vs. Rockwell International, Case # 92-CR-107,United States District Court,
    Denver, Colorado:
        Plea Agreement and Statement of Factual Basis, 26 March 1992
        Plaintiff's Sentencing Memorandum, 26 March 1992
        Defendant's Sentencing Memorandum, 26 March 1992
        Supplemental Sentencing Memorandum, 26 March 1992
        Information, 26 March 1992
        Plea Agreement and Statement of Factual Basis, 26 March 1992
        Plea Agreement, 26 March 1992
        Probation Report, Rockwell International
        Order Approving Plea Agreement, 1 June 1992
        Order Regarding Release of Grand Jury Documents, 26 January 1993
        Order Regarding Redacted Report of Special Grand Jury 89-2, 26 January
        1993
        Redacted Report of Special Grand Jury 89-2
        Unredacted Report of Special Grand Jury 89-2
Wolpe, Howard, Congressman, Chairman, Subcommittee on Investigations and
    Oversight, Committee on Science, Space and Technology, US House of
    Representatives, *The Prosecution of Environmental Crimes at the
    Department of Energy's Rocky Flats Facility*, 4 January 1993 and
    Subcommittee Hearing transcripts, Volume I, II, and III (referred to herein
    as Vol. I, _____, etc.)

Part One

"Operation Desert Glow"
Rocky Flats Nuclear Weapons Plant
Golden, Colorado, 1989-1992

Chapter One

The FBI Raids Rocky Flats. June 6th, 1989

1. General background concerning the FBI raid of Rocky Flats was devel-
    oped from Caron Balkany's interviews with the principals involved in the
    raid, and with others named on the List of Interviews. There was also wide-
    spread news coverage of the raid, including:

Paul Barrett, "Government's nuclear weapons plant near Denver is under inves-
    tigation," *The Wall Street Journal*, 7 June 1989.

Michael Booth, "Rocky Flats among targets of eco-terror suspects," *The Denver
    Post*, 1 June 1989.

Rebecca Cantwell, "Pact allows state to monitor flats," *The Rocky Mountain
    News*, 17 June 1989.

Janet Day and Sue Lindsay, "U.S. agents raid Rocky Flats," *The Rocky
    Mountain News*, 7 June 1989.

Department of Energy, press release, 9 June 1989.

David Johnston, "U.S. begins criminal investigation at nuclear plant," *The New
    York Times*, 7 June 1989.

The Los Angeles Times, "Nuclear weapons plant target of federal raid," 7 June
    1989.

Nan O'Neal, "FBI, EPA open investigation of Rocky Flats nuclear plant,"
    Arvada Sentinel, 7 June 1989.

The Rocky Mountain News, "Safety fears escalated with FBI's raid," 27 March
    1992.

Dusty Saunders, "'Frontline' has a chilling story on the ghost of Rocky Flats'
    past," *The Rocky Mountain News*, 26 October 1993.

Admiral James D. Watkins, Secretary of Energy, statement released 6 June 1989.

   Anonymous sources report that before he'd even heard about the FBI
raid, Secretary Watkins had decided that he wanted Rockwell out of all
Energy Department work. In fact, the Energy Department did go after
Federal Express, owned by Rockwell, within 8 days of the start of the raid,
suspending the use of their services for classified material shipments
pending investigation of Federal Express's Constant Surveillance Services.
See, internal letter, Delores Krieg, Traffic Manager, Rockwell
International, 17 June 1989.

   Documentation of the problems between Rockwell and the Energy
Department prior to the actual raid appear in:

"Rockwell has history of run-ins with regulators elsewhere," *The Denver Post*, 7 June 1989.

Peter Steeth, "Rockwell a conglomerate of diverse projects," *The Denver Post*, 7 June 1989.

US District Court, District of Colorado, "Presentence Report" for Rockwell International Corporation, 18 May 1992.

The Energy Department's efforts to blame the problems at Rocky Flats on Rockwell appear in Thomas Graf, "Energy Department freezes millions in bonuses to Rockwell," *The Denver Post*, 17 June 1989.

2.   Bryan Abas, "The Secret Story of the Rocky Flats Grand Jury," *Westword*, 30 September 1992.

3.   Dr. Carl Johnson's work on the effects of plutonium contamination in the Rocky Flats area includes:

Carl Johnson, MD, "Plutonium hazard in respirable dust on the surface of the soil," *American Association for the Advancement of Science*, Vol. 193, 6 August 1976;

————, "Offsite distribution of plutonium in the respirable dust on the surface of the soil in the vicinity of the Rocky Flats plant," report to the Jefferson County Board of Health, unpublished, 31 March 1977;

————, "Measuring plutonium concentrations in respirable dust," *Science*, Vol.196:4294, 3 June 1977;

————, "Report on death rates from lung cancer in the eight census tracts near Rocky Flats and in Golden, and in nineteen census tracts at the south end of the county," report to the Jefferson County Board of Health, unpublished, 20 November 1977;

————, "Epidemiological evaluation of cancer incidence rates for the period 1969-1971 in areas of census tracts with measured concentrations of plutonium soil contamination downwind from the Rocky Flats plant," summary of a report to the Jefferson County Board of Health, Colorado Board of Health, and the National Cancer Institute, NIH, PHS, USDHEW, unpublished, 9 February 1979;

————, letter to the Editor, *Speak Out*, rebuttal to LeRoy Moore, 28 September 1979;

————, "Cancer incidence in an _____contaminated with radionuclides near a nuclear installation," *Ambio* Vol.10:4, Royal Swedish Academy of Sciences, originally presented to the American Public Health Association, 7 November 1979;

————, "Contamination of municipal water supplies in the Denver metropolitan area by the Rocky Flats plutonium plant," presented at the annual meeting of the American Association for the Advancement of Science, 8 January 1980;

————, "Comments on the 1957 fire at the Rocky Flats plant in Jefferson County, Colorado," reported to the Conference on the Relation of

Environmental Pollution to the Cancer Problem in Colorado, at the American Medical Center and Hospital in Lakewood, Colorado, 26 September 1980;

————, "The public health impact of the Rocky Flats nuclear weapons plant in the Denver area: A case history with recommendations," unpublished and undated document;

————, "An investigation of brain cancer, melanoma and other neoplasms in employees of the Rocky Flats nuclear weapons plant in Jefferson County, Colorado," presented to the American Public Health Association, 3 November 1981;

————, "Epidemiologic of cancer incidence in people living near nuclear installations," a letter to the editor, *Health Physics*, Vol. 45:3, 18 August 1982;

————, *et al.* "Cancer incidence and mortality, 1947-1981, in the Denver standard metropolitan statistical area downwind from the Rocky Flats nuclear plant," presented to the Epidemiology Section of the American Public Health Association's 11th annual meeting, 16 November 1983;

————, "Comment" [trends in cancer incidence over time] in *The American Statistician*, Vol. 37:4, November 1983;

————, letter to The Honorable Scott Matheson, re: The N.I.H. radiation injury compensation tables, 25 June 1985;

————, Memorandum to the Colorado State Board of Health, Re: The role of CDH in the decision of Judge Matsch in the Rocky Flats case, 21 August 1985;

————, "Denver's Rocky Flats nuclear weapons plant: relocation cost vs. health cost," presented to the Environmental Health Section of the American Public Health Association's annual meeting, 19 November 1985;

————, "Beyond Chernobyl: Radiation hazards and the public's right to know," presented to the American Public Health Association's annual meeting, 1 October 1986;

————, "Before Chernobyl: Hanford, Savannah, and Rocky Flats," Letters in *AMA*, Vol. 257:2, 9 Jan 1987;

————, "Selecting presumably radiogenic cancers for compensation," Letters to the Editor [and rebuttal], *American Journal of Public Health*, Vol. 77:1, January 1987;

————, "Cancer incidence patterns in the Denver metropolitan area in relation to the Rocky Flats plant," Letter to the Editor, *American Journal of Epidemiology*, Vol. 126:1, 1987;

————, "Investigation of cancer incidence near a DOE nuclear facility: Selection of exposed populations within radionuclide-in-surface soil isopleth areas versus area selection by arbitrary quadrants and distance from the urban center," manuscript dated 21 February 1987. Reviewed in *American Journal of Epidemiology*, Vol. 126:153, 1987;

————, "Recent corroboration of independent studies of public health effects of the nuclear industry on workers environment and the public," presented at the University of Colorado School of Medicine, 15 May 1987;

————, "Some studies of low-level radiation and cancer in the United States," presented at the University of Basel, 9 June 1987;

————, "Cancer in the Denver area related to Rocky Flats: A DOE/Los Alamos report versus an independent investigation," manuscript dated 1 July 1987;

————, "Mortality among plutonium and other radiation workers at a plutonium weapons facility," Letter to the Editor, *American Journal of Epidemiology*, Vol. 127:6, 1988;

————, "Questions about the performance of the Department of Energy as an advocate for the worker and the public, and the DOE role as monitor and source of funds for studies of the health effects of radioactive materials," undated manuscript.

Information from other writers includes:

John Cobb *et al.*, "Plutonium burdens in people living around the Rocky Flats plant," US Environmental Protection Agency project summary, March 1983;

L.D. Hamilton, "Alternative interpretations of statistics on health effects of low-level radiation," a rebuttal of Johnson's findings, *The American Statistician*, Vol. 37:4, November 1983;

Bertram Wolfe, "Public has exaggerated fears of exposure to radiation," *The Denver Post*, 27 September 1986;

Gregg S. Wilkinson, et. al., "Mortality among plutonium and other radiation workers at a plutonium weapons facility," *American Journal of Epidemiology*, Vol. 125:2, 1987;

Thomas Graf, "Doctor warned of Rocky Flats danger," *The Denver Post*, 19 June 1989;

Richard Pollock, "Uncovering nuclear cancer," *In These Times*, 22-26 March 1978.

4.   Len Ackland, *Making A Real Killing* (University of New Mexico Press, 1999).

5.   Janet Day, "Flats' worst threat may lie underground," *The Rocky Mountain News*, 23 July 1989.

6.   Joseph Krupar, *FBI Interview*, 21 December 1989. Rocky Flats, like the nation's other weapons plants, used the veil of national security to bar State agencies and the Environmental Protection Agency from inspecting much of their operation. See, Application and Affidavit for Search Warrant, p. 63. Also, Memo from Energy Department Secretary James Watkins to John Layton, Inspector General, 23 February 1990.

7.   The Energy Department was known for its lack of candor, even with Congress. See, "A Report to the Committee on Appropriations, US House of Representatives," Surveys and Investigations Staff, February 1986; Sandy Graham, "Probers denied full Rocky Flats report," *The Rocky*

Mountain News, 17 April 1985; and Sandy Graham, "Rocky Flats coverup charge denied," *The Rocky Mountain News*, 9 May 1985.

8.   *The Denver Post*, " Rocky Flats at a Glance," 7 June 1989. Also, Assistant US Attorney Ken Fimberg, 1991, Affidavit, *Cypher vs. United States*, Civil Action 91-W-171 USDC, Colorado. According to Bruce DeBoskey, a Denver attorney who represented many Rocky Flats workers in personal injury claims, Rocky Flats may have been the most polluted place on the planet. See, Caron Balkany interview with Bruce DeBoskey, 18 September 2002. Also, Janet Day, "Flats' worst threat may lie underground," *The Rocky Mountain News*, 23 July 1989.

9.   The information about Adrienne Anderson comes from her interview with Caron Balkany on 26 December 2001, and from subsequent conversations.

10.   Caron Balkany interviewed Bonnie Exner on 23 June 2001.

11.   The information about Jim Stone comes from Caron Balkany's interviews with principals of the FBI investigation, from interviews by Caron Balkany and Wes McKinley with Jim Stone, and from Jim Stone's FBI interview 28 July 1987.

12 . Len Ackland, *ibid.*

13.   The background information about US Attorney Michael Norton comes from Sue Lindsay, "Norton Traveling the Road to Respect," and "Norton reflects on life in 'hot seat'," *The Rocky Mountain News*, 7 July 1989.

14.   The October 1988 Building 771 radioactive contamination incident is documented in: James Baker with Mark Miller, "A new scare at Rocky Flats," *Newsweek*, 26 June 1989; XXXX, *FBI Interview*, 14 June 1989; and Keith Fultz, Senior Associate Director, General Accounting Office, letter to the Honorable David Skaggs, House of Representatives, 27 October 1988.

15.   See, the Affidavit and Application for Search Warrant for the major areas of investigative interest.

16.   Attorney General Thornburgh's release of the sealed information was unusual because the Attorney General had been openly critical of publicizing investigations. David Johnston, "US Begins Criminal Investigation at Nuclear Plant," *The New York Times*, 7 June 1989. According to environmental crimes expert, attorney Adam Babich, unsealing the affidavit was a "highly unusual move." Search warrant affidavits are normally sealed because they rest on preliminary investigations.

      The publicity is usually not good for the investigation. In this case, the publicity started out good for aspiring gubernatorial hopeful US Attorney Michael Norton. EPA Special Agent William Smith, whose work with FBI Special Agent Lipsky had started the investigation, recalled Norton's desire for publicity and remembers him agreeing to do the FBI raid because it was "a win win" situation for Norton. See, Caron Balkany's interviews with William Smith, 27 November 2001 and 26 June 2001. As events turned out, it more like was a "lose-lose." But back in 1989, Norton looked pretty good in the press.

17. The stated reasons for unsealing the search warrant appear in the US Department of Justice, press release, "Investigation initiated at Rocky Flats," 6 June 1989. Interestingly, the Criminal Division of the Justice Department, prior to the raid, itself warned that "If the contents of the [search warrant] affidavit were to be publicly disclosed, potential defendants would be provided with a virtual road map of the areas under investigation by the government." See, undated memorandum from Martin C. Carlson, Senior Legal Advisor, to Lawrence Lippe, Chief General Litigation and Legal Advice Section, Criminal Division.

18. Later, during the Grand Jury investigation, Rockwell and the employees' union entered into a "joint defense agreement." Through it, Rockwell knew just about everything the Justice Department was investigating, and therefore most Rockwell employees were not willing to cooperate with the FBI for fear of losing their jobs.

19. The information about Dominick Sanchini comes from Special Agent Lipsky's congressional testimony and FBI interviews with Mr. Sanchini on 6 June 1989, 10 June 89, and 11 June 89, along with copies of Mr. Sanchini's notebooks and diaries.

20. According to Lipsky, Sanchini was later caught having taken home some documents, despite the "handshake agreement."

21. There are other ways Rockwell and the Energy Department could have been tipped off about the raid. The water samplers which the FBI had placed in Walnut Creek and Woman Creek, downstream from the Plant, were discovered by Rockwell a few months before the raid. Rockwell questioned EPA's Nat Miullo about them repeatedly, and although he told them it must have been placed by some neighborhood activists, it is unknown whether Rockwell accepted this explanation. The FBI/EPA joint team surreptitiously removed the samplers shortly thereafter. See, Nat Miullo, *EPA Interview*, 5 April 1989.

22. The Criminal Division at the Justice Department used the fact that headquarters controlled the investigation to require prosecutors to rewrite the affidavit so it was not as directly accusatory of the Energy Department. See, undated memorandum from Martin C. Carlson, Senior Legal Advisor, to Lawrence Lippe, Chief General Litigation and Legal Advice Section, Criminal Division, 9. Energy Secretary Admiral James Watkins was on Capital Hill the morning of the raid, doing damage control. Joan Lowry, "Flats Raid Spreads Shock Waves," *The Rocky Mountain News*, 7 June 1989.

23. The information about Mr. Whiteman's transfer appears in Memorandum of Interview, US Department of Energy, Office of Inspector General, 6 December 1990.

24. The furtive Laurel and Hardy-like drum movement is documented in Vol.

I, 618 and in XXXX, *FBI Interview*, 1 November 1990. There was other evidence that some of the people at Rocky Flats had advance notice of the raid. According to Jon Lipsky, the FBI itself thought there had been a tip off and investigated a Rockwell official at the Plant and a high-level Energy Department official for obstruction of justice. The existence of this part of the investigation was not made public; the results are unknown as well.

Chapter Two
The Whistleblower,
June 15th, 1989

25. The information concerning the whistleblowers' involvement with the FBI comes from interviews by Caron Balkany with the principals involved in the raid and with persons named on the List of Interviews; public testimony and documentation submissions by Jacque Brever and Karen Pitts to the Advisory Committee on Nuclear Facility Safety, known as the Ahearne Committee, in July, 1991; diaries kept by Ms. Brever which she used in testifying to the Grand Jury; and FBI interviews with Ms. Pitts and Ms. Brever on 15 June 1989, 16 June 1989, 17 June 1989, 12 October 1989, 17 October 1989, 31 October 1989, 1 November 1989, 22 January 1990, 21 February 1990, 22 August 1990, 22 January 1991, 11 February 1991, and 25 February 1991. The insights into the internal Rockwell response to the raid and the warnings to whistleblowers are documented in diaries kept by former Rockwell plutonium worker Jacque Brever.

    The descriptions of the Building 771 plutonium incinerator are documented in the Application and Affidavit for Search Warrant and in Caron Balkany's interviews with former EPA investigator Nat Miullo on 21 June 2001 and 27 November 2001, and with EPA investigator Bill Smith on 26 June 2001 and 27 November 2001.

26. Documentation of the 1988 shutdown of Building 771 operations and the actions of Brever and Pitts during the first revelations of the FBI investigation, in addition to Balkany's interviews, *supra*, includes:

Bruce Finley and Thomas Graf, "Rocky Flats illegally burned, dumped waste, U.S. claims," *The Denver Post*, 10 June 1989;

———— "DOE official says he knew nothing about illegal burns," *The Denver Post*, 28 June 1989;

Thomas Graf, "Investigation at Rocky Flats: management shakeup at plant reported," *The Denver Post*, 9 June 1989;

Sue Lindsay and Janet Day, "Flats burned waste secretly," *The Rocky Mountain News*, 10 June 1989;

Howard Pankratz, "Rocky Flats conspiracy alleged: FBI used spy plane in probe," 10 June 1989;

Rusty Pierce, "Flats charges include illegal waste burning: document claims chemicals put in creeks feeding water supplies," *Daily Camera*, 10 June 1989;

Gary Schmitz, "Use of officially idled incinerator for toxic waste suspected: Feds assume conspiracy, Rep. Skaggs speculates," *The Denver Post*, 9 June 1989;

Peter Steeth, "Investigation at Rocky Flats: Mismanagement a cause for contract cancellation," *The Denver Post*, 9 June 1989.

Caron Balkany's interviews with the principals involved in the raid, with persons named on the List of Interviews, and with unnamed Grand Jury sources and the FBI interviews of Ms. Brever and Ms. Pitts provide documentation for the activities inside the Grand Jury room.

27. The union steward's comments appear in his FBI Interview, 14 September 1989.

Chapter Three

The Grand Jury, August 1st, 1989

28. Oath and Instructions to the Grand Jury, Special Grand Jury 89-2.

29. Ken Fimberg's sworn testimony that Karen Pitts and Jacqueline Brever were "not very reliable sources" is in Vol. III, 194.

Chapter Four

The Justice Department Ends the Grand Jury Investigation, March 26th, 1992

30. Norton and Fimberg's public statements concerning the plea bargain are found in the court filings and in statements issued by Michael Norton, 26 March 1992; 23 September 1992 "Statement of Michael J. Norton," issued by the Justice Department; and 18 November 1992 "Supplement to Statement of Michael J. Norton," also issued by the Justice Department. Some additional public statements by US Attorney Norton about the Rocky Flats investigation appear in:

Sue Lindsay, "Norton reflects on life in 'hot seat'," *The Rocky Mountain News*, 7 July 1989.

Bill Scanlon, "Norton defends Flats' plea bargain: Deal struck with Rockwell was best solution, and he'd do it again, U.S. attorney tells law school society," *The Rocky Mountain News*, 4 March 1993.

US Attorney Michael Norton also stated that one of the difficulties with the case was that no Rocky Flats employee had ever come forward to help the Justice Department and the FBI make their case. This is an incorrect statement. In addition to Pitts and Brever, the FBI had announced back on June 16th, 1989 that it had received more than 100 calls in less than 24 hours on the FBI hotline and that "almost all" of them were from people with insider information. US Attorney Norton is quoted in *The Denver Post* by Peter Chronis, "Norton: feds Balked at Flats Jury report," 4 March 1993. Bob Pence, head of the Colorado FBI office, contradicted this assertion in *The Rocky Mountain News* in an article by Janet Day, "Flats Hotline Gets 100 calls in First Day," 16 June 1989.

31. Emphasis supplied. Norton's statement appears at Vol. I, 1081.

32. The Justice Department was often misleading in its statements that criminal fines would be indemnified by US taxpayers. US Attorney Norton stated that ". . . it seemed probable that taxpayers would end up paying for any fine that would be imposed." Vol. I, 110. Ken Fimberg made similar sworn statements. Ultimately, Edith Holleman, questioning him during the Wolpe congressional hearings, got Fimberg to admit that the Energy Department had never before indemnified a contractor for criminal penalties. Vol. I, 1587. And the Energy Department, during the plea negotiations, had agreed not to indemnify any criminal penalties stemming from Rocky Flats. Department of Energy Memo, 4 September 1991.

    Additionally, there are considerable legal arguments against indemnification of criminal penalties, so the repeated statements that indemnification of criminal penalties was a major factor in Norton's decision to settle the case are dubious. See, Vol. I, 1093 and "For the first time ever, DOE will not pay or reimburse fines," *The Rocky Mountain News*, 6 July 1997, and Sue Lindsay, "Closed testimony latest page in Flats saga," *The Rocky Mountain News*, 6 July 1997.

33. Order, 25 September 1992.

34. The *Westword* article breaking the Grand Jury story is "The Secret Story of the Rocky Flats Grand Jury," Bryan Abas, 30 September 1992.

35. Judge Finesilver's request that the Grand Jury be investigated is documented in *US News and World Report*, "Just Desserts," Douglas Pasternak with Ancel Martinez, 14 December 1992 and in his letter to Michael Norton dated 16 October 1992.

36. Norton's request to the FBI to investigate the Grand Jurors appears in *Time*, "Sometimes it Takes a Cowboy" Michael Lemonick, 25 January 1993.

37. Shortly after the Grand Jury's press conference, Judge Finesilver did a partial about face and released the Grand Jury Report to the public. Only it wasn't the Grand Jury Report written by the 23 members of Special Grand Jury 89-2. Instead, Judge Finesilver had allowed the US Attorney's Office to remove portions of the Report, and to insert their own argument about why the Report was wrong. The prosecutors' arguments that the Report was wrong were longer than the Report itself. The revised and redacted and rewritten Grand Jury Report was almost impossible to follow. See, Order Regarding Redacted Report of Special Grand Jury 89-2, 26 January 1993.

Other newspaper coverage of the Grand Jury appears in:

"Rocky Flats grand jury seeks special prosecutor," *Hazardous Materials Intelligence Report* , 27 November 1992;

Sue Lindsay, "Judge won't release Rocky Flats report," *The Rocky Mountain News*, 26 September 1992;

————, "Flats jury asks Clinton for special prosecutor," *The Rocky Mountain News*, 19 November 1992;

Editorial, "An angry jury deserves a hearing," *The New York Times* 1 December 1992;

Mark Obmascik, "Flats grand jury rebuffed-panel wanted DOE, Rockwell employees indicted," *The Denver Post*, 30 September 1992;

————, "Flats jurors ask for probe-letter to Clinton requests special prosecutor," *The Denver Post*, 19 November 1992;

Bill Scanlon, "Judge releases grand jury paper on Rocky Flats," *The Rocky Mountain News*, 27 January 1993;

Matthew Wald, "Bomb plant grand jury seeks inquiry into handling of case," *The New York Times*, 19 November 1992.

38. The documentation of the Grand Jury's quest for congressional immunity so they could reveal what the prosecutors had done in the Grand Jury room appears in:

Adriel Bettelheim, "Gag Flats grand jury, Skaggs says," *The Denver Post*, 17 November 1993;

Patricia Calhoun, "It bombed in D.C.," *Westword*, 19-26 January 1994;

————, " Grand Illusions," *Westword*, 16 November 1999;

C. Rustnock Hoover, "Flats jurors may testify in Congress," *Daily Camera*, 2 December 1992;

Patricia Schroeder, U.S. House of Representatives, Affidavit in support of the petition of the members of special grand jury 89-2, 25 July 1996;

Kerri Smith, "Flats jury rocks the system-evidence called insufficient," *The Denver Post*, 2 July 1997;

Jonathan Turley, letter to Wes McKinley, 29 March 1994;

———— and Bette Bushell, U.S. District Court (Colorado), "Petitioners' memorandum of points and authorities in support of the petition of member of special grand jury 89-2 for a sealed hearing and a subsequent order removing or modifying continued secrecy obligations," 1 August 1996;

Garrison Wells, "Did corporate lobby silence Flats jurors?-major companies afraid of precedent," *The Denver Business Journal*, 7-13 January 1994.

39. Edith Holleman, in private conversations with Caron Balkany, indicated that the Wolpe subcommittee didn't have time to fight the immunity battle before the term expired, and that it had made a strategic decision not to pursue testimony from the Grand Jurors since the Justice Department had indicated it would put up an intense battle about the subject.

Part Two
The Citizens' Investigation Begins, 1997

Chapter Five
The Cowboy Gets Legal Counsel, 1997

40. Dr. Arjun Makhijani, Dr. John Till, and Dr. LeRoy Moore have discussed the less protective clean-up standards utilized at for the former weapons plant with author Balkany. The Rocky Flats National Wildlife Refuge Act was signed into law by President Bush in December 2001. The National Wildlife Refuge Administration Act, 16 USC 668dd, provides that ". . . wildlife-dependent recreational uses are the priority general public uses of the system and shall receive priority consideration in refuge planning and management."

Laurie Shannon, Planning Team Leader, US Fish and Wildlife Services, has stated that horse riding, hiking, interpretative tours for school children, wildlife photography, and hunting are all under consideration. See, Caron Balkany's interview with Laurie Shannon, 9 July 2002. The Rocky Flats National Wildlife Refuge Act doesn't include any requirements about the amount of clean-up the Energy Department must do at the Refuge. The Fish and Wildlife Service of the Department of the Interior will just take the land in whatever condition the Energy Department gives it to them. Interestingly, Gale Norton, President GW Bush's selection for head of the Department of Interior which will be overseeing the Refuge, was the Attorney General of Colorado at the time of the Rocky Flats plea bargain.

41. Newspaper articles, with Grand Jury information often provided by Justice Department officials, quickly followed publication of the initial *Westword* article on the Grand Jury Report:

"Rocky Flats Fallout-Congress cuts a deal with the justice department," *Westword*, 7-13 October 1992;

"Dingell's justice probe is justified," *The Wall Street Journal*, 22 July 1993;

"The jury that wouldn't stay quiet; the pollution that wouldn't go away," *Covert Action*, Winter 1993-94;

Patricia Calhoun, "The jury is out," *Westword*, 4-10 November 1992;

Linda Himmelstein, "Finger-pointing at Rocky Flats: 'runaway' grand jury in DOJ case," *Legal Times*, 2 November 1992;

Justice Department, "Environment Division under fire," *The DOJ Alert*, Vol. 2 No. 10, October 1992;

Michael Lemonick, "Sometimes it takes a cowboy," *Time*, 25 January 1993;

Sue Lindsay, "Norton barred indictments in Flats case," *The Rocky Mountain News*, 30 September 1992;

Douglas Pasternak with Ancel Martinez, "A grand jury and its bitter denunciation of 'a deal'," *U.S. News & World Report*, 14 December 1992;

Kelly Richmond, "Key panel takes Flats case: Subcommittee set to probe allegations," *The Denver Post*, 5 June 1993;

Ryan Ross, "The secrets of the Rocky Flats grand jury report," *Denver Digital City* News Special, 2 September 1997;

Barry Siegel, "Showdown at Rocky Flats," *The Los Angeles Times*, 8 and 15 August 1993;

Jonathan Turley, "Jurors alone can unravel Rocky Flats mystery," *The Rocky Mountain News*, 18 March 1994;

Matthew Wald, "Justice Dept. termed too lenient on bomb plant," *The New York Times*, 5 January 1993;

The Wall Street Journal, "Review & Outlook: General Dingell," 8 July 1993.

In addition, the leaked Grand Jury Report was posted on the web-site maintained by the Denver chapter of the Sierra Club, and the redacted Grand Jury Report, with Justice Department argument added, was released by Judge Finesilver on 26 January 1993. None of the Grand Jury Reports - official or revised by the Justice Department - catalogs the evidence or testimony.

42. Many of the facts set forth in Wes McKinley's letter are also found in the government's sentencing memorandum.

43. Information concerning Dr. Carl Johnson's firing appears in:

Timothy Lange, "They fired Dr. Johnson," *Westword*, Vol. 4:19, 28 May-11 June 1981;

LeRoy Moore, letter to Dan Rather suggesting Dr. Johnson's forced resignation as a topic for "Sixty Minutes," 3 June 1981;

Rocky Flats Action Group, "Johnson fired as Jeffco Health head," *Action: The Voice of nuclear criticism and education in Colorado*, Vol. VI:III, June/July 1981;

Paul Krehbiel, "Johnson seeks reinstatement," *Citizens Healthwatch*, Jan-March 1982;

Carl Johnson, MD. vs. Jefferson County Board of Health, 662 P. 2d 46 (Col. 4/18/98)

44. Oath of the Grand Jury.

45. The sentencing memorandum, the plea bargain, the Justice Department's internal review of the Grand Jury investigation, Caron Balkany's interviews with Ken Fimberg/Scott and with "A Justice Department Prosecutor," and congressional testimony from Fimberg at Vol. III, 194, establish Justice's position that the midnight burning allegations had been a mistake; that the infrared expert had changed his testimony; that the midnight burning had not occurred; and that Karen Pitts and Jacque Brever were not very reliable sources of information.

Additionally, see:

Bill Scanlon, "Flats case bedeviled prosecutors; U.S. attorneys say they relied on evidence," *The Rocky Mountain News*, 6 October 1992;

———, "The Good, Bad, and the Unknown from Rocky Flats," *The Rocky Mountain News*, 5 December 1989.

46. FBI Case Status Form, 15 March 1989.
47. These uncontrolled nuclear reactions are incredibly dangerous. They could leave widespread radioactive contamination.
48. Congressman Tom Udall from New Mexico is a cousin of Congressman Mark Udall of Colorado, who, with Senator Wayne Allard, wrote and sponsored the legislation establishing the Rocky Flats National Wildlife Refuge.

Chapter Six

Citizens' Investigation Analysis: How the Justice Department Stonewalled Congress, 1992

49. Bonnie Exner provided background for the environmentalists' reaction to the plea bargain in her interview with Caron Balkany on 23 June 2001.
50. Jennifer Haines, *Bread and Water: A Spiritual Journey*, (Orbis Books, 1997).
51. Bob Roach had worked with environmental activists for many years and was trusted by the Colorado activists to take their concerns seriously.
52. Documentation of the Justice Department's actions under the Reagan and Bush administrations can be found in "Criminal Environmental Prosecution by the United States Department of Justice, Preliminary Report," prepared for The Honorable Charles E. Schumer, Member of Congress, by The Environmental Crimes Project, Jonathan Turley, Director, The National Law Center, The George Washington University, 19 October 1992, and in "Damaging Disarray, Organizational Breakdown and Reform in the Justice Department's Environmental Crimes Program," a staff report prepared for the Subcommittee on Oversight and Investigations of the Committee on Energy and Commerce, US House of Representatives, December 1994.

See, also:

The Bureau of National Affairs, Inc., "Environment, DOJ environmental enforcement criticized at House oversight subcommittee hearing," *Daily Report for Executives*, 4 November 1993;

Sue Lindsay and Janet Day, "Pursuing environmental crime new ground for prosecutors," *The Rocky Mountain News*, 19 June 1989.

Despite the statutes Congress enacted, criminal enforcement of environmental laws wasn't really working either. The Justice Department's interference under the Reagan and Bush I administrations with the EPA's

gressional investigations in the late 80s and early 90s.

53. Named after its Chairman, then-Congressman Howard Wolpe from Michigan, the inquiry's formal name was Hearings Before the Subcommittee on Investigations and Oversight of the Committee on Science, Space and Technology, US House of Representatives. In 1992, led by staff attorney Edith Holleman, this congressional subcommittee undertook an inquiry into the Justice Department's handling of the Special Grand Jury investigation of environmental crimes at Rocky Flats. The Report is on the website at www.Ambushedgrandjury.com.

54. The Justice Department's refusal to comply with congressional subpoenas is documented throughout the Wolpe hearing transcripts. The Justice Department's refusal to produce the FBI agents for congressional testimony, or to allow Congress to question the FBI or the Justice Department about their decision making process, and the Wolpe subcommittee's refusal to concede this issue fundamental to its oversight responsibilities, are documented throughout the hearing transcripts in Vol. I and II, and in:

Congressional Report 103-882, "Report on the Activity of the Committee on Energy and Commerce for the 103d Congress," 2 January 1995;

John Dingell, letter to Hon. William Barr, Attorney General, 6 July 1992;

————, letter to Hon. Janet Reno, Attorney General, 12 January 1994;

Charles Doyle, Public Law Specialist, Congressional Research Service, memorandum to House Subcommittee on Investigations and Oversight, Re: refusals to disclose to Congress on the basis of Rule 6(e) (matters occurring before the grand jury), 9 September 1992;

Charles Mandigo for John Collingwood, FBI letter to Howard Wolpe, Subcommittee on Investigation and Oversight, 9 September 1992;

Office of General Counsel, statement to the clerk regarding subcommittee authority to question FBI witnesses, Vol. I, 31;

Kelly Richmond, "Justice Dept. probed on Flats-easy-on-polluters charge investigated," *The Denver Post*, 5 June 1993;

James Rowley, "U.S. to review its prosecution of polluters," *The Rocky Mountain News*, 9 June 1993;

Jonathan Turley, "We need to unearth environmental felons," *The Wall Street Journal*, 11 March 1993.

55. Lipsky's testimony about the Building 771 incinerator appears in Vol. I, 734-861 and 940. His testimony concerning the settlement negotiations with Rockwell are at Vol. I, 526. Lipsky's testimony concerning his disagreement with the plea bargain and the instructions to him to stop investigating criminal liability of individuals is at Vol. III, 7, 30-36 and Vol. I, 542.

56. Sanchini, the head of Rockwell at Rocky Flats, died of bladder cancer in late 1990.

57. At Rocky Flats, the last straw may have snapped when the Energy

Department's Albuquerque office gave Rockwell a $8.6 million perform-
ance bonus in May, 1987, ranking its management "excellent" and its
health and safety "very good", despite all the evidence to the contrary.
Rockwell's connections with its so-called oversight managers in the Energy
Department's Albuquerque Office were so tight that when Energy
Department headquarters stepped between them after the raid in 1989 and
decreased a bonus award issued by the Albuquerque Office, Rockwell
actually sued to get the bonus back. Rockwell's position was that only the
Energy Department Office in Albuquerque had anything to say about its
bonuses, not Energy Department headquarters in Washington.

Richard Starostecki, from the Energy Department, later stated, "When
it comes to award fees, that's really under the direct control of, in this case,
Bruce Twining. [Energy Department Albuquerque Area Office] He can
unilaterally make decisions on award fees. I can see that there's a problem
with the award fee system." Advisory Committee on Nuclear Facility
Safety to the U.S. Department of Energy, "Final Report on DOE Nuclear
Facilities: A Report to the Secretary of Energy," November 1001.

The documentation concerning the 1987 bonus and Rockwell's lawsuit
—*Rockwell International vs. The Department of Energy*, Case # 91-1362,
US Court of Federal Claims—to attempt to enforce the bonus when Energy
Department headquarters lowered it, includes:

Thomas Graf and Beth Frerking, "Rockwell won't drop suit against U.S. Energy
Dept.," *The Denver Post*, 23 September 1989;

Award Fee Performance Evaluation Reports, 1 October 86 through 31 March,
1987; Base Fee and Award Fee History, 1987-88;

Correspondence, Energy Department Albuquerque Operations Office to
Dominick Sanchini, Rockwell, 8 December 1988; 27 September 1989; 20
September 1989; 23 February 1990;

General Accounting Office, "DOE's Award fees at Rocky Flats Do Not
Adequately Reflect ES&H Problems," October, 1989.

See, also, Robert Kowalski, "Rockwell 'had heck of a deal'," *The
Denver Post*, 25 October 1989 for documentation of the bonus process.
Also, Peter Steeth, "Pullout won't hurt Rockwell profits," *The Denver Post*,
23 September 1989, and Linda Rothstein, "Yes, Haste Makes Waste, *The
Bulletin of Atomic Scientists*, 5 May 1995. According to XXXX, an Energy
Department Safety Officer at the time of the FBI raid, in a 26 April 1991
FBI interview, Rockwell realized several benefits beyond the fees and
awards, including: access to classified technology and weapons delivery
systems for future development and a minimum amount of corporate overhead.

58. Lipsky's congressional testimony in Vol. III, 10-12, 32, 89-91 details the
special handling instructions for the "responsible corporate officers" at
Rockwell and the Energy Department. Ken Fimberg says the instructions

about the responsible corporate officer doctrine were from Barry Hartman, Associate Attorney General, not from the Attorney General himself, and weren't anything different from what he would have done anyway, as a matter of fairness. Vol. III, 163.

The Justice Department has no documents concerning the application of the "responsible corporate officer" doctrine to Rocky Flats. Letter, 21 September 1992, from W. Lee Rawls, Assistant Attorney General, to the Honorable Howard Wolpe.

59. A noted environmental attorney and former government prosecutor observed: "[D]efendants seek to convince the courts that convictions should only be appropriate only where the government has proof that the defendant acted deliberately, with knowledge of the law. To date, the appellate courts have generally rejected that view." Helen J. Brunner, "Environmental Criminal Enforcement: Retrospective View," Criminal Enforcement of Environmental Laws, *Environmental Law*, Vol. 22: 1315, 1992, at 1327. See also, the United States Supreme Court's observation that "...federal courts have consistently approved jury instructions that allow conviction upon a showing only that the defendant acted intentionally to transport, treat, store or dispose of the waste material.... In effect, these courts have adopted the argument long proffered by the government that, because these statutes are designed to protect the public health and welfare, persons dealing with potentially harmful materials must be presumed to be aware of the regulations. *USA vs. International Minerals and Chemical Corporation*, 402 US 558 (1971).

60. Dick Thornburgh, Attorney General, U.S. Department of Justice, *Ethics Handbook*, "Foreword," 21 March 1989. The other information concerning US Attorney General Thornburgh comes from Jon Lipsky, Vol. III, 91, and from Janet Day, "Thornburgh in Probe Despite Holdings," *The Rocky Mountain News*, 19 June 1989 and from U.S. Environmental Protection Agency, "Rocky Flats," *Report of Investigation*, 9 February 1989, and attorney Rob Hager, long-time nuclear activist.

61. Michael Norton, letter to Howard Wolpe, 2 October 1992.

62. Howard Wolpe, Subcommittee on Investigations and Oversight, letter to Michael Norton, 2 October 1992. The background on Mike Norton's brush with contempt of Congress is documented in Lispky's interviews with Caron Balkany; in the Wolpe congressional hearing transcript; and in John Brinkley, "Norton avoids contempt charge-Justice Department agrees to allow U.S. attorney to discuss Flats investigation in private," *The Rocky Mountain News*, 6 October 1992.

63. Norton's quoted testimony appears at Vol. I, 1064,1074, and Vol. III, 321.

64. However, the prosecutors had written at least two draft indictments and sent them to headquarters. It is unlikely that draft indictments get written about "marginal, questionable" cases. Ken Fimberg's testimony appears in

Vol. I, 1481-1484, and Vol. III, 115, 117, 140, 154, 163-168, and 211-212. Ken Fimberg documents the two draft indictments in his congressional testimony at Vol. I, 1349. See, also, "The Secret Story of the Rocky Flats Grand Jury," *supra* at endnote 34.

There simply wasn't enough evidence to indict Energy Department officials, Fimberg repeatedly insisted. And they hadn't indicted Rockwell individuals, either, because the cases were "marginal," "questionable," and because it wasn't fair: the Energy Department culture had promoted the law-skirting, law-breaking activities, and Rockwell individuals were simply acting consistently with what the Energy Department had asked for over the last 40 years.

Chairman Wolpe was concerned with this interpretation of culture as a defense to criminal charges. "I get real nervous about this cultural argument raised in a legal context as a matter of fairness as you've put it. . . . This is the Nuremberg kind of defense."

But Fimberg stuck to his position. It just wasn't fair.

Fimberg also fielded questions about the linkage between the plea bargain and dropping individual indictments, something prohibited by the US Attorney's Manual. Fimberg admitted that the prosecution team had discussed at the end of 1990 that they might accept a corporate-only plea, with no indictments of individuals. And he admitted that the Justice Department had discussed the fact that a settlement with Rockwell was probably unlikely if they insisted on going after individuals. And as of 1990, they all felt a settlement was the best option.

Fimberg admitted that Rockwell's attorneys were constantly making a linkage to a corporate plea and no individual indictments.

The lack of any indictments against Energy Department officials had a different explanation. Fimberg testified after Lipsky, and he told the congressional subcommittee that everyone had agreed there was not enough evidence to indict Energy Department officials.

Even Lipsky agreed, said Fimberg.

Lipsky shakes his head angrily whenever this is mentioned. "That is simply not true," he says. "I never agreed. They never asked me, because they knew I wouldn't agree."

65. Balkany's conversations with Edith Holleman provide the background for the sections on the Wolpe investigation and the Wolpe Report. An example of the problems created by the Justice Department's delay tactics is Sanchini's memo pads and the FBI's written list of questions concerning them. The congressional hearing transcript includes the FBI's questions, Vol. II, 470-529, but not the actual memo pads. This is because the FBI did not turn the diaries over to Congress until after the hearings were concluded and the Wolpe Report already released. See the 14 January 1993 letter to Edith Holleman from John Collingwood, Inspector in Charge,

Office of Public and Congressional Affairs, FBI, transmitting the memo pads. Vol. II, 99.

66. The Justice Department's official position is set forth in an April 8th, 1994 memorandum from Mark Dubester, Acting Chief, Public Corruption/Government Fraud Section, US Attorney's Office for the District of Columbia, to Associate Attorney General Webster Hubbell.

Chapter Seven

Citizens' Investigation Analysis: Wes McKinley's Congressional Campaign, 1996

67. Go to www:NIRS.org, the website for Nuclear Information and Resource Services, which spearheads the citizen campaign in the US against recycled radioactive metals.

68. LeRoy Moore, in a private communication with Caron Balkany, indicated that Alex Mayer did not walk around barefoot, but that perhaps Wes thought so because Alex wore sandals in summer. Alex also held a graduate degree, and had run his own business and was a beloved and longtime member of the peace community in the Denver-Boulder area.

69. Bryan Abas' offer to the House Energy and Commerce Committee, Investigations and Oversight Subcommittee was made on 8 June 1993. The Citizens' Investigation obtained a copy of excerpts of the Grand Jury transcript from an anonymous source in the mail. In it, Assistant US Attorney Ken Fimberg told the Grand Jury: "And if the government attorneys, if Mr. Murtha and Mr. Norton and I and others that are involved in reviewing this matter have decided that this cannot be done in good faith under the governing law, it's our obligation not to pursue criminal charges."

Foreman McKinley asked: "What happens if the Grand Jury does not follow the recommendation?"

Fimberg responded: "I am not sure what you want to do with it, but it will not be a prosecution."

Other legal experts disagree, claiming that while prosecutors have the obligation not to start an investigation if they do not in good faith believe the matter should be prosecuted, this refers to the prosecutors' discretion in filing an information or convening a Grand Jury to begin with. Once a Grand Jury decides to indict, the only thing a prosecutor should do is bring the charges as recommended by the Grand Jury and then move to dismiss them if the prosecutor feels they are not supported by probable cause. A judge should make this determination in open court. See, Linda Himmelstein, *Legal Times*, 2 November 1992.

70. Greg Lopez's article is titled "From cattle trail to campaign trail, Cowboy plans to ride for 4th District seat and spill the beans on Flats investigation,"

plans to ride for 4th District seat and spill the beans on Flats investigation," *The Rocky Mountain News*, 31 December 1995.

71. The Justice Department threats were discussed in private conversations between Caron Balkany and Edith Holleman.

Chapter Eight

The Citizens' Investigation Continues—Some Small Successes, 1997-2000

72. *Concerned Citizens for Nuclear Safety vs. Department of Energy* , etc., Case # 94-1039 M, US District Court for New Mexico.
73. Caron Balkany's interviews with LeRoy Moore, Rocky Mountain Peace and Justice Center, document the history of the Future Site Working Group.
74. *The Savannah Morning News*, 23 November 2001.
75. In this type of contract, taxpayers foot the bill for all costs, even for mistakes, plus pay a fee to Rockwell just to open the doors, plus pay bonuses based on specific performance criteria. In the 1980s, this was usually for increased production of bomb triggers. The operative contract at Rocky Flats was DOE CO4-76DP03533, and its modifications. William Rask, the Director of the Production Division for the Energy Department at Rocky Flats, and one of the high level Energy Department officials the Grand Jury had wanted to indict, gave an interview to the Energy Department Inspector General in the criminal investigation, stating that "...spending more money meant a greater percentage of the Cost Plus Award Fee (CPAF) contract money for Rockwell." See, Office of Inspector General, US Department of Energy, Memorandum of Interview, Case File No.90DN005, 4 December 1990, taken by Special Agent Robert Scherer.
76. The reports from the Government Accounting Office include: "Nuclear Health and Safety; Oversight at DOE's Nuclear Facilities Can be Strengthened," GAO/RCED-88-137, 8 July 1988; "Environmental, Safety and Health Oversight of the Department of Energy's Operation," GAO/T-RCED-88-30, 31 March 1988; "Key Elements of Effective Independent Oversight of DOE's Nuclear Facilities," GAO/T-RCED-87-93, 14 April 1987; "Environmental, Safety, and Health Oversight of DOE's Operations," GAO/T-RCED-87-12, 25 March 1987; and "DOE's Safety and Health Oversight Program at Nuclear Facilities Could be Strengthened," GAO/RCED-84-50, 30 November 1983.
77. The letter from Karen Pitts to Wes McKinley is dated 18 September 1999.
78. See, Renee B. Lettow, "Reviving Federal Grand Jury Presentments," *The Yale Law Journal*, Vol. 103:133, 1994.
79. Caron Balkany interviewed Ken Fimberg/Scott at The Hague in the summer of 2000.

80. The documentation that radiation surveys were taken shortly after the raid is in:

Peter Chronis, "Cameras, sensors to survey Flats site," *The Denver Post*, 28 June 1089;

———, "Plutonium cancer risk 'negligible'," *The Denver Post*, 28 June 1987; Janet Day, "Rocky Flats is focus of aerial survey," *The Rocky Mountain News*, 8 July 1989;

Department of Energy, "DOE aerial survey over the Rocky Flats plant," press release, ____.

   The radiation surveys are:

EG&G Energy Measurements (for the U.S. Department of Energy), "An aerial radiological survey of the United States Department of Energy's Rocky Flats plant," August 1981;

———, "An aerial radiological survey of the United States Department of Energy's Rocky Flats plant," July 1989;

———, "A multispectral scanner survey of the U.S. Department of Energy's Rocky Flats plant, Golden, Colorado," June-July 1989;

———, "In situ surveys of the United States Department of Energy's Rocky Flats plant, Golden, Colorado," August 1990, October-November 1990, and November-December 1990;

US Department of Energy Special Assignment Environmental Team, "Assessment of Environmental Conditions at the Rocky Flats Plant, Golden, Colorado," August 1989.

81. Chairman Wolpe's comments appear at Vol. I, 665.

82. John Till's conversations with Caron Balkany started in August, 2001 and continued intermittently for several months thereafter.

83. Some of the reports which we reviewed include: John Till, Principal Investigator, Radiological Assessments Corporation:

"Estimated Airborne Releases of Plutonium during the 1957 Fire in Building 71," [later re-named Building 771] August 1999;

———, "Estimated Airborne Releases of Plutonium during the 1969 Fire in Buildings 776-777," August 1999;

———, "Characterization of Releases to Surface Water from the Rocky Flats Plant," Revision 1, August 1999;

———, "Development of the Rocky Flats Plant 903 Area Plutonium Source Term," Revision 1, August 1999;

———, "Estimated Exposure and Lifetime Cancer Incidence Risk from Routine Plutonium Releases at the Rocky Flats Plant," Revision 1, August 1999;

———, "Evaluation of Environmental Data for Historical Public Exposures Studies on Rocky Flats," Revision 1, August 1999;

———, "Review of Routine Releases of Plutonium in Airborne Effluents at Rocky Flats," August 1999;

Incidence Risk from Plutonium Released from the Rocky Flats Plant, 1953-1989," September 1999;

_____, "Technical Summary Report for the Historical Public Exposures Studies for Rocky Flats Phase II," September 1999;

_____, "Radionuclide Soil Action Level Oversight Panel-Independent Calculation," February 2000;

_____, "Radionuclide Soil Action Level Oversight Panel-Technical Project Summary," February 2000.

84. According to Edith Holleman, Murtha was always trying to rein in the investigation and keep Fimberg from pressing too hard for a win.

85. On debarment issues see:

Charles Hartt, Senior Vice President, General Counsel and Secretary, Rockwell International Corp., letter to John Easton, Acting General Counsel, DOJ, "regarding pending settlement discussions...with suggested language...," 18 September 1991;

Silas Fisher, Director, Office of Procurement, Assistance and Program Management, DOE, letter to Donald Beall, Chairman and CEO, Rockwell Intl. Corp., 3 April 1992.

86. The problematic EPA enforcement history at Rocky Flats is detailed by Bryan Abas in "The State Knew it and Blew it," *Westword*, 21-27 June 1989.

87. Caron Balkany interviewed Detective Sergeant Ted Schoudt on 26 June 2001.

88. Ultimately, the court entered an order that the Energy Department could no longer burn hazardous waste at Building 771 without complying with environmental laws. The Sierra Club won a total victory, basically doing what the EPA or the State of Colorado should have done years before. "EPA and the State did not have the political courage to do it," said Adam Babich, the Sierra Club's attorney. *Sierra Club vs. Rockwell International and the Department of Energy*, Case # 89-B-1181. See, also, Mark Obmascik, "Flats violated US Laws Judge Rules," *The Denver Post*, 17 April 1990.

89. See, Janet Day, "Flats' Worst Threat May Lie Underground," *The Rocky Mountain News*, 23 July 1989.

90. A search warrant must be supported by evidence that a crime has been committed (probable cause). You can't just ask a judge for a search warrant. So the multi-page affidavit in support of the search warrant, sworn to by Lipsky, is full of facts and demonstrates that the Justice Department already had lots of evidence of the culpability of Energy Department and Rockwell officials before the search warrant was even issued and before the Grand Jury was impaneled.

91. US Attorney Norton tried this legal maneuver unsuccessfully. The US Attorney's Office filed the Motion to Stay 6 June 1989 in *Sierra Club vs. United States*, US District Court for Colorado, Case # 89-B-1181; the Motion was denied 30 June 1989. See also, Janet Day, "Poisoned Air From

Flats feared," *The Rocky Mountain News*, 8 June 1989. Interestingly, Norton also represented to the judge that he could not vouch for the accuracy of some of the pleadings filed by the US Justice Department concerning the incineration of plutonium-contaminated waste. The Affidavit and Application for Search Warrant reveals that the US Attorney's Office in Colorado had become aware of the inaccuracies in the Justice Department representations to the court by at least 6 June 1989.

92.   On 26 March 1992, at the time the sentencing memorandum was filed, the prosecutors had already read the Grand Juror's Draft Report dated 18 February 1992 and their proposed indictments, and knew that the Grand Jury disagreed. See, *Westword* and *The Los Angeles Times, op. cit.* at endnote 41.

93.   The background on the civil lawsuit by Rocky Flats' neighboring landowners and the Department of Justice artifice to obtain a clean bill of health for Rocky Flats appear in *Church, McKay vs. USA*, Civ. Action # 75-M-1162, US District Court, District of Colorado, including:
Government defendants' response to plaintiffs' pretrial statement, 29 June 1984;
Report on settlement, 16 November 1984;
Motion to enter findings,15 February 1985;
Position statement of defendant board of county commissioners of Jefferson County, Colorado, 23 April 1985;
Statement concerning motion to enter findings, 24 April 1985;
Findings of fact and conclusions of law, 3 July 1985;
Affidavit of returned material, Howard Holme, 30 September 1985;
        Exhibit 1: Church's objections to the responses of Dow, Rockwell and the U.S. to Church's interrogatories of 21 December 1976, dated 15 February 1977.

94.   The Department of Housing and Urban Development had issued warnings back in 1979 that land around Rocky Flats was contaminated with plutonium, assertedly below the applicable EPA guidance levels. There were also plans to limit the amount of development near the perimeter of the Plant in the interests of rapid evacuation in the event of another fire or other emergency.

95.   Dr. Carl Johnson's letter appeared in *The Denver Post* on 11 February 1985.

96.   The pattern of Justice Department cover-ups of crimes committed within other federal agencies appears in Vol. 1, 33-39, and includes allegations of cover-ups by the Justice Department of FBI and EPA criminal conduct.

97.   Mike Norton's assertions that the most serious crimes had been charged were made several times, including Vol. I, 1064 and Vol. III, 317.

98.   According to Professor Jonathon Turley, "The only information [about the Rocky Flats Grand Jury investigation] that remains under seal is information revealing the possible misconduct and mismanagement by the Justice

Department in this case. Rule 6(e) was never intended to shield this type of information, which belongs before Congress and the public, and not in the hands of those officials involved in the controversy." Professor Turley's comments appear in "Petitioners' Memorandum of Points and Authorities in Support of the Petition of Members of Special Grand Jury 89-2 for a Sealed Hearing and Subsequent Order Removing Or Modifying Continued Secrecy Obligations," *In re Special Grand Jury 89-2*, Miscellaneous Case #: 96-___.

Chapter Nine
Flashbacks from Wes' Journals: Inside the Grand Jury Chambers, 1989-1992

99. After the Justice Department decided that the Grand Jury Report should not be released, Judge Finesilver ruled that presentments are outmoded and that only indictments brought by prosecutors can be used to charge crimes, so the Grand Jury's presentment would be sealed along with the Report. *In re Rocky Flats Grand Jury*, 813 F. Supp. 1451 (D. Colo. 1992) This, despite the fact that the United States Supreme Court has recognized that the power of the Grand Jury predates the Constitution (much less the Justice Department) and was preserved by that document. *Blair v. United States*, 250 U.S. 273 (1919).

100. Congressional testimony from Peter Murtha, Vol. III, 226 and 239, and Mike Norton, Vol. III, 346, indicates that by October, 1991, the Justice Department had vetoed the issuance of a Grand Jury Report. The judge met with the Grand Jury in December, 1991. Judge Finesilver has not responded to requests by author Balkany for an interview.

101. Apparently, one of the concerns Ken Fimberg had about the Grand Jury's report was that it accused EG&G, which took over after Rockwell, of continuing to commit crimes. See, "Redacted Grand Jury Report," and "Analysis of Rocky Flats Grand Jury Report," Ken Fimberg to Mike Norton and Peter Murtha, 11 March 1992. The law states that a Grand Jury Report could be permissible if there were evidence of on-going criminal activity. So, if EG&G and the Energy Department had continued to commit crimes, as Rockwell and the Energy Department had done previously, this provision could be satisfied, and the court might rule that the Grand Jury Report could be made public, something Justice Department headquarters had decided should not occur.

In fact, many of the same types of problems did persist after EG&G took over. Disabling safety alarms had been a frequent complaint during Rockwell's tenure and continued when EG&G took over. This endangered workers, but sped up production. See, XXXX, *FBI Interview*, 1 March

1991, discussing a foreman's orders to de-sensitize the alarms while Rockwell had been running Rocky Flats, and News Release, EG&G Rocky Flats Inc., 28 August 1991, discussing the ongoing problem of tampering with the alarms.

Another example of the continuation of criminal activity involved the contamination by EG&G of a visiting team of experts who were conducting a safety inspection. It was almost identical to a contamination incident which had precipitated the closing of Building 771 in October 1988 when Rockwell was operating Rocky Flats.

The FBI investigated this incident; the Energy Department wrote itself memos and chastised its employees and contractors for putting production ahead of safety and for communication problems. No criminal charges were filed. Vol. I, 694-696. Karen Pitts and Jacque Brever brought this incident to the FBI's attention.

A letter from Grand Juror Ken Peck to Wes McKinley 31 March 1992 refers to similar waste storage crimes continuing after Rockwell left Rocky Flats and EG&G took over. In fact, what the regulatory agencies did is make legal the same conduct Rockwell was being prosecuted for as long as EG&G agreed to try to fix it. See, also, EG&G press release, 17 June 1992, re Notice of Violation for 56 issues from 1990-1992.

102. Wes McKinley and Clerk James Manspeaker waited several hours for US Attorney Michael Norton to come and explain how he got the copy of the draft Grand Jury Report, as Norton had agreed he would do. Norton never showed.

Chapter Ten
The Citizens' Investigation Continues, 2001

103. XXXX gave interviews to the FBI and the EPA on 26 October 1989 and 16 February 1990.

104. For instance, according to the "Assessment of Environmental Conditions at the RFP," August, 1989, US DOE Special Assignment Environmental Team [Tiger Team]: "There are deficiencies in the ambient air monitoring program for radionuclides. As a consequence, the accuracy of measured concentrations of plutonium in ambient air are questionable. These data are reported monthly and annually, and are used in calculating annual radiation dose to the public to confirm dose calculations that are made based on radioactive effluent emission data."

The team noted that equipment calibration had not been done since the 1970s and that the air emissions monitoring program does not comply with the Clean Air Act or other legal requirements and does not present an accurate picture of the radioactive air emissions. The plant did not analyze for uranium or for americium 241. The sampling equipment is more than 15 years old.

The Tiger Team observed: "The assessment of the RFP [Rocky Flats Plant] contribution to the public radiation dose as reported [by Rocky Flats as a regulatory requirement] . . . does not fully address all potential exposure pathways and radionuclides. The quality assurance and quality control practices for radiochemistry analyses in the Building 123 HS&E laboratory...cannot adequately verify the validity of analytical results. Chemistry Standards lab also non-complying. General lab for radiochemistry analysis non-complying. Information provided to the EPA concerning releases of chemicals is false. It indicates the chemicals have actually been measured, when in fact they are based on estimates and assumptions."

105. The background on the inability of the Energy Department to self-regulate was provided by former Rep. David Skaggs in an interview with Caron Balkany on 6 December 2001 and in Caron Balkany's interviews with Dr. John Till in the summer of 2001. See, Linda Cornett and Bill Scanlon, "Agents probe allegations at Rocky Flats," *Daily Camera*, 7 June 1989 and Joan Lowry, "Flats Accident Possible Says Report," *The Rocky Mountain News*, 7 October 1989.

106. Peter Murtha discussed the Unitary Executive Policy at Vol. I, 1181. Bruce DeBoskey, a Denver environmental attorney, in an interview with Caron Balkany on 19 September 2001, provided details of the Energy Department's concern over the citizen suit provisions of the environmental statutes. This is confirmed in an undated internal Energy Department memorandum to Undersecretary of Energy Mary Walker which was leaked in 1987 and which helped motivate the FBI to investigate Rocky Flats, according to Jon Lipsky, Vol. I, 399. The unnamed Energy Department official states:

> *"GC's [general counsel] real fear of the EPA being able to issue an order under RCRA is that the order would allegedly be subject to citizen suit enforcement. The order, being final and valid on its face, would be prime material for a successful summary judgment motion, GC maintains."*

107. The EPA's response to the Citizens' Investigation FOIA request included the following documents: Internal letter, Rockwell International, from C.R. Rose to W.D. Crossland, re: Building 771 main exhaust plenum utilization and upgrading, 8 April 1982; M.L. Huber, Rockwell International, Building 771 incinerator Study, 2 January 1980; Preliminary Analysis, Air Pollution Control Division, Colorado Department of Health, 11 July 1985; Unsigned, undated Incinerator History; Unsigned, Incinerator Fact Sheet, 12 November 1987.

108. Janet Day reports in *The Rocky Mountain News*, "Officials in the Dark on plutonium burning," 23 January 1987, that the State of Colorado didn't

know about the incineration of plutonium contaminated waste until 1987.

Chapter Eleven
Jacque Brever, 2001

109. Feeding the ducks radioactive waste is also documented by FBI interviews with XXXX, 17 October 1990 and with XXXX, 5 June 1990, as well as in an FBI phone interview with an anonymous female caller, 8 June 1990.
110. The list of FBI interviews is in Vol. I, 417.
111. The Energy Department's report is called "Analysis of Building 771 Incinerator," 19 June 1989, from Ronald Gersten to the Department of Energy, Acting Manager of Rocky Flats.

The main reasons the Justice Department gave for dropping the secret midnight plutonium burning charges was because the infrared analyst had changed his position, the prosecutors couldn't corroborate Pitts and Brever's testimony, and because if the incinerator had been run, lots of people would have known about it. See, Memorandum from Mark Dubester, Acting Chief, Public Corruption/Government Fraud Section, US Attorney's Office for the District of Columbia, to Associate Attorney General Webster Hubbell, 8 April 1994. No co-worker interviewed by the FBI actually admitted to being involved in the illegal work on the incinerator. However, reliance on the failure of these co-workers to incriminate themselves by admitting they had worked on the incinerator during the shutdown is questionable. These workers had already been warned about being "whistleblowers." Brever, *op. cit.*, *FBI Interview*, and XXXX, *FBI Interview*, 14 September 1989.

And none said they'd actually seen the incinerator and had first hand evidence that it hadn't been operating, or stated any mechanical reason that it couldn't have been operated the shift before. Instead, they simply provided conclusions that it had been shutdown, with no first hand information.

One of these three Rockwell employees at first stated that she remembered working with Pitts and Brever taking down the incinerator as Pitts and Brever had explained to the FBI; she recalled the same co-workers as did Pitts and the same processes, including the removal of many of the filters.

This employee admitted to working a great deal of overtime from October 1988 through April 1989, and said that the event being described could have occurred during any of that time; she wasn't sure of the date. She was sure that the incinerator had been run the day before the date when she worked with Pitts and Brever, but did not know when that was. See, XXXX, *FBI Interview*, 16 June 1989.

The date of the second interview was 14 September 1989, the same date that two co-workers intentionally contaminated Jacque Brever with plutonium and then laughed at her about it. Word was all over the Plant that Pitts and Brever were in a lot of trouble for cooperating with the FBI. Jon Lipsky had noted during the first interview that XXXX was "VERY SCARED." By the second interview, XXXX stated that she had "never worked on the incinerator in Building 771 with BREVER or PITTS in December of 1988."

112. See, Defendant Rockwell's sentencing memorandum.

113. Rockwell's position is set forth in its 7 September 1989 letter to the US Attorney's Office, Vol. III, 68-80.

114. The report stated: "Analysis of the plant liquefied gas logs shows that only normal evaporation losses (about two inches per day) occurred during the 9-10-88 to 2-24-89 period."Jon Lipsky's testimony concerning the oxygen logs is in Vol. I, 753-763,773.

115. "The December 1988 data is similar to June, July, August and September, 1988 and also the end of February and March, 1989." The Energy Department admitted that the incinerator operated in July, August, September, 1988 and February and March, 1989.

Chapter Twelve
Special Agent Jon Lipsky, 2001

116. The correspondence between the FBI and Caron Balkany is dated 16 August 2001 and 1 October 2001. There were also several telephone calls.

117. The FBI memo to Special Agent Lipsky is dated 15 August 2001.

118. Chairman Wolpe's statements about retaliation are in Vol. I, 655.

119. Barry Siegel, "Showdown at Rocky Flats," *The Los Angeles Times*, 8 and 15 August 1993.

120. "A Justice Department Prosecutor" advised Caron Balkany concerning the Justice Department's ethical position about settlement under these circumstances.

121. Starting in December, 1990, Rockwell had insisted that there be no individual indictments if the case were to be settled, and by December 1990, the Justice Department and Ken Fimberg had decided that settling the case was the right approach. Vol. III, 196. Other attorneys, including author Balkany, believe that the case is one that should have been tried not settled, that citizens had a right to know what had been going on at Rocky Flats and that a jury of Colorado citizens was the best place to decide the criminality of that conduct, not behind closed doors at the Justice Department.

122. The US Attorney's Manual requires prosecutors to conduct a complete investigation before settling charges. Also, as Ken Fimberg was to acknowledge in an affidavit filed in *Cypher vs. United States*, Civil Action

91-W-171, USDC, Colorado, 1991, a case where one of the Rockwell workers had sued him for harassment, the United States Supreme Court has ruled that "[a] grand jury investigation is not fully carried out until every available clue has been run down and all witnesses examined in every proper way. . . ."

The documentation that the prosecutors decided not to charge any individuals before the investigation had even been completed is found in testimony from Jon Lipsky at Vol. III, 30-39, and 62, in the Wolpe report. High-level Energy Department officials had not been interviewed even as of 30 April 1991. See, Norton, in Vol. I, 1063 and Vol. III, 306, and an internal EPA memo from William Smith concerning a Sixteen Month Status report on the case, 30 April 1991, Vol. I, 1133. The proffers from targets did not occur until the summer of 1991. Vol. III, 137.

123. The environmental statutes do not cover purely radioactive materials at US weapons plants. Only the Atomic Energy Act regulates them, and that is enforced by the Energy Department, not by any independent source. That left the Energy Department free to do pretty much whatever it wanted at the weapons complexes, until the EPA and the states asserted their authority to regulate wastes contaminated with both radioactivity *and* hazardous components.

124. Norton's testimony that he'd never discussed the substance of the case with Energy Department officials is at Vol. I, 1109.

125. The 28 March 1991 memo Balkany gave Lipsky is from the Energy Department General Counsel to the Deputy Secretary of the Energy Department.

126. Documentation that Rockwell required the official statements in the plea bargain is found at Vol. I, 1237. At the time the sentencing memorandum was filed, the Grand Jury's disagreement was still secret, their Report was still secret, and none of the prosecutors apparently thought their deal would come under intense public and congressional scrutiny. Afterwards, after the Report was leaked and subpoenas were issued, US Attorney Norton, without explanation, partially backed off his inaccurate statements in the sentencing memorandum, with a qualification:

". . . we found no evidence of any significant off-site physiological threat to the environment or to the public health *not already known to the regulators*, and therefore the subject of various regulatory or clean-up agreements." (emphasis supplied) See, 23 September 1992, "Statement of Michael J. Norton," issued by the Justice Department.

Even with the new and belated qualification, the statement is inaccurate, according to Grand Jury sources and Special Agent Lipsky.

127. Rockwell made good use of the Justice Department's statements that there'd been no secret midnight plutonium burning to advance its efforts to settle the case without individual criminal indictments. See, Rockwell's letter to Dick Thornburgh, US Attorney General, 6 May, 1991.

128. The Energy Department Memorandum for the Record agreeing to no debarment of Rockwell is dated the same day the Grand Jury was discharged. See, Berton J. Roth, Deputy Director, Office of Procurement, Department of Energy, Memorandum for the Record, 24 March 1992.

129. The letter from the Justice Department to Rockwell's attorneys declining to intervene in the Stone false claims lawsuit was signed the same day as the Plea Agreement. Michael Hertz, US Department of Justice to Bryan Morgan, 24 March 1992. Rockwell had been demanding for some time that the Justice Department not intervene in the Stone false claims lawsuit. Vol. III, 365-366.

130. Thane Hendrix, from EG&G, at the request of the Energy Department FOIA Office in Las Vegas, Nevada, gave the authors the information on the radiological surveys at Rocky Flats and the absence of any search for strontium.

      The articles documenting strontium in the groundwater are in *The New York Times*, 15 June 1989 and *The Rocky Mountain News*, 16 June 1989; 21 July 1989; and 12 August 1989.

131. Some newspaper articles concerning the criticality rumors and the Energy Department's efforts to deflect them are:

Staff article, "Flats denies N.Y. Times' reports of radioactivity," *The Rocky Mountain News*, 15 June 1989;

————, "DOE experts seek source of elements at Flats," *The Rocky Mountain News*, 21 July 1989;

Janet Day, "Probe dispels tales of nuclear accident, scientists find no evidence of long-ago fires, reactions at Rocky Flats," *The Rocky Mountain News*, 12 August 1989;

Department of Energy, press release, "DOE to fly aerial survey over the Rocky Flats nuclear weapons facility," 16 June 1989.

132. The status reports are dated 20 October 1989 from William Smith to the Acting Director of EPA's National Enforcement Investigation Center. The agenda for the 8 July 1990 Hartman/Norton meeting does not include discussion of falsified laboratory testing or false statements as issues of interest to the investigation.

133. Rockwell faced significant legal and monetary exposure from civil lawsuits claiming personal contamination and property damage from Rocky Flats' operations.

134. An FBI interview with Mike Bartelson, Director of Water Resources, City of Broomfield, on 6 February 1991, documents the City of Broomfield's concern about Blue Baby syndrome. The towns of Westminster and Broomfield also changed their drinking water supplies so as not to receive water from Rocky Flats. This cost millions of dollars, paid for by the Energy Department.

      Plutonium contaminated sediment is known to lie at the bottom of

Standley Lake. John Till, private conversations with Caron Balkany. And although the prosecutors emphasized and repeated that there was no off-site contamination and no problems with the drinking water supplies, prosecutor Fimberg had told Jon Lipsky that the reason there were no charges based on off-site contamination from nitrates "...wasn't because there were no nitrates in the water; he told me there were just no regulations about them." This is not accurate; the nitrate standards of the Clean Water Act had been in effect since the 1970s.

135. According to LeRoy Moore, Ph.D., of the Rocky Mountain Peace and Justice Center, the Energy Department has never adequately characterized the type or amount of waste at Rocky Flats, and has no plans to do so. This means the clean-up plans are based almost entirely on data collected in the past by the Energy Department and its defense contractors, and on assumptions. It has already been shown that at least some of the data and assumptions are incorrect.

The decades of secrecy and cheating can mislead even well-intentioned and objectively conducted studies, and can result in mistakes in development of the clean-up plans for Rocky Flats. The tritium analyses reflected in the "Technical Summary Report for the Historical Public Exposures Studies for Rocky Flats Phase II," Risk Assessment Corporation, September 1999, are an example.

Tritium is a radioactive isotope of hydrogen with a 12.5 year half-life that emits low energy beta particles as it decays. Tritiated water is its most common form when found in the environment. In the technical summary report, the dose reconstruction team estimated the dose to the public from tritium based on the assumption that there was no tritium production at Rocky Flats. This is what the team had been advised, and based on this information, Dr. Till, as principal Investigator, concluded that, "Tritium was not produced at the RFP, but it has been released accidentally from the RFP on several occasions during processing of tritium-contaminated scrap plutonium from Lawrence Livermore Laboratory." See, Technical Summary report, *ibid.*

However, the information that Rocky Flats did not produce tritium is contradicted in a 7 June 1991 interview by Special Agent Lipsky with XXXX, a chemical engineer then recently retired from Rocky Flats after approximately 40 years. XXXX stated: "Due to the ongoing practice of conducting Classified projects at Rocky Flats, tritium was produced and disposed of at the plant, in the area of the 207 ponds."

There was also a Project Rover in the 1950s, an effort to develop a nuclear powered rocket. We do not know how much if any of Project Rover was actually developed on-site at Rocky Flats. This information would be important to the development of proper clean-up methodology.

136. Private conversations between Caron Balkany and attorneys Peter

Nordberg, Bruce DeBoskey and Steve Kelly in 2002 provide the background about *Cook vs. Dow Chemical, Rockwell International, and The United States of America* Civ. Action # 90K-181, United States District Court, District of Colorado.

137. The attorneys representing the Energy Department's contractors have billed the government over $32 million in attorney's fees so far. In fact, the billing was so outrageous that two congressional hearings were held to try to hold them in line. Former independent prosecutor Ken Starr is a main partner in that law firm. See, John Brinkley, "Flats lawyers have high time at taxpayers' expense," *The Rocky Mountain News*, 13 July 1994. The congressional investigation determined that lack of Energy Department oversight let the defense contractors and their lawyers bill for pretty much whatever they wanted.

138. The testing obtained by plaintiffs' counsel in that class action indicates that: "People living near the Rocky Flats facility were exposed to radionuclides and other chemicals, such as beryllium, discharged from the plant over the period of its operation." Radford, Edward, MD, "Comments on Medical Monitoring of People Exposed to Hazards From Rocky Flats Nuclear Facility in Colorado."

139. *In Re Special Grand Jury 89-2*, Miscellaneous Case #: 96-___.

140. The study referred to is by the Colorado Central Cancer Registry, Emergency Medical Services and Prevention Division (Colorado Department of Public Health and Environment), "Ratios of cancer incidence in ten areas around Rocky Flats, Colorado, compared to the remainder of metropolitan Denver, 1980-89 with update for selected areas, 1990-95," A Report to the Health Advisory Panel on Rocky Flats,1998.

The Energy Department is paying over $600,000 to a public relations firm to publicize the results of the health studies. Katie Kerwin, "Rocky Flats PR runs up $634,000 tab," *The Rocky Mountain News*, 4 May 1994.

There is additional information about the health effects of the Rocky Flats operations in:

Associated Press, "Perverse secrecy called root of weapons plant's crisis," *The Rocky Mountain News*, 19 June 1989;

———, "Report on radiation's harm spurs nuclear plant study," 22 December 1989.

Adriel Bettelheim, "Building 771 is nerve center for facility," *The Denver Post*, 11 June 1989;

Judith Brimberg, "New studies sought on health effects of radiation exposure," *The Denver Post*, 14 April 1980, "Doctors can't answer many of the questions about exposure to pollutants allegedly coming from Rocky Flats," *The Rocky Mountain News*, 11 June 1989;

Marlys Duran, "Ex-health chief renews Flats warnings," *The Rocky Mountain News*, 7 January 1985;

Alan Gottlieb, "EPA may toughen testing of water discharges," *The Denver Post*, 29 March 1989;

Bruce Hall, "Plutonium found in teeth of children throughout Britain," *Greenpeace Nuclear Disarmament Campaign*, 1 August 1997;

Joan Lowy, "Governors urge more funds for N-plant cleanups," *The Rocky Mountain News*, 29 January 1989;

Arjun Makhijani, Bernd Franke, and Hisham Zerriffi, "Forgotten exposures: Worker doses at three nuclear materials processing plants in the 1940's and 1950's," *Science for Democratic Action*, Vol. 9, No. 1, December 2000;

Richard Martinez and David Shander, "Rocky Flats reflects values turned upside down," *The Rocky Mountain News*, 3 July 1989;

Pat McGraw, "Health study of Flats' neighbors waste of money, says DU biologist," *The Denver Post*, 29 March 1989;

Kris Newcomer, "'Exotic' wastes part of experiment?" *The Rocky Mountain News*, 18 June 1989;

Mark Udall and Wayne Allard, "Coming clean at Rocky Flats," *The Denver Post*, 12 August 2001;

Joseph Verrengia, "Doctors want Flats closed until safety board named," *The Rocky Mountain News*, 18 June 1989;

———, "Radiation still not fully understood; health threats compounded by outside," *The Rocky Mountain News*, 18 June 1989;

Mathew Wald, "Low doses of radiation risky: independent study contradicts government's current data," *The New York Times*, _____;

Eileen Welsome, "This place is a dump!" *Westword*, 27 July 2000.

141. Bernd Franke provided the analysis of the Colorado cancer incidence study.

142. See Dr. Johnson's papers at endnote 3. See, also information from other writers, including:

John Cobb *et al.*, "Plutonium burdens in people living around the Rocky Flats plant," US

Environmental Protection Agency project summary, March 1983;

L.D. Hamilton, "Alternative interpretations of statistics on health effects of low-level radiation," a rebuttal of Johnson's findings, in *The American Statistician*, Vol. 37:4, November 1983;

Bertram Wolfe, "Public has exaggerated fears of exposure to radiation," *The Denver Post*, 27 September 1986;

Gregg S. Wilkinson, et. al., "Mortality among plutonium and other radiation workers at a plutonium weapons facility," *American Journal of Epidemiology*, Vol. 125:2, 1987;

Thomas Graf, "Doctor warned of Rocky Flats danger," *The Denver Post*, 19 June 1989;

Richard Pollock, "Uncovering nuclear cancer," *In These Times*, 22-26 March 1978.

143. Goble, Robert, Ph.D., "Exposures from Releases of Plutonium and Other

Toxic Substances at Rocky Flats," 24 November 1996.

144. Clapp, Richard, MPH, D. Sc., 13 November, 1996.
145. Arjun Makhijani reports the Energy Department plans for the conversion of waste dumps to playgrounds and wildlife refuges. See, EPA's *Superfund Redevelopment Initiative* (1999); the DOD's *Fast-Track Clean up Program* (1996); and the DOE's *Accelerating the Paths to Closure Program* (1998). All three programs have a priority on placing Federal Facility Superfund sites into re-use "as expeditiously as practicable." EPA fully supports recreational use stating, "Use of a site may give a community greater recreational opportunities by providing ball fields, playgrounds, historic or cultural centers, or scenic hiking trails." See, Federal Facilities Restoration and Reuse Office Library. Downloaded 07/20/03.
146. The affidavit, which Lipsky never signed, is at www. Ambushedgrandjury.com.
147. The lawsuit against Ken Fimberg is *Cypher vs. USA*, Civil Action 91-W-171, USDC, Colorado, 1991.

Chapter Thirteen
We Prove the Justice Department Cover-Up. Now What?

148. The infrared reports can be seen at www.Ambushedgrandjury.com. They are formally known as "Emergency Report, Department of Energy Rocky flats Plant," Golden, Colorado, February 1989, and "Aerial Photographic Analysis of the Department of Energy Rocky Flats Plant," Golden, Colorado, May, 1989.
149. See, Caron Balkany's interviews and correspondence with the infrared analyst, Al Divers, on 7 November 2000, 4 March 2001, 10 April 2001, 8 August 2001, and 21 August 2001, as well as Mr. Divers' FBI interviews, 2 January 1989 and 5 January 1989.
150. "Prosecutors don't do that," said congressional subcommittee staff attorney Holleman. "They don't have to present anything but their best evidence, so it's very unusual that they would put on testimony to undermine their own witnesses. Especially right in the beginning."
151. Corroboration of the drinking and drug problem at Rocky Flats comes from Caron Balkany and Wes McKinley's interviews with Jim Stone; from an Energy Department press release dated 26 October 1990; and from interviews with Jacque Brever and Ron Avery.
152. Mark Pitts, husband of Karen Pitts, gave the FBI an interview on 18 October 1989 describing how he had seen cardboard boxes full of wet filters from Building 771. Paul Voillequi, from Radiological Assessment Corporation, described to Caron Balkany how wet filters sag, and don't fit properly. This can cause radioactive contamination to escape around the sides of the filter, and out the exhaust stack into the environment.

153. According to many experts, there is no safe level of exposure to ionizing radiation.

154. Physicians for Social Responsibility, *Dead Reckoning* (1992).

155. The Associated Press article on increased risks from low-level radiation is carried as "Report on radiation's harm spurs nuclear plant study," *The Rocky Mountain News*, 22 December 1989.

156. Karen Pitts's gave testimony at a public hearing for the Ahearne Committee in Denver on 17 July 1991 concerning her radiation badge:

> *"I exited this plant on 4/17/91. I still have my TLD [radiation detection device worn on the outer clothing] from November of 1989. It has not been counted, but I did receive a count for that badge and for 1990. I would like to know where in hell those counts came from. I was not on Plant site, I did not turn in my badge, I still have it, I still have the TLD. I still have the picture, I still have it."*

157. Go to www.IEER.org, the website sponsored by the Institute for Energy and Environmental Research, for an in-depth article on errors and problems in reporting radiation doses for nuclear workers. The admission of faulty data appears in *The Rocky Mountain News*, 18 March 1994, A. Partile, "Radiation exposures at weapons plants not monitored correctly, US now says."

158. The FBI mishandling of our FOIA request was typical of the FOIA responses from the other federal agencies. The difference with the FBI FOIA response is that we ultimately obtained the requested document—perhaps only because I told the FBI we already had a version of it—whereas with the Justice Department FOIA responses, we have received virtually none of the requested documentation. *The Denver Post* also had to wait more than three years before receiving a response to its FOIA request to the Energy Department about Rocky Flats. The newspaper got the last of the requested documents two days before EG&G's contract expired. EG&G was the company blamed for the waste which the newspaper was investigating. Mark Obmascik, "Flats withheld documents from Post FOIA request," *The Denver Post*, 2 July 1995.

159. The information about Judge Finesilver is found in Patricia Calhoun, "Grand Illusions, When it comes to Rocky Flats the Jury is still out," Patricia Calhoun, 16 November 1999, *Westword*.

160. CB Note: Ken Fimberg was perplexed that people were accusing him of covering things up at Rocky Flats. He felt he had done his best. *The Los Angeles Times* did a two part piece based on a seven hour interview with Fimberg.

"How did I turn into the bad guy?" he wonders in that article. In 1993, after the Wolpe Report was published, Fimberg's mother wrote several angry letters to Congressman Wolpe and other members of Congress, berat-

angry letters to Congressman Wolpe and other members of Congress, berating them for "mistreating" her son. Ken Finberg had applied to be US Attorney, seeking to replace Mike Norton, a Republican who would be leaving because the Democrats had taken over the White House. According to his mother's letter, Fimberg had been bitterly disappointed not to have even made the short list of recommendations for the judicial nomination commission. Ken Fimberg's mother felt that was in no small part due to the Wolpe congressional investigation into the Justice Department's handling of the Rocky Flats case. The letters from Fimberg's mother are dated 10 February 1993 to the Honorable Patricia Schroeder, US House of Representatives.

Fimberg was a golden boy, according to Edith Holleman. The congressional subcommittee had been impressed with his Harvard education, his honors degrees, his skill in a courtroom. But I wondered what it must have been like to have been Fimberg that summer and fall of 1992. A star prosecutor who had spent three years of his life dedicated to one mammoth, highly publicized case. A case with massive historical implications. But one that was more than a little political, and which surely hadn't turned out the way he'd intended.

Ken Fimberg, star prosecutor, must have been squirming on the wrong end of the congressional investigation. He was used to asking the questions, not answering them. He was used to being in control of criminal investigations, not being investigated. He was used to being the one demanding subpoenaed documents. He probably never dreamed he'd be under subpoena himself to produce even his most private memoranda and notes about a case that had suddenly made him look like a bad guy.

List of Interviews by Caron Balkany

Abas, Bryan, reporter, with Wes McKinley June, 2000
Anderson, Adrienne, environmental educator, numerous private communications
Avery, Ron, former Rockwell foreman, numerous private communications
Brever, Jacqueline, former Rockwell employee, numerous private communications
DeBoskey, Bruce, attorney, 19 September 2002
Divers, Al, infrared analyst, November 2000, 4 March 2001, 10 April 2001, 8 August 2001, and 21 August 2001
Exner, Bonnie, environmental activist, 23 June 2001
Fimberg/Scott Ken, former Assistant US Attorney, 12 September 2000, 21 September 2000, August 2000
Gerash, Walter, attorney, numerous private communications
Holleman, Edith, congressional staff counsel, numerous private communications
Liechtenstein, Ken, physician, 7 December 2001
Lipsky, Jon, FBI, numerous private communications

Makhijani, Arjun, Institute for Energy and Environmental research, numerous private conversations

Manspeaker, Jim, Clerk, US District Court, Colorado, 28 November 2001

Marshall, Tom, Rocky Mountain Peace and Justice Center, private communications

Miullo, Nat, EPA, 29 June 2001, 27 November 2001

Moore, LeRoy, Rocky Mountain Peace and Justice Center, private communications

Norton, Michael, former US Attorney, 12 June 2001

Peck, Ken , 18 August 2000, 18 June 2001

Rehder, Tim, EPA, 26 June 2001

Roach, Bob, congressional staff counsel, private communications

Schoenbeck, Margaret, Colorado Health Department, 19 December 2001

Skaggs, David, former Member of Congress, 6 December 2001

Shannon, Laurie, US Fish & Wildlife Service, 9 July 2002

Smith, Bill, EPA, 27 November 2001 and 26 June 2001

Stone, Jim, with Wes McKinley, numerous private communications

Till, John, Radiological Assessment Corporation, numerous private communications

Vollequie, Paul, Radiological Assessment Corporation, numerous private communications

A former prosecutor on the Rocky Flats investigation who was allowed to identify himself only as "Justice Department Prosecutor" 1 and 2 June, 2001

Other Sources

Pat Buffer, Employee Communications Building, "Rocky Flats Site History: events leading to the creation of the weapons complex and events at the Rocky Flats Site from the 1930's to present," 15 March 2000.

EG&G Rocky Flats, Inc., "Rocky Flats Plants Site Environmental Report for 1990."

———, "Rocky Flats Plants Site Environmental Elements 98 Report for 1991."

Daniel Ellsberg, "Two proposals on Lying, Truth-telling and Secrecy," 29 March 1998.

Arjun Makhijani and Sriram Gopal, "The Scientific Basis of Subsistence Farmer Scenario and Its Application to the Estimation of Radionuclide Soil Action Levels (RSALs) for Rocky Flats," a report prepared for the Rocky Mountain Peace and Justice Center, 1 August 2001.

US Department of Energy, "Environment, Safety and Health Progress Assessment of the Rocky Flats Plant," May 1993.

———, "Final Radionuclide Air Emissions Annual Report for Calendar Year 1998, Rocky Flats Environmental Technology Site," reviewed June 1998.

Citizens' Grand Jury Indictment

I, a Citizen Grand Juror, find that there is probable cause to believe that the US Justice Department covered up dangerous nuclear crimes at Rocky Flats Nuclear Weapons Plant during the 1989-1992 investigation of Energy Department and Rockwell International criminal activity.

_____   _____
yes   no

I further find that Rocky Flats is too contaminated to be used for recreation.

_____   _____
yes   no

I also find that congressional investigation is needed into government policies which permit lowered clean-up standards at toxic and hazardous waste sites designated for public access and recreation.

_____   _____
yes   no

I find that congressional investigation is needed into Energy Department plans to build "Rocky Flats II."

_____   _____
yes   no

_____
Name (or simply write "A Citizen Grand Juror")

_____   _____
Date   City and State

Please mail to **The Ambushed Grand Jury**, P.O. Box 2706, Grand Junction, CO 81502-2706. Or go on-line to send in your indictment at www.Ambushedgrandjury.com.